The Impact of Health Insurance in Low- and Middle-Income Countries

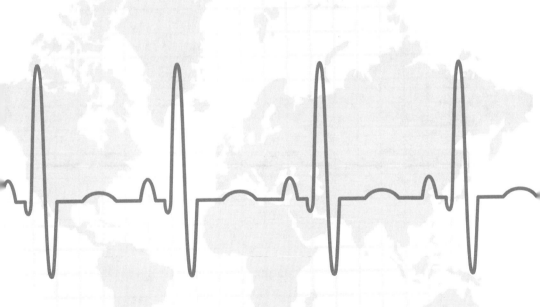

The Impact of Health Insurance in Low- and Middle-Income Countries

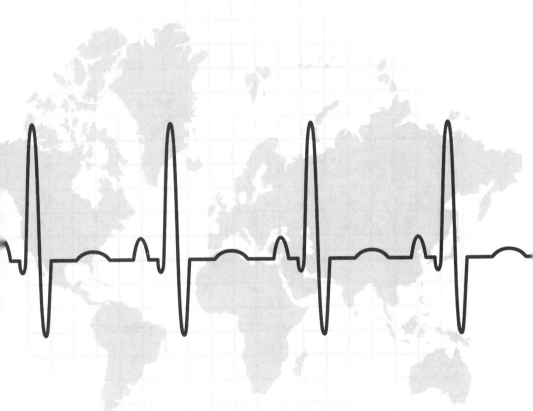

Maria-Luisa Escobar
Charles C. Griffin
R. Paul Shaw

EDITORS

BROOKINGS INSTITUTION PRESS
WASHINGTON, DC

Copyright © 2010
The Brookings Institution
1775 Massachusetts Avenue NW
Washington, DC 20036
www.brookings.edu

Library of Congress Cataloging-in-Publication data

Impact of health insurance in low- and middle-income countries / edited by Maria-Luisa Escobar, Charles C. Griffin, and R. Paul Shaw.
    p. ; cm.
  Includes bibliographical references and index.
  ISBN 978-0-8157-0546-8 (pbk. : alk. paper)
  1. Health insurance—Developing countries. I. Escobar, Maria-Luisa. II. Griffin, Charles C., 1951–. III. Shaw, R. Paul. IV. Brookings Institution.
  [DNLM: 1. Insurance, Health. 2. Developing Countries. 3. Health Policy—economics. W 225.1]
  HG9399.D442I47 2010
  368.38'20091724—dc22   2010038233

Editing and typesetting by Communications Development Incorporated, Washington, DC.

Contents

Chapter 10 Main Findings, Research Issues, and Policy Implications   178

Editors and Authors   199
Index   205

Boxes

Figures

Tables

Preface

While the underinvestment in health technology for poorer countries has become glaringly obvious and is starting to be rectified, health care financing has been an area of neglect. Yet in richer countries, public policy in health focuses almost exclusively on financing and incentive issues—and much progress has been made by those countries in improving access and care. Low- and middle-income countries continue to limp along with poorly performing public health care delivery systems, which almost all rich countries have abandoned for mixed systems financed through public purchasers or insurers financed predominately from tax revenues.

What could be done at the global level to support countries interested in undertaking fundamental reforms in health finance? One obvious candidate is health insurance, which for most low- and middle-income countries would be a paradigm-shifting change in the technology of health financing. The first question asked, however, is whether such a change could have demonstrable impacts on the take-up and impact of health services. We know little about this issue because economists' principal empirical interest in insurance has been its impact on financial risk protection, not on health benefits.

This question of insurance as a tool of health policy is the challenge addressed by this book. It is a small first step to explore whether changing the health financing method fully or partly into an insurance-based approach—that is, moving away from the supply side or direct service delivery model that dominates low- and middle-income country health financing—can have beneficial effects on health-seeking behavior and, by implication, health status.

We did not know what to expect when we set out to find countries, datasets, and analysts to shed light on this question. Our conclusion is that shifting partly or fully to insurance-like financing methods (in which payments are made to providers contingent on providing services to patients) has positive effects on the health-seeking behavior of consumers, at least in the countries covered in this book. Even in a country like Costa Rica, where 80% of the population is covered by insurance and everyone has access to hospital care when they need it (at no cost if they cannot afford it), the uninsured behave differently from the insured. The association of insurance with better health-seeking behavior—and in some cases a clear impact of insurance on better management of a family's health—is strong enough to encourage more experimentation and policy innovations.

In a few cases, particularly China and Peru, it is apparent that insurance also affects provider behavior, although that is not the focus of the book. Moreover, although we also did not expect it, there are lessons in every chapter about the nuts and bolts of design and implementation that illuminate some of the tasks reformers need to do well for a reform to work. Because the hoped-for benefits of insurance depend on how it is designed and who benefits from it, no effort should be spared to get the details right before policy reforms are put in place.

The authors of the chapters in this book retrofitted evaluations as best they could. It is surprising to us that evaluation had not been built into all of these insurance reforms from the start. How else can anyone know what is working and what needs to be changed? How else can the progress of the reform against its goals be measured? We do not end this effort with a simple call for more research but with a call for more innovations in health financing policy like those covered in this book. But pairing them with a research agenda by building in evaluation at the start is the only way to improve reforms as learning takes place and impacts become clear. We hope this book encourages health finance policy innovation, more international support for it, more learning, and feedback of that learning into constantly improving policies for better health.

Maria-Luisa Escobar
Charles C. Griffin
R. Paul Shaw

Acknowledgments

Each chapter was written by a team whom we challenged to do their best to understand the impact of health insurance reforms using available household data and their knowledge of health policy in the country they were working on. We have been impressed by their resourcefulness in securing data and finding creative ways to address econometric problems and by their willingness to persist in reanalyzing the data and rewriting their chapters as the editors and peer reviewers gave them feedback. Most of all, therefore, we acknowledge the efforts of the chapter authors to produce the fine work that is collected in this volume. Whatever success we have with this volume is due to the contributors' professionalism and commitment.

We would also like to recognize the contributions of the peer reviewers, who worked with us and the chapter authors to provide feedback not just at the end of the process but during each stage of the analytical work. We paired two peer reviewers with each set of authors, with some reviewers working with more than one set of authors. As with the chapter authors, we appreciate their persistence in reading the same manuscript several times; in delving into the data, econometric, and policy issues with the authors; and in participating in long conference calls to help move the project forward. They were an essential resource and gave their time freely, with little more compensation than the hope that they were contributing to our understanding of the potential of insurance as a health policy option for low- and middle-income countries. The peer reviewers were Anil Deolalikar, Philip Musgrove, Menno Pradhan, Jacques van der Gaag, Bill Savedoff, and Adam Wagstaff.

We have a great debt to Dan Kress of the Bill & Melinda Gates Foundation for his willingness to take risks that we could deliver a collection of empirical studies exploring the impacts of health insurance for countries where it is often not considered to be a feasible health policy option. We also thank Dan for challenging us to go beyond the typical economist's focus of financial protection to begin addressing the question of whether health insurance could be considered a viable intervention to improve health status. As a result of his prodding, each chapter attempts to discover proximate measures of outcomes, or outcomes themselves, that are affected by health insurance. While for many readers this effort may raise more questions than it answers, that is a good result, as we hope it will prompt other work. After all, health policy is dominated by physicians and public health specialists, not economists. If they are convinced that insurance is a side issue that has no direct effect on health, then it will remain a side issue. We thank Dan for insisting that we address this question of health impact. We have some tantalizing results, but much more can and should be done in this area. And we thank Margaret Cornelius, also of the Bill & Melinda Gates Foundation, both for pushing this issue along with Dan and for working with us to get everything done.

We would also like to thank the Global Economy and Development Program at the Brookings Institution, including Lael Brainard and her team, for supporting us while we were in residence at Brookings to undertake this work. On the business side, Amanda Armah has been tireless in managing the many contracts required for the work, managing the grant, and keeping us in line. Sun Kordel has backstopped Amanda and always helped us find a way past hurdles. Kyle Peppin worked with us throughout the long period of gestation of the book and helped enormously with administrative arrangements, communicating with the authors, and research. The book would not have been possible without him.

As the original editors, Maria-Luisa Escobar and Charles Griffin would like to thank Paul Shaw for joining our team midway to offer a third perspective and extra help to get the volume out after we returned to other duties at the World Bank. Paul discussed the big picture with us many times, wrote the original versions of the first and last chapters, and provided timely feedback to the authors that helped keep everyone attuned to what we were trying to achieve.

With great respect and thanks, we recognize the contributions of Bruce Ross-Larson and his team at Communications Development Incorporated—Meta de Coquereaumont, Rob Elson, Jack Harlow, Christopher Trott, and Elaine Wilson—who whittled more than 700 pages of manuscript down to something concise enough to be readable and consistently "on theme" despite all the different contributors and countries. They have made a substantial contribution to this endeavor.

Why and How Are We Studying Health Insurance in the Developing World?

Chapter 1

Maria-Luisa Escobar, Charles C. Griffin, and R. Paul Shaw

More than 2 billion people live in developing countries with health systems afflicted by inefficiency, inequitable access, inadequate funding, and poor quality services. These people account for 92% of global annual deaths from communicable diseases, 68% of deaths from noncommunicable conditions, and 80% of deaths from injuries. The World Health Organization (WHO) estimates that more than 150 million of these people suffer financial catastrophe every year, having to make unexpected out-of-pocket expenditures for expensive emergency care (WHO various years).

Within countries, the burden of dysfunctional health systems is disproportionately felt by the poorest households. Their access and use of services, such as immunizations and attended deliveries, tend to be half those of richer households. They have limited recourse to purchase quality services from private providers. Their enrollment in health insurance tends to be marginal. And they are unable to shield themselves from catastrophic health expenditures by drawing on accumulated wealth.

In view of these shortcomings, policymakers in many low- and middle-income countries are debating the virtues of scaling up health insurance to improve health outcomes. Major international conferences have been convened in Berlin (2005) on social health insurance in developing countries and in Paris (2007) on social health protection in developing countries. Regional conferences have followed, as in Africa in 2009. Related to these initiatives, the World Health Assembly passed a policy resolution whereby the WHO would advocate formally mandated social health insurance to mobilize more resources for health in low-income countries, pool risk, provide more equitable access to health care for the poor, and deliver better quality care (WHO 2005a).

All rich countries have adjusted their health finance systems to reduce out-of-pocket expenditures for health, which plunge as per capita income rises across countries (table 1.1). In terms of purchasing power parity (PPP), our preferred measure, per capita gross national income (GNI) is 29 times higher in the richest group than in low-income countries, but health spending per capita is 63 times higher. The share of gross domestic product (GDP) devoted to health more than doubles, the governments' share in the total rises, and the burden on individuals plummets as out-of-pocket spending falls as a proportion of the total. The bottom of table 1.1 shows how much this result reflects the situation in South Asia because of its large share of the total low-income population. The situation is slightly less dire in Africa, but only a bit.

Rich countries achieve these results through general revenue tax financing in support of national health insurance or subsidies for specific groups (such as the poor or the elderly), payroll taxes to support social health insurance, or, most commonly, some combination of both. Rich countries provide prepaid entitlement to health care benefits, reduce vulnerability to the expenses of care at times of illness or injury (financial risk protection), and use copayments and deductibles chiefly to manage demand rather than to raise revenue. They seek to reduce the discontinuity of care so common when people are navigating the system on their own and paying out of pocket at each point of contact. For the most part, richer countries have also separated financing from the provision of care, depend on a mix of public and private providers that are reimbursed through the insurance system, and rely increasingly on primary care providers as gatekeepers to more expensive higher level services. In a nutshell, poor countries want to mimic these successful and desirable behaviors of rich countries sooner rather than later. Mysteriously, donors have historically financed the direct delivery of health services in poorer countries with almost no attention paid to helping them build sustainable financial and purchasing institutions that could emulate some of the core successes of richer countries.

Whatever policymakers and donors want to do or think they should do to emulate successful health financing reforms, there are knowledge gaps that create enormous risks of failure for any reformer. This book attempts to begin filling some of them, but much more work remains.

The widest knowledge gap concerns the impact of health insurance on health status. Do people with health insurance in low- and middle-income countries, or

TABLE 1.1

Income and health finance indicators for select country groupings, 2007

Country group	Gross national income per capita (US$)	Per capita health expenditure (US$)	Gross national income per capita (PPP)	Per capita health expenditure (PPP)	Total health expenditure in GDP (%)	Public share of total health expenditures (%)	Out-of-pocket share of total health expenditures (%)
Low income	461	27	1,284	69	5	42	48
Lower middle income	1,752	81	4,234	182	4	42	53
Upper middle income	6,705	488	11,534	753	6	55	31
High-income OECD	39,540	4,618	37,328	4,327	11	61	14
East Asia and Pacific	2,190	96	4,946	208	4	46	48
Europe and Central Asia	6,013	396	11,123	647	6	66	29
Latin America	5,888	475	9,802	715	7	49	35
Middle East and North Africa	2,795	151	7,350	364	6	51	46
South Asia	879	26	2,535	98	4	27	66
Sub-Saharan Africa	966	69	1,858	124	6	41	35

Source: World Bank 2010.

even rich countries, have better health status indicators than those without? Evidence from rich countries suggests yes (box 1.1). But what about low- and middle-income countries? An affirmative on this issue would surely seem essential to consider health insurance as a health policy intervention rather than simply as a financial protection intervention. The vast array of people involved in health care because they want to improve health—nutrition advocates, family planning advocates, tuberculosis and AIDS activists, vaccine supporters, Millennium Development Goal supporters, health systems improvers—would have to see health insurance as an intervention that would be more effective in improving health outcomes than other directly focused options. Obviously, carrying a health insurance card by itself does not make one healthier, but if that card increases the use of appropriate services, makes a person more likely to access new proven technologies, creates incentives for providers to deliver the right services, and equalizes use among the rich and the poor, most analysts would be satisfied that it can have a powerful impact on improving health. They then can devote themselves to making sure the services work.

A second knowledge gap concerns the impact of health insurance on out-of-pocket expenditures for health. Do people with health insurance have lower out-of-pocket spending than those who do not, especially when they are struck by health emergencies? Do the uninsured poor pay a higher proportion of their income for health care than the rich? When out-of-pocket spending is the principal means of securing health care, emergencies result in people borrowing, selling assets, not getting needed care, and engaging in other coping mechanisms. A high proportion of out-of-pocket spending also leads to poorer households spending more of their income on health care than richer households do, just as they spend a higher proportion on other necessities, like food and shelter. Health insurance should address this problem, yet the empirical evidence is slight in our focus countries. The more one explores this issue, the more it becomes apparent that success depends on the design of the program and who is covered; health insurance is not a homogeneous product. A yes on reducing out-of-pocket spending would be essential to argue that health insurance can help prevent people from sliding into health-related poverty.

We can stop with those two questions. Both must be positive to even consider health insurance as a sensible health policy tool in low- and middle-income countries. There are many other practical questions of implementation, but they reside in the realm of sufficiency, not necessity, for considering insurance as a health policy option rather than just a financial protection option.

Objectives of this study and how it was conducted

This study aims to contribute to current policy debates on scaling up health insurance in low- and middle-income countries by shedding light on these two issues: its impact on measures of health status and reducing out-of-pocket spending. Four objectives guide the research and analysis.

Objective 1. Rigorously review and synthesize published and unpublished studies to determine what we know about the impact of health insurance on access and use of health services, the impacts on financial risk protection, and the methodological and data issues in ascertaining causality.

Objective 2. Undertake new country case studies to assess the impact of health insurance on access and use of health services as well as financial risk protection using the latest data sources and statistical methodologies.

BOX 1.1
Impact of health insurance on health-related outcomes in rich countries

A committee sponsored by the Institute of Medicine of the National Academies in Washington, DC, reviewed 130 research studies that consider the impact of health insurance on health-related outcomes for adults ages 18–64 (IOM 2004, updated in IOM 2009). Findings suggest that uninsured adults are less than half as likely as those insured to receive needed care for a serious medical condition. Uninsured women and their newborns receive less prenatal care and are more likely to have poor outcomes during pregnancy and delivery, including maternal complications, infant death, and low birthweight. In addition, the uninsured more often:

- Lack regular access to medications to manage conditions, such as hypertension and HIV.
- Do not receive care recommended for chronic diseases, such as timely eye and food exams to prevent blindness and amputations in people with diabetes.
- Go without cancer screening tests, which delays diagnosis and leads to premature death.

- Receive fewer diagnostic and treatment services after a traumatic injury or a heart attack, causing an increased risk of death even when in the hospital.

Findings specific to children reveal the uninsured are:

- Less likely to get routine well-child care.
- More likely to receive no care or delayed care, thus placing them at greater risk of being hospitalized for conditions such as asthma that could have been treated on an outpatient basis.
- Using medical and dental services less frequently than insured children.

However, as Gruber (2009) observes, most of these studies simply document a correlation between no health insurance and poor health. Almost none attempted to control for the endogeneity of health insurance coverage with respect to health status. He cites only a handful of U.S. studies that have adequately controlled for endogeneity, but they too show strong impacts of health insurance coverage on health.

Objective 3. Cast more light on the inclusion of the poorest quintile of the population in health insurance in low- and middle-income countries, as well as the benefits they experience compared with the uninsured poor.

Objective 4. Identify the challenges, risks, and opportunities of undertaking retrospective evaluation of health insurance in developing countries using household data.

Shedding light on these objectives requires more than applying good econometrics. Researchers require a fundamental understanding of how health systems work to know what questions to ask and what models to use to find answers. This requires familiarity with design elements that might affect the measured impacts of health insurance on health outcomes (such as enrollment criteria, benefits entitlements, and copayments). Beyond this, however, the study does not assess whether the organizational design of health insurance in different countries is the most efficient or most cost-effective arrangement in satisfying clients, providing quality care, paying providers, or being financially sustainable over the long term. These issues, while important, are complex and demanding enough to require another volume. In short, this study focuses on impacts of health insurance schemes as presently designed and implemented, not what such schemes might accomplish if implemented differently.

Reading this book may raise more questions than it answers, which is good, as we want to present the evidence available today on the topic. We began by identifying low- and middle-income countries that had experienced insurance reforms of interest. We narrowed the list according to whether data existed that could be used to measure what happened at the household level in response to these insurance reforms. We sought researchers who knew the country well and were qualified to do the work. We paired them with advisers and peer reviewers who would commit to read and advise as drafts of the chapters took shape. We tried to keep all of the individual projects advancing along the same timeline and hoped that the ensuing chaos would result in a good collection of work. We did not have the luxury of perfection in any part of this process.

There are many technical impediments to showing an impact of health insurance on anything. These are discussed in the literature review in chapter 2. For some of the chapters readers may conclude that the evidence provided does not get far past associations; in other chapters the evidence may look conclusive that causation has been established. The consistent theme that there is an impact—despite the variety of situations, data, methods, and policies examined—becomes inescapable after reading all the chapters.

Country case selection

Four considerations guided our selection of country case studies. First, we sought countries with sufficiently diverse backgrounds to shed light on the extent findings could be generalized across different contexts. Second, to gain insight into impacts of scaling up health insurance for relatively disadvantaged or poor households, we sought countries with a pro-poor orientation in the design and implementation of health insurance. Third, we sought countries with sufficiently well developed surveys or data systems that would facilitate rigorous statistical analysis of impacts of health insurance on measures of health status and financial risk. Fourth, we sought researchers with a solid knowledge of health insurance who were capable of performing complex statistical modeling to tease out causal impacts. Table 1.2 provides summary data on the seven countries in this volume. We have two giant countries in the mix, China and Indonesia; however, except for Namibia and Costa Rica, all are sizeable. The data used in the chapters are nationally representative except in Namibia, Ghana, and China. There are some important differences across countries in the state of health, income, and health spending, but perhaps the widest range lies in out-of-pocket spending, ranging from 3%–8% of total health spending in Namibia and Colombia to over 50% in China. It is low in Namibia because of good penetration of private insurance; it is low in Colombia because of high government spending, primarily through its insurance system.

Namibia. The Namibian health insurance industry is better developed than that of most Sub-Saharan African countries. It is organized primarily into nonprofit

TABLE 1.2
Indicators for the country cases, 2007

Indicators	Namibia	Ghana	Costa Rica	Peru	Indonesia	China	Colombia
Population (millions)	2.1	22.9	4.4	28.5	224.7	1,317.9	44.4
Life expectancy (years)	60	56	79	73	70	73	73
Infant mortality rate (per 1,000 live births)	32	53	10	23	32	19	17
GNI per capita (US$)	4,110	590	5,530	3,340	1,520	2,410	4,070
GNI per capita (PPP)	6,080	1,330	10,530	7,060	3,280	5,430	8,200
Health expenditures per capita (US$)	319	54	488	160	42	108	284
Health expenditures per capita (PPP US$)	467	113	878	327	81	233	516
Health expenditures in GDP (%)	8	8	8	4	2	4	6
Public share of health spending (%)	42	52	73	58	55	45	84
Out-of-pocket in total health expenditures (%)	3	38	23	32	30	51	8
Population enrolled in health insurance (%)	<30	61	88	42	36	80-90	90

Source: World Bank 2010. Data on population enrolled in health insurance are based on information from the chapters in this book.

medical aid funds—about one-third mandatory social health insurance funds and about two-thirds voluntary, private plans. Many of the funds are closed, with membership limited to employees in a particular firm or industry or to government civil servants. This has resulted in large disparities in enrollment across socioeconomic categories; only 5% of individuals in the poorest quintile are enrolled, compared with 70% of individuals in the richest quintile. While some private insurance plans aim to broaden the insured population through low cost plans, the challenge is huge because of the country's high prevalence of HIV/AIDS, estimated at 20% for people ages 15–49, concentrated largely among the poor (Feeley, Preker, and Ly 2007).

The case study assesses differences in the consequences of health shocks between the insured and uninsured—stemming from death, hospitalization, weight loss, and HIV/AIDS—specific to households in different income quintiles. The impact of health insurance has been assessed using multiple regression analysis, using 2006 survey data that include both socioeconomic and biomedical information.

Ghana. In 2003 the government passed the National Health Insurance Act, with a vision of insuring 40% of the population by 2010 and 60% by 2015. About 60% of the population was enrolled by 2008, exceeding expectations, with the success attributable to the generous benefit package and prior familiarity with enrolling households in district level mutual health organizations. Other African countries are closely watching Ghana's attempt to scale up health insurance, given the far reaching implications for raising funds, purchasing, and providing care to a largely poor population.

The case study applies a pre-post evaluation design in two districts, one classified as deprived, the other as less deprived. The impact of the health insurance reform is assessed using pre-post bivariate comparisons of key indicators, multivariate regression analysis, and a tentative application of propensity score matching analysis (tentative because of the small sample sizes), using data from a baseline household survey in 2004 and an endline survey in 2007.

Costa Rica. This country has become a benchmark of health insurance attaining wide coverage with no copayments, based on a direct delivery model. Social health insurance was introduced in 1950, and the Universal Coverage Act passed in 1961. Since then, health insurance coverage grew from about 18% in 1961 to 45% in 1971, 60% in 1975, and a high of 92% in 1990. In 2009 about 88% were covered, although the surveys used by the authors in this book put coverage closer to 81% in 2006.

The case study looks at the 19% of the population without health insurance in the 2006 surveys to establish differences in their health status and other characteristics and to investigate whether their health-seeking behavior and results are different. The impact of health insurance on health and related behaviors has been assessed using instrumental variables and data from the 2006 National Health Survey; expenditure results are based on the 2004 Income and Expenditure Survey; and a database of hospital discharges from 2006 provides a unique perspective on how the insured and uninsured use the system differently when they are sick.

Why study a country where everyone is either insured or, if they are not, have equal access to hospital care if they need it? One would not expect to see differences in financial protection in such a system for sure, but because we are interested also in health outcomes, it might be a unique opportunity to see whether not being covered by the formal insurance program has any impact even with Costa Rica's equal access provision.

Peru. With about 35% of the population covered by employer-mandated social security and other forms of health insurance, the government consolidated and began scaling up two pro-poor schemes initiated in 2001: one targeting children in public schools, the other targeting maternal and child health. Enrollees in the new consolidated program doubled from 3.6 million in 2001 to 7.3 million in 2007.

The case study assesses the impact of this publicly subsidized health insurance program that explicitly targets the poor. The impact of health insurance has been assessed with several models, using data from two household surveys: the Demographic and Health Surveys (DHS) for 2000 and 2004 (heavy on health information but light on economic data) and a nationally representative panel survey from 2004 to 2006 (with substantial economic data but limited health data).

Indonesia. With about 36% of the country's population covered by social security schemes as well as a public health insurance scheme, the government greatly increased public spending on health from about $1 billion in 2001 to $4 billion by 2007. Much of this additional spending was due to the expansion of the Askeskin health insurance program, which targets the poor.

Our case study examines changes in health status associated with movements in and out of health insurance, to shed light on how health insurance might affect health status and financial risk protection where only formal sector insurance coverage exists. The impact of health insurance has been assessed with individual fixed effect models, using panel data from longitudinal surveys in 1991, 1997, and 2000. The panel data used in this analysis provide a unique contribution even though the most recent installment of the survey was not yet available to the researchers, which would have allowed them to include the Askeskin reform in the analysis.

China. In 2002 the government announced a new national policy for rural health care, the New Cooperative Medical Scheme (NCMS), which aimed to recapture successes of China's past health policies. In the late 1970s China's Cooperative Medical System, a communal-based approach, covered 90% of China's rural population. But it collapsed after the government introduced the Household Responsibility System in 1979, and communes disappeared as a result. The revised NCMS is a voluntary scheme that gives priority to covering catastrophic health expenditures and subsidizes premiums. By the end of 2008 it was credited with reaching more than 90% of the rural population.

The case study reports on a social experiment of a community-based prepayment scheme—Rural Mutual Health Care—undertaken as an implementation of the NCMS in several counties. Operating from 2002 to 2007, the experiment aimed to contribute to knowledge on the impacts of insurance, tailored to conditions in the poorest regions of China. The impact of health insurance has been assessed using differences-in-differences statistical methods and propensity score matching, using a pre-post treatment-control study design in two of China's rural provinces. A baseline longitudinal survey was conducted, along with two more panels following the same individuals during implementation of the experiment.

Colombia. A commitment by the government in 1993 to reorganize its dual health care system (a Ministry of Health direct delivery system alongside a social security direct delivery system), to expand coverage of the population by insurance, and to offer more choice to citizens on both insurer and provider offerings, has increased coverage from 24% in 1993 to 90% in 2007. Health insurance is financed through a contributory regime by employees in the formal sector and a subsidized regime in the informal sector. A major accomplishment of government efforts to scale up health insurance is an eightfold growth of enrollment among the poorest quintiles.

The case study uses the gradual implementation and still incomplete coverage of the subsidized regime to identify differences in health outcomes between those with health insurance and those without. The impact of health insurance has been assessed with a variety of semiparametric methods—including propensity score matching, double difference, and matched double difference—and instrumental variable analysis, using data from various Colombian DHS (1995, 2000, and 2005) as well as Living Standard Measurement Survey data for 2003 and administrative data.

. . . and to the book

While there is considerably more interest in insurance as a financing option for health care even in poor countries, progress has been greatly hampered by a lack of knowledge of what the future would look like after such a reform. The first questions that arise from policymakers and reformers are:

- What country has done something like this that faces our constraints?
- What has been the impact?
- How did they implement it?
- What would they do differently in hindsight?

This book cannot explain much about how the reforms covered were implemented (the third question); that requires a different type of case study. But it does provide considerable information on the first two questions. On the fourth, each of the chapters has suggestions for what the authors think the authorities should have done in hindsight. Whether the suggestions will be taken up is another step entirely.

One thing that is essential to keep in mind in reading this book is that in no case is a perfect laboratory experiment being described. In fact, there is no chance of one being developed to assess the impact of insurance. Why? Because you can never take away from people all the other options they face. The most important other option in this book is the availability, in all cases, of free or low cost government-provided care in its own facilities. In Namibia the government system is reputed to function well and to be well financed. Yet even with this option we see substantial differences between the insured and uninsured. In Colombia, in comparisons of the insured poor against the uninsured poor, it is not that the uninsured poor have no services available because they can use the public system still in place. In Peru the insurance analyzed not only sits next to the subsidized public system, the insured are required to use the public system. So, as with all such analysis in low- and middle-income countries, there is always the unobserved impact of a free or low cost public system option (however well or poorly it functions) that confounds the results, more than likely by attenuating the impacts of insurance. For countries considering a complete switch from the supply side funding of free public services to demand side funding under insurance, we can say only that the evidence in this book is just a starting point.

The good news for reformers is that this book demonstrates—we think—that to know something about the impact of insurance, clever use of available data can obtain reasonably robust results. Moreover, to introduce health insurance as a health policy reform, it is not necessary to wait for results of randomized or social experiments. By now, we know that insurance can improve access and use of services and can protect from the risk of financial loss. We see this in the literature review and in all the cases in this book. How much and for whom depend on the specifics of the design of the insurance scheme. Despite the statistical challenges researchers face, countries can reasonably expect that by introducing a pro-poor insurance scheme they can obtain improved results for access and use of services and for financial protection. The obvious alternative is to invest in providing free services directly, but we see in Namibia, Costa Rica, Peru, and Colombia that insurance or an insurance-like alternative may have a greater impact.

Does use of more health services and improved financial protection lead to better health? The cases in this book demonstrate the difficulty in establishing that link with the available data and measures of health outcomes; even so, there are many tantalizing clues that should encourage more effort in this area. What is needed are explicit goals for health outcomes embodied in an insurance system, disaggregated measures of health outcomes that insurance (and alternatives to it) can affect, and data suitable for measuring impacts without bias. There is much more to be done on this topic and, as well, on the impact of insurance on providers. In this book for the most part we focus on the demand, or patient, side of the equation.

Queries about each chapter should be directed to the corresponding authors, whose email addresses are listed in the Editors and Authors section after chapter 10.

References

Feeley, F., A. S. Preker, and C. Ly. 2007. "On a Path to Social Health Insurance? A Look at Selected Anglophone African Countries." World Bank, Washington, DC.

Gruber, J. 2009. "Covering the Uninsured in the U.S." *Journal of Economic Literature* 46 (3): 571–606.

IOM (Institute of Medicine). 2004. *Insuring America's Health: Principles and Recommendations.* Washington, DC: National Academies Press.

———. 2009. *America's Uninsured Crisis: Consequences for Health and Health Care.* Washington, DC: National Academies Press.

WHO (World Health Organization). Various years. *World Health Report.* Geneva: World Health Organization.

World Bank. 2010. *World Development Indicators 2010.* Washington, DC: World Bank.

A Review of the Evidence

Ursula Giedion and Beatriz Yadira Díaz

Chapter 2

We used a detailed protocol to evaluate the robustness of the available evidence on the impact of health insurance in low- and middle-income countries—on access, use, financial protection, and health status (box 2.1). Of 49 quantitative studies, about half provide reasonably robust evidence. They indicate that health insurance improves access and use, seems to improve financial protection in most cases, but has no conclusive impact on health status. The third result may be related to the difficulties of establishing a causal link between health insurance and currently available information on health status.

The positive effect of health insurance on medical care use has been widely demonstrated and generally accepted. Hadley (2003), in his review of research published in the past 25 years on health insurance in the developed world, concludes that there is a compelling case for the positive correlation between having health insurance and using more medical care. Little evidence exists, however, on the impact of health insurance in the developing world, and only a few studies have tried to summarize what is available either in some regions or for specific types of health insurance.

Whether health insurance is a recommendable strategy to improve access to health care in low- and middle-income countries is hotly debated but insufficiently documented. For example, a resolution adopted at the 2005 World Health Assembly invited member states to ensure that their health financing systems include a method for

---

BOX 2.1
The key analytical question

The purpose of health insurance is three-fold: increase access and use by making health services more affordable, improve health status through increased access and use, and mitigate the financial conse-quences of ill health by distributing the costs of health care across all members of a risk pool. The key analytical question in this chapter is: What does the literature say about the impact of health insurance on access and use of health care, on health status, and on financial protection?

Evaluating the impact of health insur-ance is, methodologically, a challeng-ing endeavor. It requires econometric methods to tackle issues such as poten-tial selection bias and the bidirectional relationship between health insurance and health status. It also requires quality data on households and providers to measure outcomes of interest, to correct for differ-ences among the insured and uninsured, and to account for supply constraints—and, above all, profound knowledge of the

specific health insurance scheme being evaluated. Often one or more of these items are missing, and analysts must cope as best they can.

Some policy reforms aim to use health insurance to change supplier and pro-vider behavior as well as to create a more elastic form of financing than govern-ment tax revenue can provide. However, this review focuses on a circumscribed number of performance dimensions and does not include the literature evaluating other consequences of health insurance, such as changes in the organization of health systems or the overall efficiency of health insurance as compared with other financing mechanisms. It is limited to studies that attempt to establish a causal relationship between health insurance and health-related outcome indicators. It thus excludes studies that present descriptive statistics only or that resort to qualitative analysis when evaluating health insurance in low-income countries.

---

prepaying financial contributions for health care. But a recent joint nongov-ernmental organization briefing paper laments the lack of evidence on whether health insurance can really work in low-income countries and concludes that health insurance "so far has been unable to sufficiently fill financing gaps in health systems and improve access to quality health care for the poor" (Oxfam and others 2008).

What do we really know about the impact of health insurance in low- and middle-income countries? This chapter synthesizes the best available evidence regarding the impact of health insurance in low- and middle-income countries on access, use, financial protection, and health status. It emphasizes the results of the 10 studies that provide the most robust evidence and belong to the top quartile score after applying our quality assessment tool.[1] We extend this analysis to the second quartile whenever the evidence is especially scarce (box 2.2).

BOX 2.2
Robustness of the evidence base

The robustness of the evidence was determined on the basis of five general criteria: quality of the study design (selection of the treatment and control groups), strength of the impact evaluation methodology (mostly related to the way the potential selection bias problem was dealt with), the rigor with which each method was applied, and the quality of the discussion related to the findings of each study.

Five key issues emerge from the analysis of the robustness of the literature. First is dealing with the nonrandom variation in health insurance status (endogeneity). Second is considering the heterogeneity in impact across different population groups and insurance schemes. Third is exploring the possibility of spillover effects of health insurance. Fourth is undertaking the relevance of timing when evaluating the impact of health insurance. Fifth is being clear in

the statement of research goals, methods, and potential limitations.

The quality evaluation protocol assigns a maximum score of 100 points according to the five criteria. The scores obtained by our evidence base varied between a minimum of 11 points (least robust study) to a maximum of 83 points (most robust study).

Two-thirds of the studies reviewed scored 45 points or lower, a result that argues for continuing to support the production of quality research on the impact of health insurance in developing countries (box table 1). Note, however, that a small (but growing) number of studies provide higher quality evidence of impact. The 10 studies in the highest quartile explicitly address endogeneity and clearly describe research goals, methods, results, and the limitations of their evaluations. Several take into account the potential heterogeneity of impact across different groups and insurance schemes.

BOX TABLE 1
Distribution of the literature by score quartile

Score quartile	Score	Total	Access and use	Financial protection	Health status
Lowest	11–44	21	16	11	3
Lower middle	45–63	10	9	4	0
Upper middle	64–68	10	7	4	2
Upper	69+	10	7	3	7
Total		51	39	22	12

Source: Authors.

The top 10 studies provide the best available evidence on the impact of health insurance in low- and middle-income countries (box table 2). Unfortunately, the number of countries covered by the best

studies (China, Colombia, Costa Rica, Taiwan, and a cross-country study) is limited; all the more reason to widen and deepen the evidence base.

(continued)

BOX 2.2 (continued)
Robustness of the evidence base

BOX TABLE 2
The most robust evidence of the impact of health insurance

Country	Author	Year	Title	Access and use	Financial protection	Health status
China	Wagstaff and Yu	2007	Do Health Sector Reforms Have Their Intended Impacts? The World Bank's Health VIII Project in Gansu Province, China.	✓	✓	✓
	Wagstaff and others	2007	Extending Health Insurance to the Rural Population: An Impact Evaluation of China's New Cooperative Medical Scheme (NCMS)	✓	✓	
	Yip, Wang, and Hsiao	2008	The Impact of Rural Mutual Health Care on Access to Care: Evaluation of a Social Experiment in Rural China	✓		
	Wang and others	2008	The Impact of Rural Mutual Health Care on Health Status: Evaluation of a Social Experiment in Rural China			✓
Colombia	Trujillo, Portillo, and Vernon	2005	The Impact of Subsidized Health Insurance for the Poor: Evaluating the Colombian Experience Using Propensity Score Matching	✓		
	Giedion, Diaz, and Alfonso	2007	The Impact of Subsidized Health Insurance on Access, Utilization and Health Status: The Case of Colombia	✓		✓
Costa Rica	Dow and Schmeer	2003	Health Insurance and Child Mortality in Costa Rica			✓
	Dow, González, and Rosero-Bixby	2003	Aggregation and Insurance-Mortality Estimation			✓
Cross-country	Wagstaff and Moreno-Serna	2007	Europe and Central Asia's Great Post-Communist Social Health Insurance Experiment: Impacts on Health Sector and Labor Market Outcomes	✓	✓	✓
Taiwan	Chen, Yip, Chang, Lin, Lee, Chiu, and Lin	2007	The Effects of Taiwan's National Health Insurance on Access and Health Status of the Elderly	✓		✓
Total				7	3	7

Note: Studies are first ordered alphabetically by country, and then by year of publication.
Source: Authors.

Impact of health insurance on access and use

Overall impact

Besides providing financial protection from the economic consequences of illness, health insurance is meant to improve access (Nyman 1999). Seven of the ten studies in the top quartile evaluate the link between health insurance and access and use; nine find a positive and significant impact of health insurance on access and use. Similar results are also found when we extend our analysis to the full evidence base. A majority of the studies (39 of 51) analyze the impact of health insurance on access and use, and 28 find evidence indicating that health insurance increases access to and use of health services. This finding seems consistent with the results of previous reviews in the developed world (see, for example, Buchmueller and Kronick 2005 and Hadley 2003 for a summary of this evidence). And it seems to confirm what insurance theory predicts: health insurance reduces the price of health care and thereby promotes access and use.

The one study in the top quartile that does not present conclusive evidence on the impact of health insurance on access and use compares 28 post-communist countries in Eastern Europe and Central Asia, some of which have maintained tax-financed systems and some of which have switched to a social health insurance scheme (Wagstaff and Moreno-Serra 2007). It finds that social health insurance has had a small positive impact on some use variables but not on others. One might wonder, however, whether the heterogeneity in the social health insurance schemes (in benefits packages, institutional implementation, and so on) evaluated allows for a meaningful cross-country comparison (even after controlling for observable differences such as variations in provider payment mechanisms). In this context several studies find that an aggregate measure of health insurance may cloud the impact of health insurance by not taking into account the heterogeneity in impact across different health insurance schemes.[2]

Distributional impact of insurance on access and use

The 10 studies in the top quartile suggest that the impact of health insurance varies across populations but that these differences vary substantially across countries and settings. Some studies find that it is precisely the most vulnerable (low income and rural) population groups who benefit most (Chen 2007; Trujillo, Portillo, and Vernon 2005; Giedion, Díaz, and Alfonso 2007). Others find that only the better off are increasing access and use as a result of health insurance (Wagstaff and others 2007 on China). Still others find that the middle-income population is benefiting least (Yip, Wang, and Hsiao 2008). In some instances the impact on use across population groups varies over time and even across research and health insurance settings in the same country. This variability in results almost certainly stems from unaccounted for design elements of the programs.

For example, Wagstaff and others (2007) find little impact from China's New Cooperative Medical Scheme (NCMS) on access and use among the poor. They explain this situation by looking at the specificities of NCMS: "Given high coinsurance rates, it is perhaps not surprising that there has been no significant increase in utilization among the poorest quintile." Yip, Wang, and Hsiao (2008) present a more nuanced picture as they look at considerable heterogeneity in benefit packages, coinsurance rates, deductibles, and ceilings across counties and coverage modes. They find that one modality of NCMS combining an individual savings account for outpatient care with coverage for catastrophic care and high deductibles and ceilings has little impact on access and use. But another modality providing first dollar coverage with no deductibles but with ceilings does have an important impact on access and use, especially among the poorest and highest income groups.

The discussion and examples highlight the importance of incorporating the possible heterogeneity of health insurance schemes and the impact across different population groups into the study design and data collection. Typically household data used to study insurance programs are collected for other purposes and are difficult to use to understand the impact of insurance program design elements.

Other issues emerging from the literature

One interesting question put forward by several authors is related to the limits of the concept of use when evaluating the impact of health insurance: if health insurance is found to increase use is this necessarily good? As Nyman (1999) indicates: "The value of insurance for coverage of unaffordable care is derived from the value of the medical care that insurance makes accessible." In this perspective and given the substantial access problems in most low- and middle-income countries, observing improved access and use through health insurance will therefore generally be considered a welfare gain.

What if health insurance encourages the overuse of health services? Wagstaff and others (2007) indicate, "The aim of health insurance is to reduce risk exposure and to make necessary health care affordable . . . Theory suggests that the welfare gains in terms of access must be weighed against the potential welfare loss from demand-side and supply-side moral hazard. Further research is required to investigate the issue of whether the extra utilization [obtained through health insurance] is medically necessary or not." In our view, it can be safely assumed that in most low-income countries and many middle-income countries. The population and especially the most vulnerable ones tend to experience severe access problems and thereby underuse rather than waste and overuse health services, the literature does not sufficiently discuss this tradeoff between improved access of necessary services and the potential moral hazard issues.

Much research goes beyond simply stating whether health insurance has a positive impact on use of health services to ask more interesting questions that should be further explored. For which services is an increase found and why? Does use of preventive and curative health services increase (Waters 1999)? Does insurance induce primarily increases in low cost-effective services or, to the contrary, does it increase high cost-effective services (Dow, González, and Rosero-Bix 2003)? What do results finding a differential impact across different services say about the limits of the health benefits provided under the insurance scheme (Smith and Sulzbach 2008)? Is an increase in use accompanied by a substitution for inexpensive services by more expensive insurance-covered services (or vice versa) or by a shift from informal and self-medication to formal care (Hidayat and others 2004)? As the evidence on each of these questions is still scarce, no generalizations are possible. Further exploration of these issues would be extremely useful.

Impact of health insurance on financial protection

General impact

Providing financial protection against the economic consequences of illness lies at the heart of the adoption of health insurance. As Nyman (1999) states: "Why do people purchase health insurance? Many economists would answer that it permits purchasers to avoid risk of financial loss." It comes then as no surprise that almost half the studies included in our evidence base (22 of 51) evaluate the impact of health insurance on financial protection. However, only two in the top quartile provide evidence on the impact of health insurance on financial protection. Both evaluate China's cooperative medical schemes but at different times and in different parts of the country. Wagstaff and Yu (2007) evaluate the impact of the World Bank Health VIII project (containing an insurance component) in the Gansu province using data from 2000 (pre-program) and 2004 (post-program). They find that the project had reduced both out-of-pocket payments and the incidence of catastrophic payments, especially among the poorest. By contrast, Wagstaff and others (2007)—evaluating the impact of the NCMS in 12 of China's 30 provinces and using data from 2003 (pre-intervention) and 2005 (post-intervention)—find that it has had no statistically significant effect on average out-of-pocket spending by households, overall or on any specific type of care per contact, for either outpatient or inpatient care. Indeed, they find a hint that it may have increased the cost per inpatient episode. However, across China's provinces and counties a lot of variation exists in how the NCMS is being implemented, and the authors recognize that this heterogeneity may constitute one important limitation of their study. In contrast, Yip, Wang, and Hsiao (2008) reach contrary conclusions—indicating that a NCMS modality providing first dollar coverage has indeed reduced out-of-pocket payments and the incidence of catastrophic payments (Hsiao and Yip 2008).

As the examples illustrate once again, health insurance is not a homogeneous concept, and in-depth familiarity with the specifics of the health insurance scheme being evaluated is key to interpreting results. Avoiding generalizations across countries and even across settings in the same country seems advisable unless details of the plans can be controlled for, which is difficult if not impossible using existing data and research techniques.

Because few studies in the top quartile evaluate the impact of health insurance on financial protection, we extend our analysis to the second quartile. All studies in the second quartile find that health insurance has reduced out-of-pocket spending and the incidence of catastrophic payments. This positive evidence on the impact of health insurance on financial protection still holds when considering all studies in the evidence base and despite the fact that studies use many different indicators to measure financial protection and different model specifications to evaluate them.[3]

Distributional impact

Two studies in the top quartile (Wagstaff and Yu 2007; Wagstaff and others 2007) confirm that the impact of health insurance varies across income groups. The study evaluating the World Bank Health VIII project in Gansu province finds that health insurance seems to have had a greater impact in reducing out-of-pocket payments among the poorest. The results for China's NCMS are more complicated. It seems to have increased average out-of-pocket spending among the poorest decile but to have reduced the incidence of catastrophic spending among this group. By contrast, the NCMS appears to have increased the incidence of catastrophic spending among deciles 3–10, leaving average spending unaffected overall.

In the poorest decile no impacts on outpatient use are evident; impacts are evident only in deciles 2–10. The study also finds no impacts on inpatient use for the poorest decile; statistically significant positive impacts are found only in deciles 3–10. NCMS appears, in other words, to have increased average spending per episode among the poorest (as use has not changed) but reduced the incidence of catastrophic payments. This result is ascribed mainly to the limited extent of benefits, high copayments, and supply side incentives. Among the better off (deciles 2–10), the increase in use and the cost of care per episode seems to have offset the mitigating impact of insurance on the price of each service. As this example indicates, evaluating the impact of health insurance on out-of-pocket payments and the incidence of catastrophic payments is challenging because it is the result of sequential decisions (whether to use care, what type of care to consume, how much care, and finally the price to pay for care based on the former sequence). The positive impact of health insurance on use may, for example, offset the reduction in price per health service obtained—or health insurance may involve a substitution from informal health services to costlier formal health services.

Does health insurance necessarily reduce out-of-pocket and catastrophic payments?

Clearly not, as the distributional impacts illustrate. Interestingly, several additional studies in our evidence base (though not in the top quartile) seem to reach similar conclusions. Ekman (2007b) evaluates the impact of different health insurance schemes in Zambia[4] not only on out-of-pocket expenditure but also on the broader concept of health care–related out-of-pocket expenditure (out-of-pocket spending on transportation, food, and other costs). Being exempted from paying for care and having access to private or employment-based health insurance significantly reduces the risk of incurring catastrophic out-of-pocket expenditure. When other costs related to health care seeking are included (food and transportation, for example), the probability of suffering from the broader concept of catastrophic health care–related expenditure actually increases. The author puts forward two main reasons for this counterintuitive result. First, the sickest people self-select into the prepayment scheme and their out-of-pocket payments may have been even higher had they not been insured. (Because of data limitations the author cannot control for this unobserved heterogeneity.) Second, and more important, the prepayment scheme facilitates access, but once inside the health system prepayments may induce the consumption of more costly health services. Likewise, Trivedi (2002) finds some evidence that Vietnam's voluntary health insurance scheme increased out-of-pocket expenditures, even though the effect was no longer significant when commune-fixed effects were included in the regression.

The findings are a clear invitation to further explore how health insurance changes health care–seeking behavior in quality, quantity, type, and composition when evaluating the impact of a health insurance scheme on out-of-pocket and catastrophic payments.

Other issues

Only one study from the evidence base (Wagstaff and Pradhan 2005) goes beyond evaluating whether health insurance reduces out-of-pocket or catastrophic payments and tries to understand whether health insurance helps reduce the impact of illness on household consumption. Much more research of this type should be undertaken because it helps us understand whether health insurance can really mitigate the economic consequences of illness at the household level rather than just indicate whether out-of-pocket spending rises or falls—or whether the level might be catastrophic.

Impact of health insurance on health status

Health insurance improves health to the extent that it improves access to health services that have a positive impact on health status. Even though the evidence is still scarce, the interest from top researchers in documenting this causal link in developing countries has grown. Only about a fifth of the studies in the evidence base (12) evaluate the impact of health insurance on health status, but most of them (9) are in the top two quartiles (7 in the top, 2 in the second).

The analysis here is based on results from the nine studies in the first two quartiles. Several find no convincing evidence of an impact of health insurance on the health status measures available. The two studies of Costa Rica's social insurance scheme find only a small effect of social health insurance on child and infant mortality (Dow, Gonzalez, and Rosero-Bixby 2003; Dow and Schmeer 2003). Similarly, Giedion, Díaz, and Alfonso (2007), using data from standard Demographic and Health Surveys, find that although the Colombian subsidized health insurance scheme has greatly improved use of curative and preventive services by the poor, no convincing evidence emerges of an impact on child mortality, low birthweight, or self-perceived health status.

Chen and others (2007) use longitudinal data and a difference-in-difference methodology to show that, although Taiwan's National Health Insurance greatly increased the use of both outpatient and inpatient services, the increase did not reduce mortality or lead to better self-perceived general health status for the Taiwanese elderly. They conclude that measures more sensitive than mortality and self-perceived general health may be necessary to discern the impact of health insurance on health status. This could indeed be the case especially given that they find that health insurance increases the use of health services, which may increase awareness of health problems and thereby negatively impact self-perceived health status. Likewise, and as indicated by Giedion, Díaz, and Alfonso (2007), the mortality rate may be too blunt a measure of health to capture improvements in health status brought about by health services under the Taiwanese insurance scheme. Wagstaff and Yu's (2007) evaluation of the World Bank Health VIII project in China finds mixed evidence of an impact. While the evidence points to the project's reducing sick days, the evidence on chronic illness and self-perceived health status is not conclusive. And it is difficult to attribute any of these changes to health insurance alone since this project had several supply side interventions combined with the expansion of health insurance on the demand side.

Wagstaff and Moreno-Serra (2007) evaluate the impact of social health insurance versus a general tax-financed system in formerly communist countries in Eastern Europe and Central Asia on an extensive list of health outcomes. They find that, once they control for any concurrent differences in provider payment systems, social health insurance does not lead to better health outcomes.

Three of the nine studies find that health insurance has improved several health status measures. Wagstaff and Pradhan (2005), using panel data and matched-double-difference to evaluate the impact of health insurance on health status, find that Vietnam's health insurance program favorably affected height-for-age and weight-for-age among young school children—and body mass index among adults. This result is only suggestive because the aggregate health measures used by these authors depend marginally on better access to health care and are strongly influenced by other variables.

Wang and others (2008) find that the community-based health insurance scheme implemented in Guizhou province has had a positive effect on health status among participants. Besides using self-perceived health status, they use EQ-5D (a proprietary, standardized instrument to measure health outcomes). Their results indicate that among the five EQ-5D dimensions, health insurance significantly reduced pain/discomfort and anxiety/depression for the general population—and had positive impacts on mobility and usual activity for people above age 55. They also find that the positive impact has been greater among the poorest.

Nyman and Barleen (2007) evaluate the impact of supplemental private health insurance on self-perceived health status in Brazil. This study is an example of a way to tackle endogeneity. The authors try to establish the causality (from health insurance to an increase in health care and health) by analyzing specific subpopulations.

- *Only respondents who indicated a specific acute illness, which would presumably eliminate the influence of illness on the decision to become insured.* Thus, the authors estimate the effect of health insurance on the use of health care and on health, contingent on the respondent's reporting an acute medical problem within the last 30 days. This addresses, at least in part, the endogeneity from the self-selection of sicker individuals into health insurance.
- *Only respondents who reported a chronic health problem, which eliminates the influence of a chronic condition on the decision to become insured.* Thus, the authors determine whether supplemental health insurance generates an improvement in health status, conditional on the respondent having an acute or chronic health problem.

Results from both models indicate that supplemental private health insurance has improved self-perceived health status in Brazil. According to the authors, the finding that better self-reported health status is associated with health insurance, given the presence of acute or chronic conditions or other health problems, might reflect better control of symptoms or quicker recovery associated with the increased access to health care available with health insurance.

The results provide mixed evidence on the impact of health insurance status. The studies reviewed here use different measures of health status, so it may not be surprising that results are inconsistent and hard to compare. It is not clear which are the most suitable health status measures when evaluating the impact of health insurance. Whatever the health status indicators finally chosen, they should be directly and substantially related to the benefits provided under the health insurance scheme being evaluated. From this perspective, the current literature on the impact of health insurance on health status in low- and middle-income countries seems to still be in its infancy, perhaps related to the limited health status information available in standard household surveys.

The scarcity of the evidence on this issue is likely related, at least in part, to the methodological challenge of evaluating the impact of health insurance on health status. Besides the usual problem of unobserved confounding variables, evaluating the impact of health insurance on health status is further complicated by bidirectional causality: those insured may be healthier because they have health insurance, but they may buy health insurance in part because they are healthier, especially if access to insurance is positively related to income and type of employment.

Heterogeneity of health insurance schemes

Health insurance varies considerably in design, target groups, benefits coverage, financing mechanisms, and experience. Note that variations are observed both across and within countries. Differences in design affect not only what types of benefits are made more affordable and, therefore, what type of results we might expect but also who tends to affiliate. The latter is important since one of the most important methodological challenges in evaluating impacts of health insurance is related to the nonrandom variation in health insurance status and the need to correct for this possible endogeneity. So, to properly model the impact of health insurance, it is crucial to understand what determines affiliation with one health insurance scheme or another.

In comparing the impact of health insurance across different health insurance schemes, several studies show that health insurance is by no means a homogeneous concept and that its impact depends on the specifics of the insurance scheme. A study by Ekman (2007b), evaluating the impact of multiple health insurance schemes in Jordan, illustrates this point. Ekman first finds no impact of insurance coverage on outpatient care use, but when the type of insurance is disaggregated, it turns out that people with access to the Ministry of Health insurance program have a significantly higher probability of seeking outpatient care than do people covered under other insurance schemes. Similarly, Yip, Wang, and Hsiao (2008) find a significant positive impact of health insurance for one new rural cooperative medical scheme in China on use but only a limited impact for another type of health insurance.[5]

The implications of this heterogeneity in health insurance schemes are clear. First, the specification of the models should take this heterogeneity into account. For example, in some cases it may be necessary to run different models for different health insurance schemes,[6] to run different models for different population groups, or to include some interaction terms between the health insurance dummy variable and the groups of interest. Second, the possible heterogeneity of different health insurance schemes indicates the need for care when trying to generalize results across and even within countries.

Moving forward

Does health insurance matter in low- and middle-income countries? This review indicates that studies show consistently that health insurance improves access and use. This result is found among the 10 studies in the top quartile and among the general evidence base, a finding consistent with what has been found in the developed world. Most studies in the top quartile and those in the general evidence base indicate that health insurance mitigates out-of-pocket expenditures and reduces the incidence of catastrophic payments. We also found that studies constituting outliers in this context indicate that the specific design of health insurance schemes (high copayments and deductibles, little first dollar coverage), together with the fact that health insurance may increase use and cost per episode of care more than it reduces the price to the insured of each service (for example, by providing incentives to switch to costlier care when protected by health insurance), explain why health insurance may not always increase financial protection and reduce catastrophic costs. These results are important, as financial protection lies at the heart of any health insurance scheme.

We find no conclusive evidence of an impact of health insurance on health status. In this context some crucial issues must be answered, such as the type of health status variables able to capture changes in health status that may result from better access and use of health services resulting from health insurance. We question whether self-perceived health status measures, indicators of nutritional status, or blunt mortality information are good ways to go forward, and we suggest that researchers should perhaps concentrate more on analyzing the impact of health insurance on health services that are likely to have an important impact on health status (for example, immunizations) rather than look at health status measures directly.

What do we know about the robustness of the evidence base, and how could we improve it? Our search strategy[7] produced more than four dozen studies evaluating the impact of health insurance in low- and middle-income countries, despite the restrictive inclusion criteria. Many of these studies have been published recently, mirroring a growing interest among researchers and policymakers in health insurance as a financing option. We identified 10 studies providing the best available evidence. Almost half do not use impact evaluation methods to test the effect of health insurance and so provide only weak evidence on the impact of health insurance. There is considerable room for stronger evidence.

Several methodological recommendations emerge from this review. First, future studies should shift from purely correlational analysis to causal research that isolates the impact of health insurance from other confounding variables. Second, most studies reviewed here use retrospective standard cross-sectional household data to evaluate impact. Such data, typically available in many countries, can go a long way toward evaluating the impact of health insurance. But efforts to produce prospective data should be supported. Care should be taken, however, when randomized controlled trials are promoted as the only valid alternative to evaluate the impact of health insurance. Quasi-experimental methods can provide reasonably solid evidence, and social experiments may also suffer from limitations, often and most importantly from limited external validity.[8]

Third, the quality of a study does not depend solely on the sophistication of the method. It depends on how well researchers understand a health insurance scheme and how they use this knowledge to find the most appropriate econometric tool and the best available information to measure its impact. It is surprising that many studies reviewed here spend little time establishing a clear link between the specifics of a health insurance scheme and the method used to evaluate it. For example, endogeneity is not omnipresent and can be context specific. Similarly, local context may be an important confounding variable in some settings (for example, health insurance coverage may be highest in places that also have the most complete provider network). Looking for complementary information may be crucial in such a setting but will depend on the researcher's understanding of the circumstances. Familiarity with local circumstances thus becomes a key ingredient of quality literature in this field.

What are some of the biggest knowledge gaps? Some aspects of the potential impact of health insurance have yet to receive the full attention of researchers. These include the distributional impact of health insurance; the impact of health insurance in reducing inequality in use of services, expenditures, and financial protection; the dynamics of the health insurance over time; the variation of impact as the duration of exposure to health insurance varies; the impact of health insurance on household consumption smoothing patterns; the spillover effects of health insurance; the variation in impact across different health insurance schemes; the variation in impact across health insurance and other supply side (for example, provider payment reforms) and demand side interventions (for example, equity funds) targeted toward increasing financial protection and improving access and use; the cost-effectiveness of health insurance compared with other interventions; and the general equilibrium effect of health insurance in recognition of the interrelationship of market price and production.

As the geographic distribution of our evidence base indicates, a few countries seem to receive substantial attention from the research community (such as China, Colombia, and Vietnam). But most other countries implementing health insurance have received little attention, and some regions seem to be receiving almost none.

Even though much work remains, based on the literature reviewed here, a compelling case can be made for a positive correlation between having health insurance and two important results: using more medical care and being less exposed to the financial risks associated with illness (although the latter is sensitive to how the insurance is designed). Although it is difficult to move from the conclusion that insurance increases (or is associated with an increase in) the use of medical care to a conclusion that insurance improves health outcomes or health status, almost all the efforts to improve health in the world involve greater use of medical care: to benefit from specific procedures, to obtain immunizations, to improve knowledge and behavior, to make births safer, to improve diagnosis, to screen patients, and more. That we do not have a clear link from insurance to outcomes—or that we do not better understand why there is not a strong link—is an important challenge for the research community.

Notes

1. Box 2.2 outlines the protocol followed to evaluate the robustness of each of the articles reviewed. See the full study from which this chapter is drawn for details of the conceptual framework, methods, and all 51 studies assessed (Giedion and Diaz 2008).

2. See Ekman 2007 for an excellent example of this issue.

3. Of the 22 studies evaluating financial protection, 16 find that health insurance has improved financial protection, 4 find that health insurance has improved financial protection for some groups or for some indicators but not for all, 1 finds that health insurance has actually worsened financial protection, and 5 measure financial protection but do not provide any information on the statistical significance of their results.

4. A voluntary prepayment scheme, private or employment-based insurance, and a user fee exemption scheme.

5. They find a positive impact for a scheme operating in two western provinces that provides first dollar coverage for both inpatient and outpatient services and uses supply side interventions to improve quality and reduce inefficiencies in health service delivery, while they find no significant positive impact for another scheme common in the western and central regions of China that provides a medical savings account that combines an individual medical savings account with high-deductible catastrophic insurance and that provides mainly catastrophic insurance for expensive hospital services. Chapter 8 of this book explains the findings in detail.

6. Data from a voluntary health insurance scheme for the informal sector may have, for example, a different endogeneity problem than a mandatory social insurance scheme for formal sector workers.

7. This literature review searched studies in online databases, performed manual searches, reviewed reference lists of related papers, and inspected webpages of major international organizations and donors. To be included in the list of studies reviewed, the study must have been about a health-related insurance mechanism; must have addressed out-of-pocket spending, catastrophic health expenditure, access to care, use of health services, or health status; must have been quantitative; and must have

appeared in an academic journal or book. Of course, the empirical focus needed to be a low- or middle-income country. We reviewed papers published between 2000 and 2008 and written in English only.

8. There is a vigorous debate about the structural versus program evaluation approach in econometrics. See Deaton (2010), Heckman (2010), and Imbens (2010).

References

Buchmueller, T., and R. Kronick. 2005. "The Effect of Health Insurance on Medical Care Utilization and Implications for Insurance Expansion: A Review of the Literature." Medical Care Research and Review 62 (1): 3–30.

Chen, L., W. Yip, M. Chang, H. Lin, S. Lee, Y. Chiu, and Y. Lin. 2007. "The Effects of Taiwan's National Health Insurance on Access and Health Status of the Elderly." Health Economics 16 (2) 223–42.

Deaton, A. 2010. "Instruments, Randomization, and Learning about Development." Journal of Economic Literature 48 (2): 424–55.

Dow, W. H., K. González, and L. Rosero-Bixby. 2003. Aggregation and Insurance Mortality Estimation (Costa Rica). NBER Working Paper 9827. Cambridge, MA: National Bureau of Economic Research.

Dow, W. H., and K. K. Schmeer. 2003. "Health Insurance and Child Mortality in Costa Rica." Social Science & Medicine 57 (6): 975–86.

Ekman, B. 2007. "The Impact of Health Insurance on Outpatient Utilization and Expenditure: Evidence from One Middle-Income Country Using National Household Survey Data." Health Research Policy and Systems 5 (6).

Giedion, U., E. Alfonso, and Y. Diaz. 2007. "Measuring the Impact of Mandatory Health Insurance on Access and Use: The Case of the Colombian Contributory Regime." Working Paper. Brookings Institution, Washington, DC.

Giedion, U., Y. Díaz, and E. A. Alfonso. 2007. "The Impact of Subsidized Health Insurance on Access, Utilization and Health Status: The Case of Colombia." World Bank, Washington, DC.

Hadley, J. 2003. "Sicker and Poorer—The Consequences of Being Uninsured: A Review of the Research on the Relationship between Health Insurance, Medical Care Use, Health, Work, and Income." Medical Care Research and Review 60 (2): 3–75.

Heckman, J. J. 2010. "Building Bridges between Structural and Program Evaluation Approaches to Evaluating Policy." Journal of Economic Literature 48 (2): 356–98.

Hidayat, B., H. Thabrany, H. Dong, and R. Sauerborn. 2004. "The Effects of Mandatory Health Insurance on Equity in Access to Outpatient Care in Indonesia." Health Policy and Planning 19 (5): 322–35.

Hsiao, W., and W. Yip. 2008. "Discover New Models of Health Insurance through Social Experimentation." Presentation at the Brookings Institution, April 15, Washington, DC.

Imbens, G. W. 2010. "Better LATE Than Nothing: Some Comments on Deaton (2009) and Heckman and Urzua (2009)." Journal of Economic Literature 48 (2): 399–423.

Oxfam, Action for Global Health, Medicins du Monde, Global Health Advocates, Save the Children, and Act Up Paris. 2008. "Health Insurance in Low-Income Countries: Where Is the Evidence That It Works?" Joint NGO Briefing Paper 112. [www.oxfam.org.uk/resources/policy/ health/downloads/bp112_health_insurance.pdf].

Smith, K., and S. Sulzbach. 2008. "Community-Based Health Insurance and Access to Maternal Health Services: Evidence from Three West African Countries." Social Science & Medicine 66 (12): 2460–73.

Trujillo, A., J. Portillo, and J. Vernon. 2005. "The Impact of Subsidized Health Insurance for the Poor: Evaluating the Colombian Experience Using Propensity Score Matching." International Journal of Health Care Finance and Economics 5 (3): 211–39.

Wagstaff, A. 2007a. "The Economic Consequences of Health Shocks: Evidence from Vietnam." Journal of Health Economics 26 (1): 82–100.

———. 2007b. "Health Insurance for the Poor: Initial Impacts of Vietnam's Health Care Fund for the Poor." Policy Research Working Paper 4134. World Bank, Washington, DC.

Wagstaff, A., M. Lindelow, G. Junc, X. Ling, and Q. Juncheng. 2007. "Extending Health Insurance to the Rural Population: An Impact Evaluation of China's New Cooperative Medical Scheme." Impact Evaluation Series 12. World Bank, Washington, DC.

Wagstaff, A., and M. Pradhan. 2005. "Health Insurance Impact on Health and Nonmedical Consumption in a Developing Country." Policy Research Working Paper 3563. Washington, DC: World Bank.

Wagstaff, A., and S. Yu. 2007. "Do Health Sector Reforms Have Their Intended Impacts? The World Bank's Health VIII Project in Gansu Province, China." Journal of Health Economics 26 (3): 505–35.

Wang, H., W. Yip, L. Zhang, and W. Hsiao. 2008. "The Impact of Rural Mutual Health Care on Health Status: Evaluation of a Social Experiment in Rural China." Health Economics 18 (2): 65–82.

Waters, H. R. 1999. "Measuring the Impact of Health Insurance with a Correction for Selection Bias—A Case Study of Ecuador." Health Economics 8 (5): 473–83.

Yip, W., H. Wang, and W. Hsiao. 2008. "The Impact of Rural Mutual Health Care on Access to Care: Evaluation of a Social Experiment in Rural China." Harvard School of Public Health, Boston, MA. [www.hsph.harvard.edu/phcf/publications/Yip.Wang.Hsiao.2008 .RMHC.access.pdf].

Studies reviewed but not cited

Bales, S., J. Knowles, H. Axelson, P. D. Minha, H. D. Long, and T. M. Oanhd. 2007. "The Early Impact of Decision 139 in Vietnam: An Application of Propensity Score Matching." Vietnam, Ministry of Health, Hanoi.

Bleich, S. N., D. M. Cutler, A. S. Adams, R. Lozano, and C. J. Murray. 2007. "Impact of Insurance and Supply of Health Professionals on Coverage of Treatment for Hypertension in Mexico: Population Based Study." BMJ 335 (7625): 875–78.

Dror, D., E. Soriano, M. Lorenzo, J. Sarol Jr., R. Azcuna, and R. Koren. 2005. "Field Based Evidence of Enhanced Healthcare Utilization among Persons Insured by Micro Health Insurance Units in Philippines." Health Policy 73 (3) 263–271.

Ekman, B. 2004. "Community-based health insurance in low-income countries: a systematic review of the evidence." Health Policy and Planning 19 (5): 249–70.

———. 2007. "Catastrophic Health Payments and Health Insurance: Some Counterintuitive Evidence from One Low-Income Country." Health Policy 83 (2): 304–13.

Flórez, C. E., U. Giedion, and R. Pardo. Forthcoming. "The Impact of Health Insurance in Colombia on Financial Protection." Washington, DC: Inter-American Development Bank.

Gertler, P., and J. Gruber. 2002. "Insuring Consumption against Illness." American Economic Review 92 (1): 51–70.

Gertler, P., L. Locay, and W. Sanderson. 1987. "Are User Fees Regressive? The Welfare Implications of Health Care Financing Proposals." Journal of Econometrics 36 (1–2): 67–88.

Gotsadze, G., A. Zoidze, and O. Vasadze. 2005. "Reform Strategies in Georgia and Their Impact on Health Care Provision in Rural Areas: Evidence from a Household Survey." Social Science & Medicine 60 (4): 809–821.

Heckman, J. J., R. J. LaLonde, and J. A. Smith. 1999. "The Economics and Econometrics of Active Labor Market Programs." In O. Ashenfelter and D. Card, eds., Handbook of Labor Economics. Amsterdam: Elsevier.

Jakab, M., A. Preker, C. Krishnan, P. Schneider, F. Diop, J. Jutting, A. Gumber, M. Ranson, and S. Supakankunti. 2004. "Analysis of Community Financing Using Household Surveys." In A. Preker and G. Carrin, eds, Health Financing for Poor People: Resource Mobilization and Risk Sharing. Washington, DC: World Bank.

Johar, M. 2007. "The Impact of the Indonesian Health Card Program: A Matching Estimator Approach." Discussion Paper 2007-30. University of New South Wales, School of Economics, Sydney, Australia.

Jowett, M., P. Contoyannis, and N. Vinh. 2003. "The Impact of Public Voluntary Health Insurance on Private Health Expenditures in Vietnam." Social Science & Medicine 56 (2): 333–42.

Jütting, J. 2004. "Financial Protection and Access to Health Care in Rural Areas of Senegal." In A. Preker and G. Carrin, eds., Health Financing for Poor People: Resource Mobilization and Risk Sharing. Washington, DC: World Bank.

Khan, A. A., and S. M. Bhardwaj. 1994 "Access to Health Care: A Conceptual Framework and its Relevance to Health Care Planning." Evaluation & The Health Professions 17 (1): 60–76.

Levy, H., and D. Meltzer. 2001. "What Do We Really Know about Whether Health Insurance Affects Health?" ERIU Working Paper 6. University of Michigan, Economic Research Initiative on the Uninsured, Ann Arbor, MI.

Limwattananon, S., V. Tangcharoensathien, and P. Prakongsai. 2007. "Catastrophic and Poverty Impacts of Health Payments: Results from National Household Surveys in Thailand." Bulletin of the World Health Organization 85 (8): 600–06.

Liu, T. C., C.S. Chen, and L. M. Chen. 2002. "The Impact of National Health Insurance on Neonatal Care Use and Childhood Vaccination in Taiwan." Health Policy and Planning 17 (4): 384–92.

Liu, Y., K. Rao, and W. Hsiao. 2003. "Medical Expenditure and Rural Impoverishment in China." Journal of Health, Population, and Nutrition 21 (3): 216–22.

Lu, J. F., and W. Hsiao. 2003. "Does Universal Health Insurance Make Health Care Unaffordable? Lessons from Taiwan." Health Affairs 22 (3): 77–88.

Pagan, J. A., A. Puig, and B. J. Soldo. 2007. "Health Insurance Coverage and the Use of Preventive Services by Mexican Adults." Health Economics 16 (12): 1359–69.

Pagan, J., S. Ross, J. Yau, and D. Polsky. 2006. "Self-Medication and Health Insurance Coverage in Mexico." Health Policy 75 (2): 170–77.

Palmer, N., D. Mueller, L. Gilson, A. Mills, and A. Haines. 2004. "Health Financing to Promote Access in Low Income Settings—How Much Do We Know?" Lancet 364 (9442): 1365–70.

Penchansky R., and J. W. Thomas. 1981. "The Concept of Access: Definition and Relationship to Consumer Satisfaction." Medical Care 19 (2): 127–40.

Pradhan, M., F. Saadah, and R. Sparrow. 2007. "Did the Health Card Program Ensure Access to Medical Care for the Poor during Indonesia's Economic Crisis?" World Bank Economic Review 21 (1): 125–151.

Ranson, M. 2004. "The SEWA Medical Insurance Fund in India." In A. Preker and G. Carrin, eds., Health Financing for Poor People: Resource Mobilization and Risk Sharing. Washington, DC: World Bank.

Saadah, F., M. Pradhan, and R. Sparrow. 2001. "The Effectiveness of the Health Card as an Instrument to Ensure Access to Medical Care for the Poor during the Crisis." World Bank Economic Review 21 (1): 125–150.

Schneider, P., and F. Diop. 2004. "Community-Based Health Insurance in Rwanda." In A. Preker and G. Carrin, eds., Health Financing for Poor People: Resource Mobilization and Risk Sharing. Washington, DC: World Bank.

Sepehria, A., W. Simpsona, and S. Sarma. 2006. "The Influence of Health Insurance on Hospital Admission and Length of Stay—The Case of Vietnam." Social Science & Medicine 63 (7): 1757–70.

Sinha, T., M. Ranson, and A. Mills. 2007. "Protecting the Poor? The Distributional Impact of a Bundled Insurance Scheme." World Development 35 (8)" 1404–21.

Supakankunti, S. 2004. "Impact of the Thailand Health Card." In A. Preker and G. Carrin, eds., Health Financing for Poor People: Resource Mobilization and Risk Sharing. Washington, DC: World Bank.

Yip, W., and P. Berman. 2001. "Targeted Health Insurance in a Low Income Country and Its Impact on Access: Egypt's School Health Insurance." Health Economics 10 (3): 207–20.

Low-Cost Health Insurance Schemes to Protect the Poor in Namibia

Emily Gustafsson-Wright, Wendy Janssens, and Jacques van der Gaag

Chapter 3

Investigating alternative mechanisms of health care provision is important for African countries, where the epidemics of HIV/AIDS, tuberculosis, and malaria increase the demands on the health care sector.

This chapter, using a unique combination of household survey data and a biomedical survey with HIV test data from Greater Windhoek in Namibia, analyzes the extent to which the fairly well developed public health care sector in Namibia offers protection from health shocks to uninsured households. Namibia is in the top tier of African countries in health expenditures. Not only is government health spending high in relative terms at almost 8% of gross domestic product (GDP), but out-of-pocket expenditures are the second lowest among African countries, after South Africa. So one would expect that the beneficial role of public health care would be particularly visible in this Southern African country. Namibia is also severely affected by the HIV/AIDS epidemic. The latest estimates suggest a prevalence rate of 15% among working-age adults (UNAIDS 2008).

The goal of this study is to investigate the potential for health insurance schemes in this setting, given the recent introduction of subsidized low cost insurance with HIV treatment components in Greater Windhoek. The chapter begins with a description of health and the health sector in Namibia. Next, it examines self-reported health status, health care use, and out-of-pocket health expenditures across insurance status and consumption quintiles. It then investigates the coping strategies of uninsured and insured households that face particular health shocks, looking at a death in the family, extended hospitalization, substantial weight loss, and HIV infection. The last section discusses the scope for targeting and subsidizing private voluntary insurance schemes.

Health and the health care sector in Namibia

Namibia is a lower middle-income country with a gross national income per capita of US$6,240 in purchasing power parity (PPP) terms in 2008. The Sub-Saharan Africa average was US$1,949 (World Bank 2010). However, this number conceals enormous differences in wealth within the population. In fact, Namibia has one of the highest levels of inequality in the world, with a Gini coefficient of 0.7. The richest 10% of the population receives 65% of the country's income, and about 35% of the population lives below the poverty line of $1 a day (WHO 2004).

The Namibian population suffers from three major communicable diseases: HIV/AIDS, tuberculosis, and malaria. Adult (ages 15–49) HIV prevalence rates increased from 2.5% in 1992 to 15.3% in 2007, when there were an estimated 200,000 HIV-infected people, 14,000 of them children under age 15. The estimated number of people in need of antiretroviral therapy in that year was 59,000, which could well rise above 200,000 when infected people develop AIDS. Tuberculosis, the second major cause of deaths in hospitals, is estimated at 767 cases per 100,000 people per year, with a mortality rate of 96 per 100,000 per year (WHO 2008b). Malaria infects on average 400,000 people per year and causes 877 deaths, mainly in the north (WHO 2005). Noncommunicable diseases are increasingly responsible for morbidity and mortality among adults, especially diabetes and cardiovascular diseases (WHO 2004).

Just after gaining independence from South Africa in 1990, the Namibian health system was divided. Most health facilities were in urban areas, segregated by race. Equality gaps in access to health care existed not only between rural and urban dwellers but also between the rich and the poor. But in the last two decades, a strong political commitment to upgrade the primary health care system has made health services more responsive to the needs of the population, albeit slowly (WHO 2004).

Namibia is among the best off African countries in health spending. From 1993 to 2000, 11% of government spending was earmarked for health (WHO 2004). In 2007 it spent 7.6% of GDP on health (PPP US$467 per capita), 42% financed by the government and 58% from private payments (of which only 5.8% was out of pocket). In Sub-Saharan Africa the average is 6.4% of GDP for health (PPP US$124 per capita), 41% from government and 59% private, of which 60% was out of pocket (World Bank 2010).

The private health sector in Namibia has a well established for-profit component, providing hospital services mainly in the urban centers. Not-for-profit missionary health facilities operate in the communal areas in the north (WHO 2004). Private sources of finance include private insurance premiums and user fees in public health care facilities. Public facilities charge flat user fees, depending on the facility. The cost recovery ratio for 2001 was 2% (WHO 2004). Medicines are generally affordable due to the highly subsidized user fees. But the public sector suffers from long waiting times. And there is a critical shortage of health professionals, particularly outside urban areas.

The Namibian health insurance industry, organized primarily into either open or closed medical aid funds, is better developed than it is in most other African countries. A fund is a nonprofit entity that pays benefits directly to medical providers in proportion to the services rendered to the beneficiary. Closed funds limit membership to employees in a firm or industry. The government health fund, PSEMAS, is considered a closed fund since it is limited to those working in government. The open funds are Namibia Medical Care, Namibia Health Plan, Renaissance Medical Aid Fund, and Nammed Medical Aid Fund.[3]

Insurance enrollment in Greater Windhoek

The household survey data used in this chapter covers only Greater Windhoek (box 3.1). Insurance coverage is high for a Sub-Saharan country, with more than 30% of individuals enrolled in a medical aid fund (table 3.1). The government health

---

BOX 3.1
Data collection

The data source for this study is the Republic of Namibia Okambilimbili Survey 2006 which includes socioeconomic and biomedical parts.[1] The socioeconomic part was conducted among a representative, self-weighted sample of the Greater Windhoek population, including 1,796 households and 7,343 individuals. It includes data on basic household structure as well as extensive data on health status, health expenditures, health insurance, and willingness to pay for health insurance. The biomedical part includes a saliva-based HIV test for those ages 12 and older consenting to participate. Having such a rich household survey connected with an HIV test provides a unique dataset and opportunity to analyze these data together.

Note

1. The survey was conducted by staff of the Multidisciplinary Research and Consultancy Centre at the University of Namibia, and the National Institute of Pathology, in cooperation with the Amsterdam Institute for International Development and the PharmAccess Foundation.

TABLE 3.1
Individuals enrolled in a medical aid fund

Household characteristic	Total population	Individuals insured (%)	Total number of households	Households insured (%)
Consumption quintile				
1 (poorest)	1,404	5.3	238	14.3
2	1,381	13.6	285	28.4
3	1,396	25.9	329	40.4
4	1,390	44.0	358	55.3
5 (richest)	1,390	69.1	444	81.3
Employment status (household head)				
Employed	6,002	34.9	1,430	52.4
Unemployed	1,249	14.1	320	25.6
Employment sector (household head)				
Government and defense	951	58.2	222	93.7
Education	337	51.6	69	82.6
Health	178	49.4	38	76.3
Services	1,853	35.2	441	50.3
Transport and storage	346	33.0	70	50.0
Manufacturing	226	24.3	58	36.2
Retail and accommodation	450	17.1	107	29.9
Construction	346	15.6	103	23.3
Others (such as agriculture and mining)	1,312	24.9	321	38.3
Total	7,343	30.9	1,769	47.2

Note: Total averages by category may differ due to missing observations in some categories.
Source: Authors' calculations based on 2006 Republic of Namibia Okambilimbili Survey.

fund, PSEMAS, insured 43% of all insured individuals. Namibia Medical Care and Namibia Health Plan each insure about a third of the number that PSEMAS does.

There are large discrepancies in enrollment across socioeconomic categories. Only 5% of individuals in the poorest consumption quintile are enrolled in medical aid, while 70% of individuals in the richest quintile have medical aid benefits. Not surprisingly, the employed are more likely to be insured than the unemployed, with considerable variation by industry. Those most likely to be insured are individuals whose head of household works in government or defense. Household members with household heads who work in education and health follow close behind. The least insured industries are manufacturing, retail/accommodation, and construction. The service industry employs the most individuals in Namibia, and 65% of individuals with a head of household employed in services are uninsured.

A household is considered insured if at least one of its members is enrolled in a medical aid fund. In 47% of Greater Windhoek households at least one individual has medical insurance, a percentage substantially larger than individual coverage rates, indicating that insurance is targeted to individuals rather than to whole families. For example, 94% of households whose head is employed in government or defense have at least one insured household member. But only 58% of their household members are insured. Relative enrollment rates across socioeconomic categories are similar to individual coverage rates: the rich and the employed are much more likely to participate in a medical aid fund than poorer households.

Inequality in health status, health care use, and health expenditures

Do the insured differ from the uninsured in their health status, and among the uninsured, do the rich differ from the poor? Given their health status, do the uninsured and insured differ in their use of health care? And do the insured and the uninsured differ in their level and proportion of out-of-pocket payments as part of their overall spending?

Overall, the insured are more likely to report chronic illness, acute illness, and hospitalization (table 3.2). One interpretation is that those who are insured have insurance because they have poorer health. A negative correlation between insured status and health status could suggest cream-skimming, where insurance companies insure those in better health, which seems not to be the case here.

In examining differences across quintiles, chronic disease increases systematically with income for both the uninsured and the insured. This may be because

TABLE 3.2

Reported prevalence of chronic disease, acute illness, or injury—and incidence of hospitalization among the insured and uninsured (%)

	Insured			Uninsured		
Quintile	Chronic	Acute	Hospitalization	Chronic	Acute	Hospitalization
1 (lowest)	13.51	12.16	9.46	10.20	13.31	7.59
2	14.36	16.49	3.72	11.58	17.67	6.45
3	16.30	22.38	8.56	12.27	17.60	5.22
4	16.53	17.81	6.70	11.44	16.71	4.24
5 (highest)	20.02	19.04	6.66	14.29	13.29	1.86
Total	17.73	18.80	6.83	11.57	15.89	5.73

Note: For acute illness and hospitalization the reported prevalence reflects that the individual experienced at least one episode in the last year.

Source: Authors' calculations based on 2006 Republic of Namibia Okambilimbili Survey.

the poor have less information or awareness about their chronic conditions.[4] For acute illness, the poorest and the wealthiest are generally less likely to report an episode than those in the middle quintiles. Although little systematic information is conveyed by these data, there appear to be significant differences in reported health status: the insured and the wealthier are more likely to report both chronic and acute illness, though it is possible that the poor and uninsured may be underreporting.

Given these differences in reported health status, is there a significant difference in health care use between the insured and uninsured for those who report having had an acute illness or hospitalization?[5] The first notable difference between the uninsured and the insured is that the uninsured seek no care for acute illness more than 20% of the time, compared with 14% for the insured (table 3.3). This could mean that uninsured individuals are forgoing care because they cannot pay for the health services and the travel costs to get to a health center. Or they choose to opt out of care because they deem the care to be low quality or because of long waiting lines in public health service locations.

When services are used for illness, there is a marked difference in public or private facilities between the uninsured and the insured for both acute illness and hospitalization. Among the uninsured, government health facilities are used in 66% of the cases, while only 10% of insured individuals used government facilities for an acute illness. A mere 7% of the uninsured used private hospitals for inpatient care, compared with 63% of insured individuals. That uninsured individuals are forgoing care more often than the insured and that the uninsured are possibly underreporting illness flag the inequitable and potentially harmful health consequences for individuals lacking health insurance.

The uninsured are less likely to report an illness, but when they do report, they are also less likely to seek care. When individuals without health insurance seek care, they are more likely to do so in public health facilities.

TABLE 3.3
Use of health services for acute illness or injury and hospitalization

Type of health facility	Acute illness or injury			Hospitalization		
	Uninsured	Insured	Total	Uninsured	Insured	Total
None	20.36	14.35	18.23			
Government	66.41	10.19	46.47	93.01	36.69	71.24
Private	10.31	71.53	32.02	6.99	63.31	28.76
Traditional	2.93	3.94	3.28			

Source: Authors' calculations based on 2006 Republic of Namibia Okambilimbili Survey.

Our third question is whether there are inequities in out-of-pocket payments for health between the insured and uninsured for those who sought care and incurred expenses. In absolute terms the insured pay more out of pocket than the uninsured—up to twice as much for chronic illness and five times as much for hospitalization (table 3.4). But in relative terms, the uninsured pay more (as a percentage of per capita consumption) for both chronic and acute illness.

This finding raises another flag. Even in a public health care system that is fairly well developed and used by the uninsured, the uninsured are disproportionately affected financially by out-of-pocket health expenditures relative to the insured. People who are ill, choose to seek care, and must pay for those costs out of pocket pay twice as much as the insured for acute illness as a proportion of their total income.

These inequalities become quite stark for the bottom quintiles among the uninsured. In absolute terms people in the higher quintiles spend much more than the poor on health care, but those in the lower quintiles spend on average a higher proportion of their consumption per capita on chronic and acute illness, albeit in a less systematic pattern (table 3.5). Uninsured individuals in the bottom quintiles spend on average up to 14% of their per capita income on acute illness (quintile 2). This finding again flags the inequities surrounding insurance coverage, even in a country with a health sector in relatively good shape.

Coping with health shocks when uninsured

Despite the fairly well developed public health care system in Greater Windhoek, the uninsured and the poor seek treatment less often than the insured and the wealthy. And if the uninsured and the poor do seek treatment, they fare relatively worse financially. This section expands on the previous section by investigating in more detail the economic consequences of health shocks on out-of-pocket expenditures

TABLE 3.4

Average per capita annual out-of-pocket health expenditures

Type of illness		Insured	Uninsured
Chronic	(US$)	1,078	491
	(%)	2.7	4.0
Acute	(US$)	1,377	967.
	(%)	3.5	7.8
Hospitalization	(US$)	1,210	226
	(%)	3.1	1.8

Note: For all individuals with positive health expenditures.

Source: Authors' calculations based on 2006 Republic of Namibia Okambilimbili Survey.

TABLE 3.5

Average per capita annual out-of-pocket health expenditures for the uninsured, by quintile

Quintile	Chronic (US$)	Chronic (%)	Acute (US$)	Acute (%)	Hospitalization (US$)	Hospitalization (%)
1 (lowest)	140	5.4	291	11.1	50	1.9
2	250	4.3	806	13.9	54	0.9
3	408	3.9	849	8.2	366	3.5
4	1,123	5.6	978	4.9	182	0.9
5 (highest)	1,015	1.9	3,787	7.2	3,548	6.7
Total	491	4.0	967	7.8	226	1.8

Note: For all individuals with positive health expenditures.

Source: Authors' calculations based on 2006 Republic of Namibia Okambilimbili Survey.

and income-earning capacity for households without health insurance compared with those with health insurance. It also analyzes which coping strategies households adopt in the face of health shocks to deal with medical expenses and reduced income.

Our ability to analyze the mitigating effects of insurance is limited given the cross-sectional data, so we cannot fully deal with selection and simultaneity bias. Despite the data constraints, however, the findings here contribute to the policy debate on health insurance by highlighting the consequences of health shocks on uninsured households. Taking advantage of our unique dataset, which combines socioeconomic data and HIV tests, the results provide insights into the potential benefits of private or community-based health insurance.

Poor households use various coping strategies to buffer shocks. A decline in earned income may be partially offset by an increase in unearned income. This would be the case if the sick individual benefits from a social scheme such as a disability grant or illness compensation. Alternatively, relatives may increase remittances to the affected household. Friends, neighbors, or other community members may provide gifts and other forms of informal assistance. To deal with the remainder of the income loss, the medical expenses, and the need for care at home, households can reallocate the labor of healthy household members. Individuals may increase their labor supply by working more hours on their job or taking up a second job, or they may enter the labor market if not working for income yet. Or households can deplete their savings, sell assets to generate additional monetary resources, borrow money, or buy goods on credit. A health shock could also induce a household to reduce food and nonfood consumption or to postpone large nonmedical household expenditures. Finally, the household may decide to forgo health care altogether.

Analysis

We estimate the relationship between health shocks and the following economic variables: income, medical expenditures, labor supply, consumption, assets, and credit.[6] In particular, we estimate the following ordinary least squares regression for uninsured and insured households separately (following Wagstaff 2007):

$$y_t^h = \alpha + \beta s_{t-1}^h + \gamma X_t^h + \delta^n + \varepsilon_t^h \text{ for } i_t^h = 0, 1$$

where y_t^h is the outcome variable for household h at time t, s_{t-1}^h is a dummy variable for each of four health shocks equal to 1 if the health shock occurred to household h in the 12 months before the time of the survey t, X_t^h is a vector with household characteristics (age, age squared, gender, education of the household head, household size, and number of children) measured at time t,[7] δ^n captures neighborhood fixed effects such as the presence of health facilities or employment opportunities, and ε_t^h is an unobserved error term. A household is considered to be insured ($i_t^h = 1$) if at least one of its members is enrolled in a health insurance scheme at time t and is considered uninsured ($i_t^h = 0$) otherwise.

The analysis is at the household level. That is, we assume that household members pool their income and share the burden of medical expenditures. We are particularly interested in the coefficients β, which reflect how, given a household's insurance status, a particular health shock is associated with differences in household income, medical spending, and coping strategies.

The cross-sectional data put two important restrictions on the analysis. First, we cannot perform an impact analysis of the mitigating effects of insurance. The decision to enroll in a medical aid fund depends in part on unobserved characteristics. For example, people who are more concerned with their health could be more likely to take insurance while being less prone to health shocks because of a healthy lifestyle. Or individuals with private information on particular health care needs could be more inclined to enroll.

Indeed, we have some indications of adverse selection into private insurance schemes. Individuals with a parent who suffers from a chronic disease, which in turn increases one's own risk of developing a chronic disease, are more likely to be insured. But we do not find a significant overrepresentation among the insured of individuals who suffer from HIV/AIDS and high blood pressure, the main communicable and noncommunicable causes of morbidity and mortality in adults. Without panel data or an experimental setup of the insurance scheme, it is not possible to control for (time-invariant) unobserved characteristics that affect insurance status. Instead, we stratify the analysis by insurance status to yield insights in the relationship between health shocks and economic outcomes for the uninsured and the insured sample separately.

Second, simultaneity effects influence interpretations of our findings. Although the health shocks in our dataset occurred prior to the survey, it is possible that the direction of causality between a health shock and an outcome variable goes both ways. For example, a low earned income over the past 12 months may affect a household's vulnerability to health shocks in that same period. In that case, a significant negative coefficient β in the regression for earned income might capture either the shock's effect on income-generating capacity or the household's poverty-related vulnerability for health shocks, or both. Another source of bias may stem from omitted variables, such as latent health status. So the findings should be interpreted as correlations, not as causal effects.

Description of the variables

The analysis looks at the consequences of four types of health shocks in the 12 months prior to the survey. All health shocks relate to working-age household members only, that is, individuals ages 15–65.

The first shock is a dummy variable equal to 1 if any working-age household member reported a loss of weight in the previous 12 months. This variable is a self-reported measure of general health status. There is much evidence that losing weight (or a drop in body mass index) is significantly related to an overall deterioration of an individual's health status.[8] In 28.8% of the households at least one working-age individual reported losing weight in the past year.

The second health shock is whether a working-age member of the household is infected with HIV. This variable is based on a direct medical saliva-based test for HIV infection among individuals ages 12 and older. Due to a lengthy validation process of the saliva-based HIV test in Namibia, only 53% of the initial respondents in the relevant age range could be tracked and interviewed at the time of revisit by nurses five months after the socioeconomic survey (Janssens, Rinke de Wit, and van der Gaag 2007). Of the respondents, 20% had relocated to a newly constructed neighborhood in Greater Windhoek with improved social services and infrastructure. This concerns especially households previously living in areas with low-quality access to water, sanitation, and other facilities. Sixteen percent were not present during the revisit for reasons of holidays, leave from work, or working out of town. The remainder refused to participate in the biomedical survey. At 86%, the participation rate in the HIV test among the respondents who could be tracked is high. A correction for nonresponse based on observed characteristics suggests that the bias due to refusal would be small. However, further adjustments for unobserved characteristics indicate that HIV-positive individuals are more likely to have refused to participate in the HIV test (Janssens, van der Gaag, and Rinke de

Wit 2008).[9] In 20.1% of the fully participating households without health insurance, at least one working-age household member is infected with HIV.

The third health shock is a dummy variable equal to 1 if a working-age household member died in the 12 months prior to the survey, and 0 otherwise. On average, 5.1% of the uninsured households experienced such a death in the past year (table 3.6).

The fourth health shock is a dummy variable equal to 1 if a working-age household member was hospitalized for at least three nights in the 12 months prior to the survey. In more than one-fifth of the uninsured households, 21.3%, at least one working-age person was hospitalized for three nights or more. This cutoff excludes the less serious episodes of hospitalization, 62% of which are to give birth. The majority of women who give birth in the hospital are discharged within three days, indicating a birth without complications. The main reasons to stay in the hospital for three nights or more are for treatment (44%), surgery (21%), giving birth (20%), specialist examination (6%), or acute illness or injury (5%).

TABLE 3.6
Health shocks for uninsured and insured households

Uninsured households	Total (n=948) Mean (#)	Quintile 1 (n=207) Mean	Quintile 2 (n=207) Mean	Quintile 3 (n=199) Mean	Quintile 4 (n=161) Mean	Quintile 5 (n=84) Mean	Difference across quintiles (x^2) p-value	
Weight loss	.288 (272)	.348	.232	.297	.288	.313	.140	
HIV/AIDS	.199 (104)	.271	.238	.135	.125	.129	.017**	
Death	.051 (48)	.068	.073	.030	.044	.048	.313	
Hospitalization	.213 (201)	.367	.242	.181	.125	.108	.000***	
Insured households	Total (n=821) Mean (#)	Q1 (n=31) Mean	Q2 (n=78) Mean	Q3 (n=130) Mean	Q4 (n=197) Mean	Q5 (n=360) Mean	Difference across quintiles (x^2) p-value	Difference uninsured vs. insured (F-statistic) p-value
Weight loss	.239 (197)	.290	.359	.231	.222	.222	.111	.021**
HIV/AIDS	.137 (55)	.143	.186	.178	.148	.095	.370	.014**
Death	.038 (31)	.000	.038	.046	.035	.039	.824	.177
Hospitalization	.204 (168)	.194	.256	.223	.212	.183	.608	.649

*** significant at $p < 0.01$; ** significant at $p < 0.05$.

Note: Information on HIV/AIDS infection is available only for 524 uninsured households and 402 insured households. Information on consumption quintile is missing for 90 uninsured households and 25 insured households.

Source: Authors' calculations.

The four health shocks are significantly more likely to occur in the poorest quintiles than in the middle or highest quintiles, as calculated with one-by-one F-tests, (except for the first quintile in the insured sample that includes relatively few observations) (see table 3.6). The overall chi-square value across quintiles is statistically significant for hospitalization and HIV infection among the uninsured households. Death and hospitalization are equally common for uninsured and insured households. But the uninsured households are significantly more likely to have a working-age household member who suffered weight loss in the past year or who is HIV infected.

The outcome and coping variables are all measured at the level of the household. But the results do not substantially change if we measure income, expenditures, and consumption on a per capita basis (see table A3.1 in the appendix).

The results of the regressions by insurance status are in table 3.7. The first column confirms the descriptive statistics. Uninsured households that experience a health shock face significantly higher out-of-pocket expenditures for health than do uninsured households without such a shock. Health insurance, by contrast, appears to protect households from high medical expenses.

The consequences of weight loss and HIV infection

Losing weight is an important indicator of worsening health status, with potentially far reaching consequences for the affected household. Indeed, weight loss is the only shock variable associated with both high medical expenditures (column 1) and substantially lower earned income (column 2). The lower earnings may be caused by an ill household member's reduced capacity to work. Conversely, it is possible that the lower levels of earned income are to some extent responsible for the weight loss. That is, the poorest may be most likely to become ill in the first place. But adult weight loss is also significantly correlated with lower labor productivity in the household, both in the number of working members and in the average months worked (column 4 and 5). This suggests that the health shock reduces a household's income-earning capacity. For households with health insurance, we do not find a significant correlation between weight loss and reduced income.

Households without health insurance seem to have two main strategies to cope with the combination of high expenditures and low income. Their unearned income (column 3) and their use of credit (column 8) are both significantly higher than those of households without an adult losing weight. A closer look at the components of unearned income shows that informal support, such as assistance from relatives and friends, helps in coping with health shocks. A second significant source of unearned income is maintenance grants.

TABLE 3.7

The economic consequences of health shocks

Uninsured (n=948)

	Ln Medical expenditures	Ln Earned Income	Ln Unearned income	Labor (number of workers as percentage of working-age household members)	Labor (average number of months worked)	Ln Annual food consumption	Ln Annual nonfood consumption	Credit and borrowing	Assets
Weight loss	.707 [.197]***	-.572 [.283]**	.530 [.251]**	-.049 [.030]	-.718 [.334]**	-.005 [.051]	.009 [.074]	.063 [.033]**	.005 [.034]
HIV-infected household member	-.082 [.259]	.148 [.328]	.181 [.331]	.042 [.039]	.491 [.416]	-.117 [.078]	-.273 [.112]**	-.098 [.042]**	-.143 [.048]***
Death in the household	.642 [.338]*	.231 [.512]	.130 [.436]	.005 [.044]	-.012 [.512]	.057 [.125]	-.036 [.139]	.022 [.059]	-.100 [.051]*
Hospitalization for at least three nights	.916 [.213]***	.208 [.237]	.616 [.328]*	.007 [.024]	.047 [.263]	-.058 [.056]	-.146 [.078]*	-.044 [.034]	-.105 [.041]**

Insured (n=821)

	Ln Medical expenditures	Ln Earned income	Ln Unearned income	Labor (number of workers as percentage of working-age household members)	Labor (average number of months worked)	Ln Annual food consumption	Ln Annual nonfood consumption	Credit and borrowing	Assets
Weight loss	.322 [.252]	.225 [.260]	.374 [.332]	-.015 [.021]	-.148 [.305]	.035 [.053]	.076 [.071]	.053 [.041]	.081 [.051]
HIV-infected household member	.670 [.385]*	.002 [.256]	-.462 [.553]	.046 [.031]	.629 [.387]	-.008 [.075]	-.239 [.102]**	.017 [.079]	-.169 [.084]**
Death in the household	.455 [.354]	.562 [.528]	.588 [.766]	.041 [.049]	.431 [.611]	-.101 [.109]	.417 [.114]***	.176 [.105]	.057 [.107]
Hospitalization for at least three nights	.244 [.236]	.212 [.209]	.652 [.363]*	.005 [.023]	-.021 [.283]	.037 [.055]	.161 [.069]**	.040 [.038]	.051 [.061]

*** significant at $p < 0.01$; ** significant at $p < 0.05$; * significant at $p < 0.10$.

Note: Numbers in brackets are robust standard errors adjusted for clustering at the PSU level. Dependent variables are at household level totals. Results for per capita dependent variables are similar. The regressions also include head of household characteristics (age, age squared, sex, education), household size, number of children, and neighborhood fixed effects. The credit and borrowing column gives marginal probabilities from a probit estimation instead of an ordinary least squares regression.

Source: Authors' calculations.

The results for HIV infection merit further explanation. Medical expenditures and earned income are not substantially different when it comes to having an HIV-infected household member. What could cause this absence of impact for one of the most devastating diseases that exists?

A first explanation is that coverage of antiretroviral treatment is high in Namibia, with about 66% of eligible antiretroviral treatment patients on treatment in March 2007.[10] Nonetheless, a further look at the coping strategies of affected households suggests that the disease is significantly correlated with lower expenditures for nonfood items (column 7) and declining ownership of assets (column 9). HIV-affected households are also less likely to have borrowed money, potentially due to reduced access to credit. A similar pattern is discernable among the insured households. In fact, medical expenditures of HIV-infected households with health insurance are significantly higher than those without HIV. This suggests that health insurance may increase demand for treatment among the insured but is not fully covered by private insurance packages.

A second explanation is that HIV infection is not a health shock per se. At an average incubation period of about eight years, most HIV-positive individuals have not developed AIDS yet. So they are currently not ill and still able to function normally for a number of years. Once HIV-infected individuals start developing AIDS, they will either get treatment and be able to work—or not get treatment and die within one or at most two years. In other words, most of the HIV-affected households will not yet suffer any of the negative health consequence of AIDS.

But at some point an individual's immune system will be damaged to such an extent that the person develops AIDS. This is often accompanied by substantial weight loss. Indeed, at the individual level the .061 correlation coefficient between HIV status and weight loss is not perfect but is statistically highly significant (p-value .003). Of HIV-negative individuals, 13% experienced a drop in weight in the past 12 months compared with 19% of HIV-positive individuals. Thus, losing weight partly proxies for a more developed state of HIV/AIDS which *will* lead to additional health problems, medical costs, and a decreasing capacity to work. Over time, more Namibians infected with HIV will develop AIDS. Without treatment, the consequences for households will be large because of the increasing pressure on one's own coping strategies and on the capacity of social networks to keep providing informal assistance.

Coping with a death in the family

A death in the household leads to substantial medical expenditures for uninsured households (column 1) but does not affect earned income in the past year (column 2). The latter finding cannot be due to the perverse effect that the death of a household member with a below-average contribution to household income might actually increase per capita income. We are looking not at per capita household income but at total household income. Columns 4 and 5 suggest that the latter finding is also not due to an increase in labor supply of other household members to offset the drop in earnings. The coefficients on a death shock in the labor regressions are small and not statistically significant. A potential explanation could be that terminally ill individuals return to their parental home to die. In that case, the household will report a deceased family member. But earned income is not affected because prior to his or her terminal stage, the individual did not contribute to household income either.

We do not find evidence of increased remittances and other sources of unearned income for households confronted with a death in the family (column 3)—or of increased use of credit (column 8) to pay for the medical costs or the funeral for example. Annual food consumption of those with a deceased household member (column 6) is not substantially different from the consumption levels of other households. By construction, the extrapolated weekly food expenditures do not capture a drop in consumption half a year earlier if it was followed by a subsequent recovery before the previous week. We find substantially higher expenditures on nonfood items for the insured who experience a death, but not for the uninsured. It is possible that uninsured households compensate for the medical and death-related costs by subsequently reducing consumption of other nonfood items. The asset score is substantially lower for uninsured households with a death in the family but not for the insured (column 9). This suggests that selling assets is one way for uninsured households to cover death-related (medical) expenditures.

Coping with the consequences of hospitalization

Hospitalization results in high medical costs for uninsured households. Earned income does not appear to be affected by hospitalization, perhaps indicating that recovery after treatment is swift enough to prevent income from dropping substantially. This interpretation is supported by the insignificant coefficient on the labor outcome variable. Overall, hospitalizations are more prevalent among the lower quintiles (see table 3.6). So it is unlikely that any negative effects of hospitalization on income are offset by a positive correlation between income and seeking hospital treatment.

Two findings stand out. First, both uninsured and insured households show significantly higher unearned income if a household member has been hospitalized for at least three nights. Further analysis of the underlying components of unearned income shows that this is related to two main sources. The first is help for medical expenses from relatives, friends, or employers. The second is social security (such as three-month unemployment, maternity leave, or a maintenance grant). Individuals who expect to receive informal assistance from others could be more likely to become hospitalized. If households with a strong social network are better able to afford hospitalization, they might be more likely to seek inpatient treatment when needed.

A second finding is that both annual nonfood consumption and the asset score are significantly lower for uninsured households with a hospitalization shock than for those without one. One way for uninsured households to cope with high hospitalization costs may be to postpone large nonfood expenditures and to sell durables. Households with health insurance on the other hand report higher nonfood expenses if one of their members has been hospitalized.

Scope for targeting

Despite the relatively accessible public health care system in Greater Windhoek, households without health insurance suffer from large medical expenditures after the death, hospitalization, or weight loss of an adult household member. Although gifts and support from others help them overcome part of the financial burden, findings indicate that households without health insurance must resort to additional coping strategies, such as selling assets, reducing nonfood consumption, or taking out loans. For households with access to private health insurance, the economic consequences of health shocks are far less pronounced.

The results do not show substantial effects related to HIV infection, but for advanced cases the consequences can be serious. Losing weight is in part a proxy for a more advanced state of AIDS if the patient is not receiving antiretroviral therapy. Weight loss is not only associated with high medical costs but also with substantially lower labor productivity and earned income. Remittances from others are significant but not sufficient to compensate for all consequences of the health shock, as the higher use of credit among affected households suggests.

This finding is particularly worrisome in view of the high HIV prevalence rates in Namibia. As more infected people without insurance develop AIDS over time, the public sector and social support networks will come under increasing pressure. Table 3.8 shows the HIV infection rates of working-age adults across socioeconomic categories. It should be interpreted with some caution, because the sample is not representative for Greater Windhoek due to the loss of respondents. But it clearly shows four patterns. First, prevalence rates are significantly higher among the poorest quintiles. Second, they are significantly higher for individuals who have

TABLE 3.8

HIV infection rates among working-age adults in biomedical Republic of Namibia Okambilimbili Survey sample 2006

	Number of observations	HIV infection rate (%)
Consumption quintile		
1 (poorest)	379	13.2
2	366	12.6
3	370	8.1
4	385	6.8
5 (richest)	306	6.2
Education level		
No education	129	15.5
Primary incomplete	208	13.9
Primary complete	123	13.0
Secondary incomplete	806	10.3
Secondary complete	444	5.2
Higher education	182	6.0
Employment status		
Employed	1,053	11.1
Unemployed	838	7.8
Industry		
Manufacturing	37	8.1
Construction	63	15.9
Retail and accommodation	106	11.3
Transport and storage	40	2.5
Services	345	9.6
Government and defense	135	18.5
Education	50	8.0
Health	35	5.7
Other	239	11.3
Individual insurance status		
Insured	553	8.1
Uninsured	1,342	10.2
Total	1,895	9.6

Note: Includes only working-age adults ages 15–65 with reliable HIV results.

Source: Authors' calculations based on 2006 Republic of Namibia Okambilimbili Survey.

not completed secondary education, especially for those without education at all. Third, HIV infection is more prevalent among the employed, especially among workers in government and defense. Fourth, HIV infection is higher among individuals without health insurance.

A high percentage of households involved in government or defense have at least one household member covered by health insurance (see table 3.1). But other sectors severely affected by HIV, such as the construction, retail, and accommodation sectors, show some of the lowest insurance coverage rates. Moreover, the poorest and least educated are most likely to be infected and least likely to be insured. For the uninsured the economic consequences of arriving at a more developed state of HIV/AIDS are potentially large and reach beyond the affected household into its social support network.

Our findings on the inequitable impacts of health shocks on the uninsured in Namibia are particularly pertinent because of the recent introduction of low cost subsidized health insurance products with an emphasis on HIV/AIDS treatment in Greater Windhoek. These products are among a set of programs initiated by two Dutch organizations, PharmAccess Foundation (PharmAccess) and the Health Insurance Fund, which currently provide low cost voluntary health insurance products for low-income workers in Africa using private sector insurance companies and health maintenance organizations.

A 2004 pilot program introduced this concept of health financing in Greater Windhoek. The Okambilimbili (butterfly) project focused on supporting Diamond Health Services, a newcomer in the Namibian private health care industry. This network of service providers offered an affordable primary health care product that included HIV/AIDS counseling and treatment (highly active antiretroviral treatment, HAART) and the treatment of tuberculosis and malaria to the uninsured employed population. The program emphasized selling insurance through employers rather than to individual workers. Initially, the product was meant to be subsidized through PharmAccess, so the costs for employees would be kept low. In the end, however, premiums were subsidized up to 50% by employers.

When it was recognized that engaging the wider medical aid fund industry was needed to scale up access to HIV/AIDS treatment, PharmAccess initiated negotiations with the private medical aid fund industry. By the end of 2005 three affordable health care packages for low- and middle-income employees were available on the Namibian market: primary health care, HAART, and basic hospitalization. New employer-subsidized insurance products were launched in May 2006. To share the risk for the insurance industry due to the high HIV/AIDS prevalence in Namibia, PharmAccess supported a risk equalization fund, HEALTH-IS-VITAL, which became the key part of the PharmAccess program. In this fund the employer-based insured and the previously uninsured groups contribute monthly premiums to a risk pool with a defined set of HIV/AIDS treatment benefits. Thus they share the financial risk of high medical costs related to HIV/AIDS treatment. In addition to subsidizing the risk equalization fund, part of the Okambilimbili project budget has been allocated to a treatment literacy campaign, which enables project partners to focus on awareness raising, treatment education, advocacy, support, and information sharing.

There is substantial demand for the new low cost insurance schemes. Of the 25 companies approached to participate in the new products, 24 agreed. All their employees have been tested for HIV, and HIV/AIDS treatment and counseling are included in all new types of low cost insurance packages. Even though the majority of individual participants belong to the third and fourth income quintiles, substantial subsidies remain necessary to keep the schemes affordable. The participating companies contribute to the costs at a 50% employer subsidy of the premium for the employees. At present, more than 30,000 people are benefiting from the new insurance products.

Our findings suggest that those lacking private health insurance are substantially affected by health-related shocks when they are forced to resort to coping strategies, which may leave them with a weak asset base. The initial success of this low-cost health insurance program provides some encouragement for the protection of more individuals from the impacts of health shocks, such as those related to HIV/AIDS.

Conclusions

Despite widely available and relatively well financed public care, the economic consequences of health shocks can be severe for uninsured households who resort to a variety of coping strategies to deal with high medical expenses and reductions in income, such as selling assets or taking up credit. HIV infection is not directly related to severe negative outcomes, but weight loss, a known correlate with advanced AIDS, is. According to our findings, the poor in Greater Windhoek are significantly more likely to be HIV infected and less likely to be covered by health insurance, resulting in significant exposure to health and financial risks.

One alternative to address poor health outcomes and catastrophic health expenditures in developing countries is to invest more in the public health care system. But we find here that the strong public health care system in Namibia still leaves the poor and uninsured unprotected from health shocks. Another alternative is to invest in private health insurance. To date, there is a proven market for the new low income insurance products being offered in Namibia for those with a regular income. In the program, both employers and employees are willing to participate in the new insurance schemes. The employees mostly belong to the third and fourth income quintiles, and so do not represent the poor. But these households are not rich either, given the high inequality in Namibia.

It is unlikely that the current insurance packages combined with low levels of subsidy can reach the two lowest quintiles. So, to penetrate these groups with insurance, the way forward would be to design tailor-made health insurance products with substantially higher subsidies. Financing for such products would most likely come in a combination of donor and government funds.

We could not estimate the actual impacts of the newly introduced Namibian health insurance schemes due to the cross-sectional data, but data from follow-up surveys will allow for such analysis. For now, however, we can conclude that there is a strong correlation between being uninsured and the negative consequences of health shocks. In light of these findings, particularly in a country such as Namibia with a fairly well developed public health care system, we should continue a serious evidence-based debate on private health insurance as a potential mechanism to provide not only financing for the increasing health care demands facing Africa, but also protection against the significant negative economic consequences resulting directly from health shocks.

TABLE A3.1

Economic outcome and coping variables (uninsured households)

Variable (definition)	Number of observations	Mean	Standard deviation	Minimum	Maximum	Mean uninsured	Mean insured	Difference (p-value)
Health expenditures								
= Natural logarithm of total medical expenditures by the household in the 12 months prior to the survey, excluding the premia for health insurance.	1,749	2.94	2.87	0	11.98	2.44	3.52	.000***
Earned Income								
= Natural logarithm of total income earned in the 12 months prior to the survey by all household members, including income from wage, from own business, and from agriculture.	1,770	9.06	3.85	0	14.40	7.94	10.37	.000***
Unearned income								
= Natural logarithm of total unearned income in the 12 months prior to the survey, including gifts and remittances from relatives, friends, employers, and others; old-age pensions; disability grants; maintenance grants; workman's compensation; social security (three-month employment, funeral, maternity leave); income from rent; and any other sources of unearned income.	1,754	3.04	3.94	0	12.52	3.14	2.94	.293
Food consumption								
= Natural logarithm of total annual household consumption (purchased, received, produced) of food items in the 12 months prior to the survey, through an extrapolation of food consumption in the past week to the entire year.	1,747	9.35	0.82	6.47	12.34	9.05	9.69	.000***

(continued)

TABLE A3.1 (continued)

Economic outcome and coping variables (uninsured households)

Variable (definition)	Number of observations	Mean	Standard deviation	Minimum	Maximum	Mean uninsured	Mean insured	Difference (p-value)
Ln Nonfood consumption								
= Natural logarithm of total annual household consumption (purchased, received, produced) of food and of nonfood (nonmedical) items in the 12 months prior to the survey, through an extrapolation of food consumption in the past week and monthly nonfood expenditures in the past month to the entire year.	1,657	10.35	1.32	5.69	15.11	9.62	11.14	.000***
Labor supply[a]								
= Total number of months that household members worked for income in the 12 months prior to the survey divided by the total number of working-age household members.	1,742	6.59	4.01	0	32	5.69	7.64	.000***
Assets								
= The first score from a factor analysis of 28 types of assets.	1,760	0.00	0.97	-1.22	3.81	-0.50	0.58	.000***
Credit								
= Dummy variable equal to 1 if in the 12 months prior to the survey any household member bought goods on credit or got a cash loan from any institution or any person, and 0 otherwise.	1,770	.353	.478	0	1	.241	.484	.000***

*** significant at $p < 0.01$.

a. Labor supply of children under age 15 is not included as a potential coping variable because the incidence of child labor is extremely low in Greater Windhoek.

Source: Authors.

TABLE A3.2

Consequences of health shocks for uninsured and insured households including income quintiles in regression

Uninsured (n=948)	Ln Medical expenditures	Ln Earned Income	Ln Unearned income	Labor (number of workers as percentage of working-age household members)	Labor (average number of months worked)	Ln Annual food consumption	Ln Annual nonfood consumption	Credit and borrowing	Assets
Weight loss	.775 [.202]***	-.544 [.281]*	.632 [.262]**	-.049 [.030]	-.781 [.319]**	.021 [.039]	.035 [.047]	.067 [.035]**	.010 [.032]
HIV-infected household member	-.005 [.275]	.091 [.330]	.367 [.338]	.040 [.037]	.466 [.394]	-.023 [.057]	-.175 [.079]**	-.095 [.041]**	-.113 [.046]**
Death in the household	.580 [.315]*	.017 [.547]	.095 [.440]	-.008 [.048]	-.060 [.533]	.029 [.095]	-.017 [.080]	.030 [.061]	-.088 [.046]*
Hospitalization for at least three nights	1.034 [.198]***	.184 [.242]	.586 [.330]*	.007 [.024]	.031 [.267]	-.020 [.050]	.006 [.050]	-.035 [.037]	-.072 [.039]*

Insured (n=821)	Ln Medical expenditures	Ln Earned Income	Ln Unearned income	Labor (number of workers as percentage of working-age household members)	Labor (average number of months worked)	Ln Annual food consumption	Ln Annual nonfood consumption	Credit and borrowing	Assets
Weight loss	.379 [.238]	.196 [.234]	.429 [.341]	-.015 [.021]	-.149 [.305]	.030 [.043]	.071 [.043]	.053 [.041]	.083 [.047]*
HIV-infected household member	.756 [.409]*	-.056 [.283]	-.344 [.556]	.044 [.031]	.598 [.393]	.009 [.067]	-.204 [.068]***	.030 [.083]	-.140 [.080]*
Death in the household	.180 [.346]	.381 [.522]	.279 [.710]	.023 [.051]	.220 [.633]	-.197 [.111]*	.234 [.109]**	.147 [.108]	-.048 [.101]
Hospitalization for at least three nights	.132 [.224]	.341 [.209]	.713 [.367]*	-.003 [.023]	-.101 [.280]	-.016 [.043]	.051 [.048]*	.038 [.039]	.009 [.055]

*** significant at $p < 0.01$; ** significant at $p < 0.05$; * significant at $p < 0.10$.

Note: Numbers in brackets are robust standard errors adjusted for clustering at the PSU level. Dependent variables are at household level totals. Results for per capita dependent variables are similar. The regressions also include head of household characteristics (age, age squared, sex, education), household size, number of children, and neighborhood fixed effects. The credit and borrowing column gives marginal probabilities from a probit estimation instead of an ordinary least squares regression.

Source: Authors' calculations.

Notes

1. The authors thank Adam Wagstaff, Robert Sparrow, Aparnaa Somanathan, Ingrid de Beer, and Michael Grimm for comments and suggestions on earlier drafts of this chapter.
2. WHO 2004.
3. Feeley and others 2006
4. We also found a significant difference between the insured and uninsured for each age group, indicating that age is not the determining factor in this difference.
5. We would have liked to examine differences across consumption quintiles also, but frequencies at that level of disaggregation are so low that analysis of that data would not be robust.
6. We do not have data on savings. Nor do we have information on whether a household decided to forgo care in relation to the specific health shocks that we examine here.
7. Our results do not substantially change if we also include income quintile as a control variable.
8. See, for example, Wagstaff (2007) and references therein.
9. To calculate prevalence rates adjusted for bias due to nonresponse, Janssens, van der Gaag, and Rinke de Wit (2008) use a Heckman selection model. The explanatory variables also include a substantial number of biological markers for HIV infection such as coughing, tuberculosis, and sexually transmitted diseases, as well as attitudes toward and knowledge of HIV/AIDS.
10. UNAIDS 2008.
11. Labor supply of children under age 15 is not included as a potential coping variable because the incidence of child labor is extremely low in Greater Windhoek.

References

Beegle, K., J. de Weerdt, and S. Dercon. 2008. "Adult Mortality and Consumption Growth in the Age of HIV/AIDS." *Economic Development and Cultural Change* 56 (2): 299–326.

Ekman, B. 2004. "Community-based Health Insurance in Low-Income Countries: A Systematic Review of the Evidence." *Health Policy and Planning* 19 (5): 249–70.

Ekman, B., N. T. Liem, H. A. Duc, and H. Axelson. 2008. "Health Insurance Reform in Vietnam: A Review of Recent Developments and Future Challenges." *Health Policy and Planning* 23 (4): 252–63.

Feeley, F., I. de Beer, T. Rinke de Wit, and J. van der Gaag. 2006. "The Health Insurance Industry in Namibia." Baseline Report. Boston University, Boston, MA, and Amsterdam Institute for International Development and PharmAccess Foundation, Amsterdam.

Fox, M. P., S. Rosen, W. B. Macleod, M. Wasunna, M. Bii, G. Foglia, and J.L. Simon. 2004. "The Impact of HIV/AIDS on Labour Productivity in Kenya." *Tropical Medicine and International Health* 9 (3): 318–24.

Gaag, van der J., and V. Stimac. 2008. "Towards a New Paradigm for Health Sector Development." AIID Discussion Series 08-02/1. Amsterdam Institute for International Development, Amsterdam.

Gertler, P., and J. Gruber. 2002. "Insuring Consumption against Illness." *American Economic Review* 92 (1): 51–70.

Janssens, W., T. Rinke de Wit, and J. van der Gaag. 2007. "Bio-Medical Baseline Report 2006–2007: Okambilimbili Health Insurance Project in Windhoek, Namibia." Amsterdam Institute for International Development and PharmAccess Foundation, Amsterdam.

Janssens, W., J. van der Gaag, and T. Rinke de Wit. 2008. "Pitfalls in the Estimation of HIV Prevalence Rates." AIID Research Series 08-03. Amsterdam Institute for International Development, Amsterdam.

Sekhri, N., and W. Savedoff. 2005. "Private Health Insurance: Implications for Developing Countries." *Bulletin of the World Health Organization* 83 (2): 127–34.

Thirumurthy, H., J. Graff Zivin, and M. Goldstein. 2005. *The Economic Impact of AIDS Treatment: Labor Supply in Western Kenya.* NBER Working Paper 11871. Cambridge, MA: National Bureau of Economic Research.

UNAIDS (Joint United Nations Programme on HIV/AIDS). 2008. "Epidemiological Fact Sheets on HIV and AIDS: Namibia, 2008 Update." Joint United Nations Programme on HIV/AIDS, Geneva.

Wagstaff, A. 2007. "The Economic Consequences of Health Shocks: Evidence from Vietnam." *Health Economics* 26 (1): 82–100.

Wagstaff, A., and M. Lindelow. 2008. "Can Insurance Increase Financial Risk? The Curious Case of Health Insurance in China." *Health Economics* 27 (4): 990–1005.

World Bank. 2010. *World Development Indicators 2010.* Washington, DC: World Bank.

WHO (World Health Organization). 2004. "WHO Country Cooperation Strategy, Republic of Namibia, 2004–2007." World Health Organization, Geneva.

———. 2005. "Namibia Country Profile: Overview of Malaria Control Activities and Programme Progress." World Health Organization, Geneva.

———. 2008a. "TB Country Profile: Namibia." World Health Organization, Geneva.

———. 2008b. *World Health Statistics 2008.* Geneva: World Health Organization.

Ghana's National Health Insurance Scheme

Slavea Chankova, Chris Atim, and Laurel Hatt

In 2003 Ghana introduced a National Health Insurance Scheme (NHIS) that aimed to cover the entire population with affordable access to basic health services within five years. This chapter provides an overview and analysis of the evolution of the NHIS in the first years of its operation, and the results from an impact evaluation on the effect the NHIS has had on use and out-of-pocket expenditures for health care. The evaluation was conducted in two districts in Ghana, using a pre-post evaluation design.

In its first three years of operation, the NHIS caused an increase in the use of curative health care services and improved financial protection against out-of-pocket expenditures for health care. It did not increase the use of maternal health care, which remains an area where nonfinancial barriers to access may overshadow the effects of increased financial protection. High population coverage has ensured better access to health services for the majority of Ghana's people, but the NHIS has not achieved equitable enrollment. Better targeting for poor people needs to be developed to achieve 100% coverage of the population.

Three key factors, taken together, threaten the financial sustainability of the scheme over time: rapidly rising enrollment, the generous benefit package, and a fairly constant insurance revenue base. The challenges to sustainability identified in this study may threaten the successes achieved in the early years of implementation and need to be addressed without delay.

Ghana's health system

Ghana's health profile is characteristic of most low-income Sub-Saharan African countries. Communicable diseases still constitute the major causes of morbidity and mortality. Malaria accounts for 40% of outpatient visits and has a high mortality rate (13%), affecting mostly young children. Other diseases in the top 10 most common causes of death include respiratory tract infections, skin disease and ulcers, diarrheal diseases, anemia, and hypertension. Pregnancy and related complications are also among the top 10 and, with yellow fever and meningococcal meningitis, are major public health concerns (Ghana Health Service 2007).

Ghana's Ministry of Health leads the health sector and is responsible for policy development, planning, donor coordination, and resource mobilization. The health system was restructured beginning in 1993, with an emphasis on decentralizing from the regional and national levels to district administrations and district health management teams. The Ghana Health Service, an autonomous executive agency under the ministry responsible for implementation of national policies and service delivery, was established in 1996 as part of these reforms. It is organized in five levels: national, regional, district, subdistrict, and community.

Services are available in the public, private (for-profit, mission, and nonprofit), and informal sectors. Private providers—a coalition of nongovernmental organizations, the Christian Health Association of Ghana, Catholic mission hospitals, and private for-profit providers—account for 40% of patient care (WHO 2008).

Health care financing

After Ghana won independence from colonial rule in 1957, its new government was committed to a welfare state system that included "free health care for all." User fees for health services were low and not aimed at cost recovery: nominal fees of 20 pence for hospital visits had existed before independence and continued to be charged thereafter (Dzakpallah 1988). But the general thrust of government policy was for equitable social development, manifested in a policy to make health care easily accessible to all at the point of use.

In 1969 the first post-independence government attempted to institute partial cost recovery in health and education (Dzakpallah 1988). Such fees quickly made the government unpopular, ushering in conditions that led to its removal from office after only a few years in power. This experience also led subsequent governments to shy away from any meaningful health financing reforms, including alternative ways of financing health, such as insurance.

During the 1970s health facilities and services entered a long period of decline. Inadequate resources were allocated to rehabilitate existing facilities falling into disrepair or to build new ones for rural populations that lacked reasonable access. Characterizing the decline were severe shortages of essential medicines and other supplies, badly paid and demoralized staff, illegal under-the-table payments by patients, and other similar signs of service deterioration. Some efforts at reform during this period floundered partly because a succession of military dictatorships lacked the legitimacy to push through painful changes.

User fees and exemptions

With the era of President Jerry Rawlings, which spanned most of the 1980s and all of the 1990s, health financing reform returned to the political agenda in a serious way. In 1985 the "cash and carry" or user fee system was established, aiming to recover up to 20% of operational nonsalary costs from patients. From the outset, the system was perceived as burdensome (Singleton 2006), and several studies showed its deterrent effect on use by the poor (Waddington and Enyimayew 1989, 1990; Nyonator and Kutzin 1999). In 1997 the government introduced fee exemptions for children under age 5, pregnant women, the elderly (older than age 70), extreme indigents, and those suffering from certain communicable diseases. In theory the patient's ability to pay for the services would be assessed by the doctor after examination. But in practice the facilities' incentive was to collect fees whenever possible, and patients were often asked to pay a "consultation fee" at the registration desk (Atim and others 2001).

Fee exemption policies for children under age 5, pregnant women, and the elderly also faced various difficulties from the start: unclear or nonexistent guidelines, uneven application, and inadequate budgetary allocations (Atim and others 2001). These persistent difficulties aggravated the problems of access for vulnerable people.[1] It was reported that "many patients were observed to have difficulty with paying for their health care (especially admission) costs. Many did not turn up at the hospital until it was too late or their illness had advanced to a more complicated phase. Some others who got admitted and were treated subsequently absconded without paying for their treatment. Many simply could not afford to pay for their care" (Atim and Sock 2000).

Growth of risk pooling

Against this background some stakeholders began to explore alternatives to user fees, especially community-based health insurance schemes. The first was the Nkoranza District Health Insurance Scheme, started in 1992 by the Catholic Diocese of Sunyani, which managed the Nkoranza District Hospital. This was basically a facilitiy cost-recovery scheme—a well informed provider's response to patients' observed inability to pay for care.

Other stakeholders, including the Ministry of Health, soon began to explore the possibilities of setting up similar schemes elsewhere in the country. A new model, the mutual health organization, was introduced around 1999, partly inspired by experience in francophone Africa. The model was based on social solidarity, community ownership, and democratic control, as opposed to the provider-driven model typified by the Nkoranza scheme. This model spread rapidly in the country, expanding from 3 schemes in 1999, to 47 in 2001, 159 in 2002, and 258 in 2003 (Atim and others 2001; Atim and Apoya 2003).

The factors that led to the rise and rapid growth of such schemes, especially the many problems with the user fee system, did not escape the notice of politicians. The leading opposition political party soon took up the issue and promised to do away with user fees if they came to power in the 2000 election (Rajkotia 2007; Singleton 2006), which perhaps played a crucial role in its victory. But only in the third year of the new government, with the approaching election of 2004, was a law rushed through establishing the NHIS.

The new national scheme

The NHIS was established under the National Health Insurance Act of 2003, which set out three distinct types of health insurance schemes to be established and operated in Ghana: district mutual health insurance, private commercial health insurance, and private mutual health insurance. Schemes must apply to the National Health Insurance Authority, which has the mandate to register, license, and supervise all schemes.[2] All public health facilities in the country are automatically accredited, but private health facilities have to apply for accreditation by the authority in order to participate. By December 2008, 1,551 private providers of different categories had been accredited (Ghana National Health Insurance Authority 2008).

The authority also manages the National Health Insurance Fund (NHIF), which is financed primarily by a sales tax levy (a 2.5% earmarked addition to the value added tax) and 2.5% of formal sector workers' contributions to the Social Security and National Insurance Trust Fund (SSNIT) (Parliament of the Republic of Ghana 2003). The NHIF provides a subsidy to the district mutual schemes to reinsure them against random fluctuations in claims expenditures, to support programs that improve access to health services, and to cover the cost of health care for indigents and other "exempt" groups deemed worthy of being subsidized.

The NHIS provides an extremely generous benefits package, covering more than 95% of the disease conditions that afflict Ghanaians, including outpatient and inpatient care, deliveries (including complications), diagnostic tests, generic medicines, and emergency care. The district mutual schemes must adhere to this standard benefit package.

To become a member, an individual needs to register with the nearest district mutual scheme or through an agent, then wait up to six months to begin using services. Payment of appropriate premium and registration fees is required for those not exempt.[3] In general, premiums are meant to be based on income and capacity to pay, with a nationally determined floor of 72,000 cedis a year (just over US$5).[4] Districts are authorized to set premium levels, which range in practice from 72,000 cedis to 480,000 cedis across the country (Asenso-Boadi 2009).[5] Groups exempt from paying premiums include SSNIT contributors (by virtue of their 2.5% contribution to the National Health Insurance Fund[6]) and pensioners; people ages 70 and older; children under age 18; indigents; and pregnant women (as of 1 July 2008, after the final set of household data used in this chapter had been collected).

Health care providers participating in the national scheme periodically send claims for scheme member service use to the district mutual scheme managers, who in turn send the claims to the national authority for settlement. The national scheme reimburses providers through the same path, from the national fund to the district mutual scheme, which then pays the providers. In exceptional circumstances, the national fund may send repayment directly to a provider.

Early successes and challenges

The national scheme has produced significant achievements during its short existence, notably, the remarkable growth of its membership. There were 145 district mutual schemes in operation at the end of 2008. Total membership was just more than 12.5 million, or 61% of the population, surpassing the NHIS target of 40% (Ghana National Health Insurance Authority 2008). About 70% of the members are in the premium-exempt categories (table 4.1), as only "informal sector adults" pay the annual premium.

While official country data show that an estimated 40% of the population lives below the national poverty line, indigents account for only 2.4% of members. The NHIS means test for indigents is strict, requiring that the person be unemployed with no visible source of income, be homeless, and have no identifiable support from another person (Republic of Ghana 2004). This narrow definition reduces the incentives of scheme managers to try to identify such persons.[7] As a result, the NHIS benefits are out of reach for many poor people, although premium exemptions for children and the elderly blunt that problem somewhat.

TABLE 4.1
National Health Insurance Scheme membership, 2008

Category of membership	Total	Percent of population
Informal sector adults	3,727,454	29.8
Ages 70 and older	866,956	6.9
Under age 18[a]	6,305,729	50.4
SSNIT contributors	811,567	6.5
SSNIT pensioners	71,147	0.6
Pregnant women[b]	432,728	3.5
Indigents	302,979	2.4
Total registered	12,518,560	61.3

a. Children under age 18 were initially exempt only if their parents or guardian were scheme contributors. Since 1 September 2008, however, children under age 18 have been exempt in their own right (known as "decoupling").

b. The exemption for pregnant women became effective on 1 July 2008 for up to four prenatal visits, delivery care, and one postnatal visit, as well as all other minimum medical benefits needed during the 12 months following initial registration.

Source: Ghana National Health Insurance Authority 2008.

There have also been well documented delays in issuing member identification cards after people have registered. In principle, the cards should be available by the end of the waiting period for the scheme, but delays well beyond this period are frequent. There is also some evidence that insured people regard the health care they receive to be of poorer quality than that of noninsured people (Asenso-Boadi 2009). There have been reports of negative provider attitudes and practices, such as illegal fee collection and possibly deliberate delays in seeing insured patients (World Bank 2007). Weak performance incentives for NHIS-accredited providers have been cited as one cause for poor quality care. In addition, supply has not kept pace with the increased demand for health services resulting from NHIS coverage, and this may compromise the quality of care (Ghana Ministry of Health 2008).

Some argue that the scheme's generous benefit package, reimbursement systems used by the NHIS for claims (initially fee-for-service and now diagnosis-related groups), and weak capacity for verifying provider claims at the scheme level gave providers incentives to provide more (or more expensive) drugs and services than necessary to insured patients—and to submit fraudulent claims (Rajkotia 2007; Garshong 2008). NHIS management reports many cases of misapplication of tariffs and spurious reimbursement claims by providers (Asenso-Boadi 2009). Delays in claims payment and the substantial workload for providers to process claims, also well documented, have caused problems for providers (Asenso-Boadi 2009; World Bank 2007).

Evaluation of the National Health Insurance Scheme

In 2004 the United States Agency for International Development–funded Partners for Health Reform*plus* project, in collaboration with the Health Research Unit of the Ghana Health Service, initiated an evaluation of the NHIS. The study focused on the following research questions:

- Who has enrolled in the NHIS?
  - Do enrollment rates differ across socioeconomic groups?
  - Is there evidence of adverse selection in NHIS enrollment?
  - How well targeted have exemptions been?
- What is the impact of the NHIS on the use of health services?
- What is the impact of the NHIS on out-of-pocket expenditures for health care?

The study was designed as a pre-post evaluation. (The appendix contains a more detailed discussion of study methods). Two districts were selected as study sites: Nkoranza (in the Brong Ahafo region) and Offinso (in the Ashanti region). A baseline household survey was conducted in September 2004, prior to NHIS roll-out. In September 2007, more than two years after launch of the NHIS, an endline household survey was conducted in the same study sites to measure the effects of NHIS implementation. The endline survey did not cover the same households as the baseline. The baseline and endline surveys collected information on socio-demographic characteristics of households; health insurance membership; health care use; and payments associated with injury or illness in the two weeks prior to the survey, hospitalization in the 12 months prior to the survey, and delivery in the 12 months prior to the survey.

At baseline 23% of the individuals in the sample were members of a community-based health insurance scheme (35% in Nkoranza and 0% in Offinso), whereas at endline 35% across both districts were enrolled in the NHIS (45% in Nkoranza and 25% in Offinso). The baseline and endline samples of individuals were similar in distribution by age group, sex, and urban/rural location (see table A4.4 in the appendix).

A significantly larger proportion of the endline sample belonged to a female-headed household, a household headed by an individual with some education (rather than no education), and a household in the top two pooled wealth quintiles. A smaller proportion of the endline sample was from households headed by a farmer, while a higher proportion was from households headed by a skilled worker or a government employee (see table A4.4 in the appendix). These differences between the survey samples imply some overall improvement in the socioeconomic status of the two districts' population in the three years between the baseline and endline surveys.

The proportion of individuals reporting illness or injury in the two weeks before the survey declined from 4.3% to 3.1% ($p = 0.03$, statistically significant at the 97%

level). There was no significant change in the distribution of these illness/injury episodes by type of condition or in the proportion that were due to accidents. There was some decrease in the proportion of individuals reporting hospitalization during the 12 months prior to the survey (2.4% to 1.9%) and in the proportion of women ages 15–49 reporting a birth in the 12 months prior to the survey (12% to 11%), though neither difference was statistically significant (see table A4.4 in the appendix).

Determinants of enrollment in the National Health Insurance Scheme

Enrollment in the NHIS in 2007 increased with wealth quintile: 52% of those in the top wealth quintile were enrolled in the NHIS, compared with 18% in the poorest quintile. This pattern of enrollment across wealth quintiles holds within age groups, including the age groups exempt from premiums (table 4.2). Increasing rates of enrollment with higher wealth quintiles are also observed within groups defined by occupation of the head of household. (These data were collected before the 2008 changes that unconditionally exempted all children and pregnant women from paying enrollment premiums.)

Probit regression analysis indicates that enrollment in NHIS was more likely if the individual was female, had a reported chronic illness, or belonged to a household headed by a female or a household participating in a community solidarity group (table 4.3). Likelihood of NHIS enrollment increased with education of the head of household and wealth quintile. Children and the elderly (particularly those ages 70 and older) were more likely to enroll than adults ages 18–49, which reflects the age-based premium exemption policies. Residents of Offinso were less likely to enroll than those of Nkoranza, possibly because of the higher premiums charged by the scheme in Offinso. Also, prior experience with community-based health

TABLE 4.2

Individuals with National Health Insurance Scheme insurance coverage, by wealth quintile and age category, 2007 endline survey (%)

Wealth quintile	Age category					Total
	0–4	5–17	18–49	50–69	70+	
Poorest	15	20	15	19	40	18
Middle-poor	29	31	25	32	50	30
Middle	37	43	33	48	62	40
Middle-rich	30	44	32	40	63	39
Richest	51	55	43	62	82	52
Total	31	38	30	41	58	35

Source: Authors' calculations.

TABLE 4.3

Predictors of individual enrollment in National Health Insurance Scheme 2007 sample only (multivariate probit model results)

Variable	Total sample		Nkoranza		Offinso	
	Enrolled in National Health Insurance Scheme (coefficient)	Marginal effect	Enrolled in National Health Insurance Scheme (coefficient)	Marginal effect	Enrolled in National Health Insurance Scheme (coefficient)	Marginal effect
Male	-0.108*** [0.032]	-0.0391	-0.108** [0.044]	-0.0426	-0.107** [0.046]	-0.0319
Age group (reference: ages 18-49)						
0-4	0.107** [0.041]	0.0393	0.052 [0.051]	0.0204	0.193*** [0.058]	0.0608
5-17	0.301*** [0.037]	0.111	0.210*** [0.033]	0.0833	0.436*** [0.058]	0.136
50-69	0.295*** [0.058]	0.112	0.127* [0.073]	0.0505	0.527*** [0.081]	0.181
70+	0.869*** [0.111]	0.336	0.597*** [0.147]	0.232	1.189*** [0.162]	0.438
Education of the head of household (reference: no education)						
Primary	0.204* [0.107]	0.0735	0.120 [0.125]	0.0473	0.351* [0.183]	0.103
Secondary or higher	0.418** [0.171]	0.160	0.450*** [0.151]	0.178	0.449 [0.292]	0.151
Household wealth quintile (reference: poorest quintile)						
Poor-middle quintile	0.247* [0.125]	0.0921	0.388** [0.181]	0.154	0.106 [0.191]	0.0324
Middle quintile	0.489*** [0.127]	0.186	0.504*** [0.170]	0.199	0.598*** [0.193]	0.203

Variable	Total sample		Nkoranza		Offinso	
	Enrolled in National Health Insurance Scheme (coefficient)	Marginal effect	Enrolled in National Health Insurance Scheme (coefficient)	Marginal effect	Enrolled in National Health Insurance Scheme (coefficient)	Marginal effect
Middle-rich quintile	0.483*** [0.153]	0.183	0.647** [0.254]	0.253	0.331* [0.185]	0.106
Richest quintile	0.833*** [0.145]	0.318	0.972*** [0.224]	0.369	0.751*** [0.191]	0.256
Offinso district	-0.589*** [0.063]	-0.211				
Urban	-0.124 [0.074]	-0.0439	-0.029 [0.101]	-0.0116	-0.270*** [0.083]	-0.0742
Female household head	0.122* [0.067]	0.0449	0.192** [0.074]	0.0763	0.019 [0.120]	0.00563
At least one household member part of community solidarity scheme	0.251* [0.127]	0.0944	0.218 [0.184]	0.0866	0.307* [0.157]	0.0995
Self-reported chronic condition	0.400*** [0.113]	0.154	0.367*** [0.096]	0.145	0.382 [0.230]	0.128
Constant	-0.905*** [0.116]		-0.917*** [0.120]		-1.590*** [0.240]	
Observations	11,622	11,622	5,740	5,740	5,882	5,882

*** significant at $p < 0.01$; ** significant at $p < 0.05$; * significant at $p < 0.10$.

Note: Numbers in brackets are standard errors.

Source: Authors' calculations.

insurance in Nkoranza may have increased knowledge of insurance, its costs and benefits, and administrative procedures connected with participation. Regression analyses run for each district separately show that determinants of NHIS enrollment were generally the same (see table 4.3).

About half the households that paid premiums to enroll in NHIS stated that the source of payment was income from harvest, 22% said that they used a gift from a friend or a relative, and 14% said that they used their savings. The main reason for nonenrollment in the NHIS, cited by households where no one was enrolled, was that the premiums were unaffordable (76%); fewer than 2% cited lack of confidence in scheme management as a reason.

Adverse selection

We found some evidence of adverse selection in enrollment: those with self-reported chronic illness were more likely to enroll. In the study sites about 4% of individuals reported having a chronic illness. Of those, 55% were enrolled in NHIS, compared with 34% of those who did not report a chronic illness ($p < 0.01$). This pattern was observed in each of the wealth quintiles. In contrast, self-assessed general health status did not appear to be associated with NHIS enrollment. Among households where some but not all members were enrolled in NHIS, only 4% said that they chose to insure only the sick/ill members.

We did not find substantial evidence of adverse selection in enrollment related to pregnancy: 36% of women who had a delivery in the 12 months prior to the study were insured at time of delivery, compared with 33% of women who did not have a delivery ($p = 0.45$). But this difference was larger for women from the top two quintiles, indicating that some wealthier women might have been enrolling for the delivery coverage. The 2008 reforms exempting pregnant women from premiums were intended to encourage pregnant women, especially those from poorer quintiles, to use health services.

Premium exemptions for National Health Insurance Scheme enrollment

How did the rules for premium exemption for government employees, children under age 18, and people ages 70 and older work in the two study districts? Overall, 64% of those enrolled in NHIS reported that they were exempt from premiums. This figure matches national figures on the share of exempt members. Nearly all NHIS members in the two districts had paid a registration fee (97%).

Although government employees are supposed to be automatically enrolled in the NHIS and exempt from paying NHIS premiums, this was not the case in our two study districts. Among the heads of household who were government employees,

70% were enrolled in the NHIS. All of them had to pay a registration fee, and 42% paid a premium that ranged from 55,000 cedis to 170,000 cedis. Age-based exemptions have worked as intended in the two study districts but have not benefitted disproportionately those in the lowest wealth quintile. Among NHIS members, 99% of children under age 18 and 98% of people ages 70 and older had been exempted from paying the premium (table 4.4). In general, this was the case in each of the wealth quintiles. But for people ages 18–69, NHIS members from the poorest quintiles were not more likely to be exempt than those from wealthier quintiles.

Multivariate analyses confirm that, among NHIS members, premium exemption was more likely among children and the elderly (than adults ages 18–49) and individuals from households headed by a government employee. But NHIS members from the poorest wealth quintile were less likely to be exempt than those from wealthier quintiles. Those with chronic illness were less likely to benefit from an exemption than those without such illness.

Effects of National Health Insurance Scheme implementation on health care use and spending

This section presents the impact of NHIS implementation on use and out-of-pocket spending for health care using multivariate regression in the pooled pre-post data. We report results for three types of health events: illness/injury in the two weeks prior to the survey, hospitalization in the 12 months prior to the survey, and delivery in the 12 months prior to the survey.

We report bivariate pre-post comparisons of care-seeking and expenditure indicators and adjusted regression model coefficients and marginal effects for the key

TABLE 4.4

Receipt of exemptions from National Health Insurance Scheme premiums, by age category and quintile (%)

| Age category | Wealth quintile | | | | | Total |
	Poorest	2	3	4	Richest	
0–4	100	100	100	100	100	100
5–17	100	100	98	100	99	99
18–34	3	10	7	2	8	6
35–49	0	2	2	1	8	4
50–69	5	11	9	8	18	11
70+	94	97	100	98	97	98
Total	64	65	59	62	60	62

Source: Authors' calculations.

variable of interest, *implementation of NHIS*, a dummy variable with a value of 0 for observations from the baseline 2004 survey (when the NHIS was not available) and a value of 1 for observations from the endline 2007 survey (when the NHIS was already implemented). The marginal effect for an indicator shows the change (from baseline to endline) in the likelihood of a positive outcome for the indicator, controlling for other potential confounders, including the individual's age, sex, and presence of chronic illness; education, occupation, and sex of the head of household; household wealth quintile; and urban location and district. In addition, the models for health care for illness/injury in the two weeks prior to the survey include self-reported severity of the condition, and the models on maternal care include parity.

TABLE 4.5

Change over 2004–07 in health care utilization and expenditures for illness/injury in the two weeks prior to the survey

		Bivariate comparison		Results from multivariate regressions[a]	
	Baseline 2004[b]	Endline 2007[b]	Signficance	Coefficient[b]	Marginal effect
				Probit regression model	
Sought care at a modern health care provider	N=413[b]	N=411[b]		N=814[b]	
Total	37%	70%	***	1.006*** [0.152]	0.382
Nkoranza	47%	74%	***	0.917*** [0.158]	0.334
Offinso	22%	64%	***	1.347*** [0.377]	0.487
Self-treated or sought care from informal/traditional providers	N=413[b]	N=411[b]		N=814[b]	
Total	76%	44%	***	-0.884*** [0.123]	-0.328
Nkoranza	70%	40%	***	-0.886*** [0.150]	-0.340
Offinso	84%	51%	***	-0.958*** [0.247]	-0.309
Had positive expenditures on treatment	N=413[b]	N=411[b]		N=814[b]	
Total	87%	57%	***	-1.025*** [0.142]	-0.310
Nkoranza	87%	44%	***	-1.504*** [0.177]	-0.478

Health care for illness/injury in the two weeks prior to the survey

The proportion who sought care from a modern provider nearly doubled, from 37% at baseline to 70% at endline ($p < 0.01$; table 4.5). Multivariate regression results confirm this finding, showing a 38 percentage point increase in the likelihood of seeking care between baseline and endline (see table 4.5). The proportion seeking care from an informal provider (such as a chemical seller, pharmacist, herbalist, or traditional healer) or self-treating at home fell significantly, from 76% to 44% ($p < 0.01$; see table 4.5).

These positive changes in care-seeking in the period when the NHIS was implemented were accompanied by a substantial reduction in the likelihood of incurring out-of-pocket spending for health care: average spending for treatment fell from

TABLE 4.5 (continued)

Change over 2004–07 in health care utilization and expenditures for illness/injury in the two weeks prior to the survey

| | Bivariate comparison | | | Results from multivariate regressions[a] | |
	Baseline 2004[b]	Endline 2007[b]	Signficance	Coefficient[b]	Marginal effect
				Probit regression model	
Offinso	86%	76%	*	−0.403** [0.153]	−0.092
Average out-of-pocket expenditures on treatment	N=413[b]	N=411[b]		N=814[b]	
Total	24,437	14,455	**		
Nkoranza	25,260	7,689	***		
Offinso	23,229	25,047			
				Log-linear regression model	
Out-of-pocket expenditures on treatment (among those who had positive expenditures)	N=361[b]	N=226[b]		N=580[b]	
Total	28,131	25,545		0.017 [0.264]	
Nkoranza	28,875	17,381		−0.414 [0.361]	
Offinso	27,020	32,991		0.427* [0.244]	

*** significant at $p < 0.01$; ** significant at $p < 0.05$; * significant at $p < 0.10$.

Note: Numbers in brackets are standard errors.

a. Adjusted regression coefficients and marginal effects for dummy variable that takes the value 0 for 2004 and 1 for 2007 observations.

b. Total sample; sample sizes for Nkoranza and Offinso are smaller.

Source: Authors' calculations.

24,437 cedis to 14,455 (p = 0.02). At baseline, 87% of the ill/injured incurred out-of-pocket spending on treatment, compared with only 57% at endline (p < 0.01). When spending on transportation to the health facility is included, the proportion that incurred spending fell by a smaller amount between baseline and endline, but the difference remains significant (88% to 71%, p < 0.01). There was no significant change in the average amount paid by those who incurred positive out-of-pocket expenditure.

Hospitalization in the 12 months prior to the survey

Results from multivariate analyses show a statistically significant decrease, by less than one percentage point, in the likelihood of hospitalization for illness or injury from 2004 to 2007 (table 4.6). We do not have a measure of the need for hospitalization, so the interpretation of this result is ambiguous: it might be due to earlier care-seeking for illness or increased use of preventive care associated with the NHIS; but the decrease could also reflect supply side factors (such as deterioration of infrastructure for inpatient care) or random fluctuations in illness severity.

TABLE 4.6

Change over 2004–07 in probability of hospitalization and in expenditures for hospitalization episode in the 12 months prior to the survey

	Bivariate comparison			Results from multivariate regressions[a]	
	Baseline 2004	Endline 2007	Significance	Coefficient	Marginal effect
				Probit regression model	
Hospitalized in 12 months prior to the survey	N=9,554[b]	N=11,770[b]		N=20,660[b]	
Total	2.44%	1.87%		–0.168** [0.076]	–0.007
Nkoranza	1.89%	1.60%		–0.104 [0.071]	–0.003
Offinso	3.45%	2.15%		–0.209 [0.126]	–0.012
Paid some amount for hospitalization (among individuals hospitalized in the 12 months prior to the survey)	N=203	N=194		N=396	
Total	87%	43%	***	–1.817*** [0.289]	–0.548
Nkoranza	71%	23%	***	–1.489*** [0.368]	–0.543
Offinso	100%	55%	***	c	
Average out-of-pocket expenditures for hospitalization	N=203	N=194			
Total	357,262	199,488	*		

However, there was a significant positive impact of NHIS implementation on financial protection from the potentially catastrophic expenditures associated with hospitalization. Average out-of-pocket spending for hospitalization decreased from 357,262 cedis to 199,488 (p = 0.08). The proportion of hospitalized individuals who incurred any out-of-pocket spending for their inpatient treatment was halved, from 87% to 43% (p < 0.01) (see table 4.6). Pooled probit regression analysis shows a decline of 55 percentage points in the likelihood of incurring hospitalization expenditures between 2004 and 2007. There was no significant change in the amount paid by those who incurred positive hospitalization expenditures.

Maternal health care

There were no significant changes in the proportion of women who had at least four prenatal care visits, delivered in a health facility, or delivered by Caesarean section (table 4.7). The proportion of deliveries that took place in a health facility was 54.4% in 2004 and remained virtually unchanged (54.9%) in 2007.

TABLE 4.6 (continued)
Change over 2004–07 in probability of hospitalization and in expenditures for hospitalization episode in the 12 months prior to the survey

| | Bivariate comparison | | | Results from multivariate regressions[a] | |
	Baseline 2004	Endline 2007	Significance	Coefficient	Marginal effect
Nkoranza	347,668	171,007			
Offinso	365,393	216,201			
				Log-linear regression model	
Out-of-pocket payment for hospitalization (among those who paid a positive amount for hospitalization)	N=145[b]	N=65[b]		N=209[b]	
Total	411,814	468,007		0.286 [0.292]	
Nkoranza	488,832	746,825		0.404 [0.490]	
Offinso	365,393	398,889		0.419* [0.225]	

*** significant at p < 0.01; ** significant at p < 0.05; * significant at p < 0.10.

Note: Numbers in brackets are standard errors.

a. Adjusted regression coefficients and marginal effects for dummy variable that takes the value 0 for 2004 and 1 for 2007 observations.

b. Total sample; sample sizes for Nkoranza and Offinso are smaller.

c. Not applicable because all who were hospitalized in Offinso at baseline paid for hospitalization.

Source: Authors' calculations.

TABLE 4.7

Change over 2004–20 in utilization of and expenditures for prenatal and delivery care, among women who had delivery in the 12 months prior to the survey

	Bivariate comparison			Results from multivariate regressions[a]	
	Baseline 2004	Endline 2007	Significance	Coefficient	Marginal effect
				Probit regression model	
Had four or more prenatal care visits	N=298[b]	N=312[b]		N=606[b]	
Total	73%	68%		-0.250 [0.179]	-0.083
Nkoranza	75%	67%		-0.290 [0.222]	-0.096
Offinso	71%	70%		-0.243 [0.302]	-0.080
Delivery in modern facility	N=298[b]	N=312[b]		N=606[b]	
Total	54%	55%		-0.121 [0.117]	-0.047
Nkoranza	63%	57%		-0.145 [0.109]	-0.055
Offinso	42%	52%		-0.003 [0.281]	-0.001
Delivery by Caesarian section	N=298[b]	N=312[b]		N=606[b]	
Total	6%	6%		0.024 [0.176]	0.003
Nkoranza	8%	7%		-0.007 [0.228]	-0.001
Offinso	4%	6%		0.392 [0.300]	0.001
Paid for prenatal care	N=298[b]	N=312[b]		N=606[b]	
Total	88%	55%	***	-1.158*** [0.170]	-0.352
Nkoranza	84%	43%	***	-1.214*** [0.138]	-0.422
Offinso	94%	70%	**	-1.234** [0.507]	-0.205
Average out-of-pocket expenditures for prenatal care	N=298[b]	N=312[b]		N=606[b]	
Total	49,671	42,782			
Nkoranza	42,446	18,298	***		
Offinso	61,212	74,704			
Paid for delivery[c]	N=298[b]	N=312[b]		N=606[b]	
Total	74%	47%	***	-0.885*** [0.145]	-0.326

TABLE 4.7 (continued)

Change over 2004-20 in utilization of and expenditures for prenatal and delivery care, among women who had delivery in the 12 months prior to the survey

	Bivariate comparison			Results from multivariate regressions[a]	
	Baseline 2004	Endline 2007	Significance	Coefficient	Marginal effect
				Probit regression model	
Nkoranza	77%	43%	***	-1.020*** [0.212]	-0.374
Offinso	69%	53%		-0.768*** [0.165]	-0.280
Average out-of-pocket expenditures for delivery	N=298[b]	N=312[b]		N=606[b]	
Total	108,217	75,481			
Nkoranza	106,017	53,037	***		
Offinso	111,754	105,009			
				Log-linear regression model	
Out-of-pocket expenditures for prenatal care (among women who had positive expenditures)	N=248[b]	N=155[b]		N=400[b]	
Total	54,399	75,641	**	0.072 [0.143]	
Nkoranza	48,215	38,533		-0.227 [0.243]	
Offinso	63,408	109,239	***	0.438** [0.181]	
Out-of-pocket expenditures for delivery (among women who had positive expenditures)	N=221[b]	N=135[b]		N=353[b]	
Total	146,642	158,930		0.091 [0.134]	
Nkoranza	138,591	122,559		-0.136 [0.128]	
Offinso	160,896	197,968		0.597** [0.262]	

*** significant at $p < 0.01$; ** significant at $p < 0.05$.

Note: Numbers in brackets are standard errors.

a. Adjusted regression coefficients and marginal effects for dummy variable that takes the value 0 for 2004 and 1 for 2007 observations.

b. Total sample; sample sizes for Nkoranza and Offinso are smaller.

c. Total sample N = 590.

Source: Authors' calculations.

But there was a substantial reduction in the proportion of women who incurred out-of-pocket expenditures for maternal care between baseline and endline. While 88% of women had some prenatal care expenditures at baseline, only 55% reported expenditures at endline ($p < 0.01$). Average spending on prenatal care fell from 49,671 cedis to 42,782, though the change was not statistically significant ($p = 0.41$). Among those who paid a positive amount, expenditures increased significantly, from 54,399 cedis to 75,641. This increase was driven by the sample in Offinso district.

Average spending for delivery care fell from 108,217 cedis to 75,481 ($p = 0.12$). The proportion of women who had to pay some amount for their delivery fell from 74% to 47% ($p < 0.01$), and multivariate probit analysis indicates a significant decrease of 33 percentage points. There was no significant change in the amount paid for the delivery among the women who had to pay a positive amount.

Differences in health care use and payment comparing National Health Insurance Scheme–insured and uninsured in 2007

Below we present comparisons of insured and uninsured individuals within the 2007 survey only. Simple comparisons of insured with uninsured do not control for self-selection into the insurance scheme. Differences between these two groups should not be interpreted as "causal" or due solely to insurance. Propensity score matching can reduce the effect of endogeneity and give a closer approximation of the individual effects of NHIS enrollment. Unfortunately, small sample sizes in this study and the lack of an appropriate comparison population put severe limitations on propensity score matching methods. While at best indicative, we provide an overview of the propensity score matching results because they generally confirm the results we show from the pre-post analyses and allow for an individual-level (rather than population-level) interpretation.

Health care for illness/injury in the two weeks prior to the survey

Bivariate and probit analyses indicated that individuals insured by the NHIS were about twice as likely to seek formal care for illness/injury and about half as likely to self-treat or seek informal/traditional care, compared with the uninsured. Among those ill/injured in the two weeks prior to the survey, the insured paid 72% less than the uninsured for treatment (7,259 cedis and 25,682 cedis respectively, $p < 0.01$). About 86% of the uninsured had positive expenditures on treatment, compared with 38% of those insured by the NHIS at time of illness ($p < 0.01$). Enrollment in NHIS also appears to have reduced mean expenditures in the subgroup of ill/injured individuals with positive expenditures for treatment. Multivariate regression analysis indicates an 85% decrease in expenditures among those with positive expenditures. Propensity score matching corroborates these results, but shows attenuated differences between NHIS-insured and uninsured individuals.

Hospitalization in the 12 months prior to the survey

Individuals covered by NHIS were significantly more likely to be hospitalized than those not covered by insurance. We were not able to fit a propensity score matching model to our data to investigate how much of this difference might be attributed to the greater access to needed health care provided by NHIS insurance coverage, as opposed to adverse selection or unobservable individual characteristics associated with enrollment and likelihood of hospitalization.

Coverage by the NHIS at the time of hospitalization was associated with substantially reduced hospitalization expenditures. On average, the insured paid 8,010 cedis for their hospitalization, compared with 477,418 cedis by the uninsured ($p < 0.01$). Nearly all uninsured individuals who had been hospitalized incurred positive expenditures for the hospitalization (99%), compared with only 5% of those covered by NHIS at the time of hospitalization. Results from propensity score matching also point toward a substantial insurance effect on hospitalization expenditures.

Maternal health care

Among women with a delivery in the 12 months prior to the survey, those enrolled in the NHIS were significantly more likely than the uninsured to have four or more prenatal care visits, to deliver in a modern health care facility, and to deliver by Caesarean section. Results from propensity score matching indicate that for each of these indicators much of the difference between insured and uninsured women might be attributed to the effects of insurance coverage, rather than merely selection bias. A recent study using data collected specifically for analysis using propensity score matching finds a strong positive impact as well (Mensah, Oppong, and Schmidt 2010). This finding contrasts with our pre-post analysis, which did not indicate any increase in use of maternal health services as NHIS was implemented.

NHIS coverage had a substantial effect on maternal care expenditures: 81% of uninsured women had positive prenatal care expenditures, compared with only 13% of women covered by the NHIS during their pregnancy ($p < 0.01$). On average, insured women paid about one-tenth as much as uninsured women for prenatal care (6,293 cedis and 69,710 cedis, respectively; $p < 0.01$). Average expenditures for delivery care among uninsured women were 115,189 cedis, compared with 17,138 cedis for insured women ($p < 0.01$), and women covered by the NHIS at time of delivery were 70% less likely to have positive expenditures for delivery care than uninsured women ($p < 0.01$).

Results from propensity score matching indicate that enrollment in the NHIS provided financial protection to women who obtained prenatal and delivery care.

Policy implications

The NHIS is not achieving equitable enrollment or ensuring well targeted exemptions

Results from the two study districts show that enrollment in the NHIS increased with wealth quintile: 52% of those in the top wealth quintile were enrolled, compared with 18% in the poorest quintile. In addition, the evaluation confirms that exemptions for the indigent have not been well targeted toward the poorest of the poor. NHIS members from the poorest wealth quintile were in fact less likely to be exempted than members from wealthier quintiles. Inadequate information flows and other barriers may be preventing some intended beneficiaries from benefiting fully from the law. Many formal sector employees paid NHIS premiums, even though they should fall in the "exempt" category. But age-based exemptions have worked as intended in the two study districts. Children under age 18 and the elderly were more likely to enroll, and nearly all insurees under age 18 and over age 70 enrolled without paying the premium.

Adverse selection is a concern

Individuals with a chronic illness were more likely to enroll, implying that the waiting period recommended by NHIS regulations for membership has not eliminated adverse selection. There was no significant evidence of adverse selection related to expected delivery, though higher rates of enrollment associated with pregnancy might be considered "socially beneficial."

NHIS has had a positive impact on the use of modern health care

Use of curative health care services at modern health facilities increased substantially with the NHIS, while there was a significant decline in self-treatment and the use of informal/traditional care. These positive effects on care-seeking for illness are likely largely attributable to NHIS implementation. Hospitalization rates declined over the period of the study, but the interpretation of this result is ambiguous because we do not have a measure of need for hospitalization in our data.

Little impact on use of maternal health services

NHIS implementation was not associated with increased use of maternal health care services, which may reflect the importance of nonfinancial barriers to formal care-seeking for delivery care. These barriers (such as poor quality in facilities, cultural preferences to deliver at home, and lack of transportation) deserve further research and need to be addressed through nonfinancial interventions as well.

Positive impact on financial protection
NHIS implementation was associated with substantial improvements in financial protection for health care, including lower out-of-pocket spending on outpatient curative care, hospitalization, and delivery care. The changes were substantial for potentially catastrophic expenditures on hospitalization, where the proportion of patients who had positive expenditures for inpatient curative care was halved, and average expenditures fell 44%. In addition, average spending for delivery fell 30% and the proportion of women with positive delivery expenditures fell from 74% to 47%.

Challenges for the future
In 2003 the rush to keep the campaign promise of abolishing user fees led to a number of questionable design decisions during the creation of the NHIS. These design problems, as well as district-level implementation challenges, could derail the substantial achievements documented in this evaluation. Key concerns include the following.

Financially unsustainable benefit package and subsidies
To give people the feeling that the user fee system had been effectively abolished as promised, the 2003 law provided for a generous but arguably unsustainable benefit package. This was accompanied by subsidies to enroll large segments of the population without requiring any premiums or co-payments. In essence, this means the NHIS has become primarily a tax-funded social health insurance system. In 2006, 76% of National Health Insurance Fund income was from the national health insurance (value added tax) levy, 24% was from SSNIT contributions of formal sector workers, and only 0.01% was from premiums paid by informal sector members (Ghana Health Service 2007).

Principal income source is not related to number of enrollees
The NHIS, unlike other typical social insurance systems, has an income base that is not directly or principally linked to the number of enrollees. The large majority of NHIS members are not social security or informal sector contributors but individuals who do not pay any form of premium. All other things being equal, available revenue for the scheme will remain basically constant over time, despite

increases in enrollment. An International Labour Organization actuarial simulation concluded that an imbalance between NHIS revenues and expenditures was likely to arise within four to five years of the scheme's initiation as membership figures rose—and would appear even sooner, the faster the uptake of the NHIS by exempted groups (Yankah and Léger 2004).

Government guarantees, reinsurance, and moral hazard

A further consequence of the politically driven process behind the NHIS is that the government is seen by schemes and their managers as having such a huge stake in the schemes that it dare not allow a scheme to fail or be unable to provide services to its members. Schemes therefore do not have a strong sense of responsibility or attention to sustainability. Moreover, the reinsurance aspect of the National Health Insurance Fund has turned into a blanket guarantee against all losses rather than random fluctuations. Schemes do not have an incentive to run any surpluses.

Previously existing user fee exemptions, including those to address equity, remain in limbo

The NHIS law failed to detail how the scheme would interface with existing exemption schemes, leading to various implementation problems at facilities. For pregnant women, this was resolved by adding them to the NHIS exempt groups in 2008. Providing exemptions to indigents has proved more challenging.

The supply of care may not be keeping pace with expanding demand resulting from NHIS coverage

This emerging concern was documented in a 2007 Ministry of Health independent review of the health sector: "There is a growing need for capital investment, to address deterioration of existing health infrastructure, provide staff accommodation and infrastructure in deprived areas, expand and improve the quality of existing facilities to meet increased demand created by the NHIS, and replace or upgrade vehicles and equipment" (Ghana Ministry of Health 2008). Increased demand without investment in increased supply may lead to worsening of quality of care over time, which would compromise the gains in health services use in the early years of the NHIS. Timely investment in expanding and improving existing health care infrastructure is essential.

Appendix: Details and methods of the evaluation

Study sites
Ghana's administrative classification lists Nkoranza as a "deprived" district and Offinso as "less-deprived." Both are predominantly rural, with agriculture as the primary economic activity. Table A4.1 summarizes health services availability in the two districts.

At the time of the baseline survey in 2004, the community-based health insurance scheme covered about 34% of the district population in Nkoranza. The scheme was managed by the district's mission hospital and covered primarily inpatient services, including Caesarean sections. In 2005 this scheme was transformed into a districtwide mutual health scheme under the NHIS, serving the entire district and covering a broader range of health services and providers. In Offinso there were no community-based health insurance schemes in operation before the districtwide scheme of the NHIS was established in 2005. Table A4.2 summarizes the characteristics of the health insurance available in the study sites during the period of the study.

Sample selection
The study used cross-sectional sampling, with different samples of households selected at baseline and endline. A two-stage cluster sampling design was used, first selecting a sample of municipalities, then selecting a sample of households within the municipalities. In each municipality the total sample was proportional to the total number of households in the municipality, and approximately equal samples of insured and uninsured households were selected.[8] The baseline sample covered 1,805 households, and the endline sample consisted of 2,520 households. Table A4.3 summarizes the resulting sample sizes.

TABLE A4.1
Health services provision in study districts, 2007

	Nkoranza	Offinso
District population	128,960	138,676
Area (square kilometers)	2,300	1,254
Number of public health posts and health centers	12	7
Number of mission clinics	0	2
Number of private clinics	1	4
Number of hospitals	1	2

Source: 2000 Population and Housing Census.

TABLE A4.2

Coverage of healthcare services by health insurance in study sites

	Baseline 2004	Endline 2007	
District	Nkoranza	Nkoranza	Offinso
Type of health insurance	Health insurance scheme (community-based)	District mutual health insurance scheme (under NHIS)	District mutual health insurance scheme (under NHIS)
Percent of population registered (administrative data)	34%	45%	36%
Registration fee	None	Previous Nkoranza scheme members: 20,000 cedis (US$2.15) New members: 30,000 cedis (US$3.23)	SSNIT contributors: 50,000 cedis (US$5.38) Other members: 20,000 cedis (US$2.15)
Premium payment[a]	Annual premium: 30,000 cedis (US$3.61) per individual for first year, 20,000 cedis (US$3.01) annual renewal	Annual premium: 80,000 cedis (US$8.60)	Annual premium: 150,000 cedis (US$16.13)
Enrollment and premium and fee payment requirements	Entire household enrollment encouraged	Payment by installment allowed but upfront payment encouraged	Payment by installment allowed but upfront payment encouraged
Participating providers	Only district hospital (mission health facility)	Primary, secondary, and tertiary health facilities in public, private, and mission sector	Primary, secondary, and tertiary health facilities in public, private, and mission sector
Benefits covered			
Outpatient visit	Only treatment of dog and snake bites	✓	✓
Prenatal care		✓	✓
Hospital admission	✓	✓	✓
Normal delivery		✓	✓
Delivery by Caesarian section	✓	✓	✓
Postnatal care		✓	✓
Drugs and supplies	Only for inpatient care	✓	✓

a. Current old Ghanaian cedis, converted at dollar exchange rate at time of each survey.
Source: Authors.

Data collection instruments

The data collection instruments included a household characteristics questionnaire and a health care questionnaire. The household questionnaire collected information on sociodemographic characteristics and composition of households, and details on

TABLE A4.3
Sample sizes from household surveys in Nkoranza and Offinso

	Baseline 2004	Endline 2007
Number of households	1,805	2,520
Number of individuals	9,554	11,770
Individuals reporting illness and injury in the two weeks prior to the survey	413	411
Individuals reporting hospitalization in the 12 months prior to the survey	203	208
Women reporting delivery in the 12 months prior to the survey	298	312

Source: Authors' calculations.

individual health insurance membership. The health care questionnaire was administered to those who had been ill or injured in the two weeks prior to the survey, those who had been hospitalized in the 12 months prior to the survey, and women who had had a delivery in the 12 months prior to the survey. It collected information on self-treatment, health care–seeking (formal and informal or traditional care) and payments associated with care. For individuals ill or injured in the two weeks prior to the survey, the data on out-of-pocket expenditures included payments for informal/traditional care and itemized expenditures on formal care, including consultation, lab tests, drugs, x-rays, hospitalization charges, other facility-care expenditures, and unofficial payments to health providers. For individuals hospitalized in the 12 months prior to the survey, the questionnaire asked about total out-of-pocket expenditures for the hospitalization. Women who had had a delivery in the 12 months prior to the survey were asked how much they paid for prenatal care during the entire pregnancy and how much they and their family paid for the delivery.

Analytical methods
Sampling weights reflecting the probability of selection in the sample were assigned to each household and used in all analyses presented here. Data on household assets and housing quality were used to construct wealth indexes at baseline and endline, using principal components analysis (Filmer and Pritchett 2001).[9] The indexes differentiated households in five asset-based wealth groups (wealth quintiles) in each time period. A separate pooled wealth index was developed for the analyses using the pooled data (across baseline and endline samples).

The methods explored include pre-post bivariate comparisons of key indicators related to our research questions; multivariate regression analyses on pooled pre-post data to measure the effects of NHIS implementation on these indicators, controlling for other potentially confounding variables; multivariate regression analysis in the 2007 sample to identify characteristics associated with individual NHIS

TABLE A4.4
Sample characteristics (%)

Variable	Pre-post comparison			2007 sample only		
	2004	2007	p-value[a]	Not insured	Insured under National Health Insurance Scheme	p-value[a]
Sample size (number of individuals)[b]	N=9,554	N=11,757		N=6,794	N=4,963	
Have health insurance	23	35	<0.01	–	–	–
Age			<0.01			<0.01
0–4	15	15		16	13	
5–17	34	35		34	38	
18–49	39	36		39	30	
50–69	8	9		8	10	
70+	3	5		3	8	
Missing	1	0		0	0	
Male	48	47	0.34	48	44	0.01
Reported chronic illness[c]	–	4	–	3	6	<0.01
Self-assessed health status[c]	–	–				0.24
Very good	–	63		63	62	
Good	–	36		36	35	
Average	–	1		1.1	1.9	
Poor	–	0		0.3	0.4	
Household head's level of education			0.01			0.02
No education	42	34		36	29	
Primary/Junior secondary	50	57		56	58	
Secondary or higher	8	9		7	13	
Household head's current occupation			<0.01			0.19
Not working	9	8		9	9	
Farmer/fisher	77	69		71	64	
Government worker	3	5		4	7	
Artisan/trader	14	15		13	17	
Other	0	3		2	3	
Head of household is female	25	32	<0.01	30	35	0.08
Urban location	15	12	0.29	12	13	0.47
Asset index quintiles[d]			<0.01			<0.01
Poorest quintile	27	16		27	11	
Poor-middle quintile	22	20		22	17	

TABLE A4.4 (continued)
Sample characteristics (%)

Variable	Pre-post comparison			2007 sample only		
	2004	2007	p-value[a]	Not insured	Insured under National Health Insurance Scheme	p-value[a]
Sample size (number of individuals)[b]	N=9,554	N=11,757		N=6,794	N=4,963	
Middle quintile	21	18		17	21	
Middle-rich quintile	16	23		18	21	
Richest quintile	14	23		15	29	
At least one household member in a community-solidarity group[c]		12		10	15	0.03
Reported illness or injury in two weeks prior to the survey	4	3	0.03	2	5	<0.01
Hospitalized in 12 months prior to the survey	2	2	0.15	1	3	<0.01
Gave birth in 12 months prior to the survey (women ages 15–49 only)	12	11	0.22	10	12	0.45
Mean household size	7	6	<0.01	6.32	5.93	0.10

a. Statistical significance of difference in means (t-test or chi-square).

b. Sample size is smaller for some variables because of observations with missing data.

c. Question not asked at baseline.

d. Quintiles developed from pooled baseline and endline data shown for pre-post comparison. Quintiles developed from endline-only data shown for endline comparison.

Source: Authors' calculations.

enrollment; and propensity score matching analyses in the 2007 data to measure the effect of individual NHIS membership on key indicators, addressing the potential endogeneity of insurance enrollment.

Limitations of the study

Our study results have five important limitations. First, the study included only 2 of Ghana's 138 districts, which limits the generalizability of study results regionally or nationally. Second, the pre-post design of our study means that the effects of NHIS implementation measured may be confounded by the effect of other health-related policy interventions that may have occurred in the study districts in the three years between baseline and endline data collection. Third, the lack of panel data or an instrumental variable constrains our ability to account for endogeneity when measuring the impact of individual NHIS membership on use of care

(Waters 1999). Fourth, the study does not have data on changes in the quality of health care in the study sites, which could be influenced by NHIS implementation and may be a potential confounder of the use and financial protection effects. Fifth, sample sizes for some of our key indicators of health care use and spending are small (particularly for rare health-related events, such as hospitalization) and limit our ability to detect the effects of NHIS implementation.

Notes

1. For instance, the 2004 Health Sector Review (Ghana Ministry of Health 2008) found that, because of insufficient funding, only 67% of facilities' claims for free services in 2004 were reimbursed by the Ministry of Health.

2. The availability of substantial subsidies for the district mutual schemes led to the demise of virtually all previously existing nondistrict mutual health organizations, after the law was implemented. The members of the previous nondistrict schemes became integrated into the district mutual schemes, providing skills and personnel for their operation. The regions where district mutual schemes are most developed today—the Brong Ahafo, Eastern, Ashanti, and Northern regions—were also those where the previous mutual health organizations were most highly developed.

3. District mutual schemes organize regular sensitization exercises in the communities to increase enrollment. Terms of premium payments are decided by each scheme. Members who pay premiums directly to the schemes (informal sector adults) may pay their dues upfront at the beginning of the scheme year, or by installments in accordance with arrangements reached with the scheme managers.

4. On 1 July 2007 the Ghanaian cedi was redenominated and is now worth 10,000 old cedis. We report all currency amounts in old cedis. Expenditures in 2007 were adjusted for inflation (40% over three years), so all expenditures are reported in 2004 old cedis.

5. Setting premium rates is largely at the discretion of district mutual scheme managers, who take into account the premium guidelines given by the National Health Insurance Authority—not below 72,000 cedis and graduated according to income if possible—and use their knowledge of incomes in the community and how much people typically pay for health services to decide on the premium for their scheme (Ghana Health Service 2009).

6. Before the NHIS was introduced, public servants were entitled to a package of free health care benefits, more limited than the NHIS package. They had to pay for services out of pocket and then seek reimbursement, which typically took months to process and was frequently below the amount incurred due to annual budget ceilings (Atim and others 2001).

7. By this definition, it is doubtful that any but the homeless beggars in Accra and other major urban centers could qualify to receive benefits, and it rules out many of the poor in the rural areas where taboos, family pride, and social solidarity systems prevent even poor relatives from being cast out to the streets.

8. In Offinso the baseline sample was selected using systematic random sampling in each selected municipality.

9. The variables used in the index are type of cooking fuel, main source of drinking water, type of toilet, type of floor, people per room, has electricity, and ownership of radio, television, fridge, phone, bicycle, motorcycle, and car.

References

Asenso-Boadi, F. 2009. "Ghana's National Health Insurance System: Design, Implementation Perspectives." Presentation on behalf of Ras Boateng, at the African Health Economics and Policy Association Conference, 10 March, Accra.

Atim, C., and M. Sock. 2000. "An External Evaluation of the Nkoranza Community Financing Health Insurance Scheme, Ghana." Technical Report 50. Partnerships for Health Reform Project and Abt Associates Inc., Bethesda, MD.

Atim, C., S. Grey, P. Apoya, S. J. Anie, and M. Aikins. 2001. *A Survey of Health Financing Schemes in Ghana.* Bethesda, MD: Partners for Health Reformplus Project and Abt Associates Inc.

Atim, C., and P. Apoya. 2003. *A Survey of Mutual Health Organizations in Ghana, November 2003.* Bethesda, MD: Partners for Health Reformplus Project and Abt Associates Inc.

Dakpallah, George. 1988. "Financing of Health Services: Effects of Cost Recovery Mechanisms on Health Services in Developing Countries—Case Study of Ghana" MSc. Thesis. University of Wales, Swansea.

Filmer, D., and L. H. Pritchett. 2001. "Estimating Wealth Effect without Expenditure Data—or Tears: An Application to Educational Enrollments in States of India." *Demography* 38 (1): 115–32.

Garshong, B. 2008. "Evaluating the Effects of the National Health Insurance Act in Ghana: Summary of In-depth Interviews with District Mutual Health Organizations in Six Districts." Unpublished manuscript.

Ghana Health Service. 2007. *Annual Report 2007.* Accra: Ghana Health Service.

———. 2009. *Evaluation of the Ghana National Health Insurance Scheme.* Bethesda, MD: Health Systems 20/20 Project and Abt Associates Inc.

Ghana Ministry of Health. 2008. "Independent Review, Health Sector Programme of Work 2007." Accra: Ghana Ministry of Health.

Ghana National Health Insurance Authority. 2008. *National Health Insurance Authority Status Report: Operations, December 2008.* Accra: Ghana National Health Insurance Authority.

Ghana, Republic of. 2004. National Health Insurance Regulations, 2004 (L.I. 1809). Accra.

Mensah, J., J.R. Oppong, and C.M. Schmidt. 2010. "Ghana's National Health Insurance Scheme in the Context of the Health MDGs: An Empirical Evaluation Using Propensity Score Matching." *Health Economy* 19 (Suppl.): 95–106.

Nyonator, F., and J. Kutzin. 1999. "Health for Some? The Effects of User Fees in the Volta Region of Ghana." *Health Policy and Planning* 14 (4): 329–41.

Parliament of the Republic of Ghana. National Health Insurance Act, 2003 (Act 650).

Rajkotia, Y. 2007. *The Political Development of the Ghanaian National Health Insurance System: Lessons in Health Governance.* Bethesda, MD: Health Systems 20/20 Project and Abt Associates Inc.

Singleton, J. L. 2006. "Negotiating Change: An Analysis of the Origins of Ghana's National Health Insurance Act." Honors Project. Macalester College, Department of Sociology, St. Paul, MN.

Waddington, C., and K. A. Enyimayew. 1989. "A Price to Pay: The Impact of User Charges in Ashanti-Akim District, Ghana." *International Journal of Health Planning and Management* 4 (1): 17–47.

———. 1990. "A Price to Pay, Part 2: The Impact of User Charges in the Volta Region of Ghana." *International Journal of Health Planning and Management* 5 (4): 287–312.

Waters, H. 1999. "Measuring the Impact of Health Insurance with a Correction for Selection Bias—A Case Study of Ecuador." *Health Economics* 8 (5): 473–83.

WHO (World Health Organization). 2008. "Country Cooperation Strategy: At a Glance." World Health Organization, Geneva.

World Bank. 2007. "Project Appraisal Document on a Proposed Credit to the Republic of Ghana for a Health Insurance Project." World Bank, Washington, DC.

Yankah, B., and F. Léger. 2004. "Financial Analysis of the National Public Health Budget and of the National Health Insurance Scheme." ILO Discussion Paper 4. International Labour Organization, Geneva.

Impact of Health Insurance on Access, Use, and Health Status in Costa Rica

James Cercone, Etoile Pinder, Jose Pacheco Jimenez, and Rodrigo Briceno

Chapter 5

Costa Rica, as a middle-income country that has largely achieved universal health coverage, allows for analysis of the differences in behavior and care for the small share of citizens who remain uninsured. This chapter sheds light on the impact of being covered by insurance in a country where access is guaranteed even if uninsured and on the costs and benefits of covering the last 10%–20% of the population with insurance or other approaches.

A country of 4.5 million people, Costa Rica has a per capita gross domestic product (GDP) of US$5,600 (US$10,700 in purchasing power parity terms), and in 2007 it spent about 7.1% of GDP on health care. In 2008 the infant mortality rate was less than 10 deaths per 1,000 live births, and average life expectancy was 80 years for women and 76 years for men. Average life expectancy exceeds that of the United States by a year, even though U.S. GDP per capita is four times that of Costa Rica.

Costa Rica has mandatory health insurance coverage, established in 1941, and a comprehensive primary health care model that reaches all citizens. The Caja Costarricense del Seguro Social (the Caja) is an autonomous government institution that is both insurer and provider of care. Nearly 90% of the country's 4.5 million people are covered. The health insurance system is based on traditional Bismarkian social insurance, with an expanded role of the central government to cover the uninsured population. It provides equal access to health care services, irrespective of income or contribution. The formal sector contributes

14.75% of payroll income to sustain the system. The poor and indigent are covered by the "noncontributory" and "insured by state" regimes, which have led to equal access to health services for the poor and wealthy, something not seen in any of Costa Rica's neighboring countries. In addition, the absence of copayments removes another possible barrier to equal access.

Main characteristics of the Costa Rican health system

Structure

The Costa Rican health system includes a wide range of entities; the most relevant for this study are the Ministry of Health, the National Insurance Institute (INS), and the Caja. The ministry oversees the performance of the essential public health functions and exercises the stewardship role in the health sector, while the INS offers protection against occupational risks and traffic accidents as well as accident liability and a voluntary insurance plan for health care.

The Caja is the key institution for this study. It manages and organizes mandatory health insurance and is an autonomous institution with technical, administrative, and functional independence. It manages the compulsory health insurance funds that come from payroll taxes and provides the highest proportion of health care services in the country, covering roughly 90% of the population with a broad package of services. Besides health services, it provides social security protection to insured individuals and poor households through the Disability, Old Age, and Funeral regime. In Costa Rica there is an administrative purchaser-provider split between the financial network and the provider network of the Caja. Nearly all provision is through the Caja network; however, the Caja also contracts with private providers and nongovernmental organizations for some services.

The network of providers belongs to the Caja, which is organized as a pyramid-style network with primary care at the bottom and tertiary hospital care at the top. Primary care consists of 104 health regions and 953 basic care teams (Equipos Básicos de Atención Integral en Salud, or EBAIS). Each EBAIS covers 3,500–4,000 people and consists of a general practitioner, an auxiliary level nurse, and a primary care technician. All members must be registered with a primary care provider. Recently, the Caja has expanded its purchasing options, and some primary care services, such as minor surgeries and diagnoses, are purchased from nonpublic agents.

Secondary care consists of 10 major clinics, 13 suburban hospitals, and 7 regional facilities specializing in hospital services. Tertiary care has three general hospitals and five specialized hospitals (women, children, geriatrics, psychiatry, and rehabilitation). General and regional hospitals have a set number of people in their catchment areas, so clients cannot freely select their hospital—that is, every person must register in the hospital in the zone where he or she lives.

The health care sector also has a private subsector, which has expanded substantially in recent years, exemplified by its increasing number of medical professionals. In the 1990s the share of medical staff in the private sector increased from 10% to 24%. Household surveys show that about 30% of the population uses private health services at least once a year.

Eligibility and coverage

According to the constitution and founding laws of the Caja, mandatory health insurance in Costa Rica covers the risks of illness, maternity, disability, aging, and involuntary unemployment. The insurance also partly covers financial burdens due to maternity, widowhood, orphanage, and burial. All wage-earners must be covered by health insurance, which also covers the workers' dependents. Coverage for poor families and the indigent is defined by the Caja board of directors and is financed by the government from general tax revenues. All pensioners are automatically covered by health insurance.

Health insurance was originally established to protect workers against the risk of illness, maternity, and labor injuries, and initially no other group was covered by the insurance. The mandatory health insurance scheme has evolved over time. In 1961 congress established universal health insurance for workers and their families. The system expanded rapidly in the 1960s, when coverage almost tripled to half the population. In 1975 health insurance was expanded to cover agricultural workers. In 1978 the Caja created the voluntary health insurance scheme for independent workers. In 1984 it created the special regime, funded from general tax revenues, to cover the indigent. In 1993 all provision of care was moved to the Caja, and the Ministry of Health became the regulator and coordinator of the sector. The fundamental difference between Costa Rica and the rest of Latin America is that Costa Rica unified its public delivery system under social security, eliminating the parallel system operated by the Ministry of Health.

In the 2000s the approval of the Act for the Worker's Protection set the mandatory enrollment of independent workers. Recent decisions by the Caja board have aimed at expanding coverage to specific vulnerable groups. For instance, the benefits of health insurance can now cover a brother or sister of a contributory member if he or she is disabled or taking care of their parents.

Roughly 88% of Costa Rica's residents have health insurance. Coverage increased from 60% in 1975 to a high of 92% in 1990. Since then, coverage rates have remained at 86%–88%.

The Caja law establishes universal coverage of health services—that is, no person can be denied health care services even if uninsured. Emergency services are free to both the insured and the uninsured. If uninsured persons go to a public facility, two possibilities arise. First, they can pay for the services. Second, if they lack resources and are deemed indigent, they can become insured by the state.

The process of affiliation and access to the health insurance system

Any person living in Costa Rica may become affiliated with the social health insurance scheme in any one of at least five ways.

- *As a formal or self-employed worker.* Health insurance is mandatory in Costa Rica for all categories of paid workers. Until 1999 this obligation was defined for formal salaried workers only. Since then, the Workers' Protection Act established that self-employed workers must also be affiliated with the Caja program. Migrants are covered by the same legislation as citizens or residents. The contribution rate for formal employees is a 14.75% payroll tax and is 10.25% of reported income for independent workers.

- *As a pensioner.* All pensioners, either members of the contributory or noncontributory schemes, are automatically affiliated with the national health insurance program. Noncontributory pensioners receive a pension from the state even though they never contributed. Contributions are set at 14% for pensioners.

- *As state-covered members.* Under this program, affiliation is usually defined at demand—that is, the uninsured person first receives health care services at the public facility, then is requested to pay for the services or to become enrolled by the state, based on a means test applied by the Caja. The program is funded by special taxes on luxury goods, liquor, beer, cola, and other similar imported goods. It accounts for about 12% of the insured.

- *As a voluntary member.* A special option gives individuals the possibility to enroll in the insurance program if they do not belong to any of the other groups. In this option, the person enrolls and pays a regular fee of about $25 a month. There is no difference in the package of services this category receives.

- *As an indirect member.* Dependents of members are automatically covered. Spouses and children studying until age 25 are covered by the direct member. As mentioned above, some additional options exist, such as dependency status for a contributing member's brother or sister who is taking care of his or her parents and is older than 60.

If a person cannot be included in any of the five groups, the chances of being insured are essentially nil because of the absence of private health insurance options prior to 2009. The Free Trade Agreement with the United States opened the Costa

TABLE 5.1
Payroll fees by insurance scheme, 2006

Type of health insurance	Contribution by type of contributor (%)				
	Employee	Employer	State	Pension regime	Total
Salaried	5.50	9.25	0.25	–	15.00
Independent	4.75	–	5.50	–	10.25
Voluntary	4.65	–	5.50	–	10.15
Contributory pensioner	5.00	–	0.25	8.75	14.00
Noncontributory pensioner	–	–	0.25	13.75	14.00
Insured by state	–	–	14.00	–	14.00

— not applicable.
Source: Caja Costarricense del Seguro Social.

Rican insurance market, a public monopoly since 1924, allowing international insurance companies to establish, operate, and sell insurance plans.[1] Currently, the INS, the public insurance monopoly, operates one health insurance scheme with approximately 10,000 affiliates nationwide.[2] Some transnational companies have insured their employees in the past through international health insurance programs, allowing their workers to obtain health care in private hospitals and clinics.

Table 5.1 summarizes sources of revenue for the Caja. The contributory portion of the system accounts for about 76% of revenues. For poor households, the Caja actuarial department estimates the number of poor households based on a household survey. Then it estimates an average premium, based on average wages and the application of a 14% payroll tax rate to that average. The number of estimated poor people times the average premium determines the expected global contribution from the state.

Who are the uninsured?

An analysis of the National Health Survey (ENSA 2006) shows significant differences in the sociodemographic profiles of the insured and uninsured in Costa Rica (table 5.2; see box 5.1 for a description of the data and methodology used in the analysis). According to the survey, 81% are insured and 19% are not. The uninsured are less likely to be female (54% of the insured are female, compared with 46% of the uninsured) and less likely to be married (32% of the insured are married, compared with 20% of the uninsured). No significant difference in average age exists between the two groups, yet the age structure is substantially different (figure 5.1). Adults ages 19–54 comprise 50% of the insured but 62% of the uninsured. Adults ages 55 and older comprise 16% of the insured but 12% of the

TABLE 5.2

Sociodemographic statistics for the insured and uninsured, 2006

Variable	Definition	Insured N=3,988 (81.30%)		Uninsured N=917 (18.70%)		Difference insured– uninsured	Signifi- cance
		Mean	Standard deviation	Mean	Standard deviation		
Age	Years	31.323	20.310	30.778	18.036	0.545	
Sex	Female	0.536	0.499	0.458	0.498	0.078	***
Income	Per capita monthly household income (US$)	159.11	153.77	134.95	145.90	24.16	***
	1st quintile	27.41	16.78	26.30	18.16	1.11	
	2nd quintile	71.31	11.31	73.13	11.81	-1.81	
	3rd quintile	115.17	14.77	114.77	13.40	0.41	
	4th quintile	185.39	26.17	183.68	23.60	1.71	
	5th quintile	401.86	190.82	378.27	225.25	23.59	
Civil status	Married	0.322	0.467	0.200	0.400	0.122	***
Household head	Household head	0.214	0.410	0.236	0.425	-0.022	
Education	Primary	0.487	0.500	0.472	0.499	0.015	
	Secondary	0.377	0.485	0.420	0.494	-0.043	**
	University	0.113	0.317	0.096	0.295	0.017	
Employment	Self-employed	0.086	0.280	0.172	0.377	-0.086	***
Size of firm	Small firms have <10 workers (0=small, 1=big)	0.073	0.260	0.021	0.145	0.052	***
Nationality	Costa Rican	0.967	0.179	0.894	0.308	0.073	***
Urban status	1 = urban	0.684	0.465	0.662	0.473	0.022	

*** significant at $p < 0.01$; ** significant at $p < 0.05$.
Source: ENSA 2006.

uninsured. These statistics suggest that there can be self-selection of the healthy into uninsured status even in a system with universal coverage.

The uninsured are more likely to have completed secondary education and to work for a small company with fewer than 10 employees. They are significantly more likely to be independent workers—17% of uninsured are self-employed, compared with 9% of the insured—and to have a lower monthly income ($135 for the uninsured, compared with $159 for the insured). The uninsured are also more likely to be immigrants (11% of the uninsured, compared with 3% of the insured). Immigrants tend to work in low paying informal sector jobs, and their employers

BOX 5.1
Data and methodology

We use data from three sources: the nationally representative National Health Survey (ENSA 2006), the administrative database of hospital discharges for 2006 (Caja Costarricense del Seguro Social 2006), and the nationally representative Income and Expenditure Survey (IES 2004). For ENSA there are a total of 7,522 households. We removed 54 with missing insurance status as well as 1,409 public employees and their dependents and 1,154 pensioners (because neither group has a choice whether to be insured, and our population of interest is those who have a choice). For the hospital data we also removed public employees and pensioners, which reduced the number of discharges from 326,583 to 267,325. We deleted these observations because the only people with the ability to avoid enrolling are the self-employed and private employers who choose illegally not to enroll themselves or their employees.

Our strategy for identifying the impact of insurance was to find instrumental variables that would explain affiliation with the Caja but not health or financial protection behavior. Depending on the dataset, we used a subset of the following for this purpose: size of firm where the individual is employed (we used the mean size within a household), sector of economic activity, occupation type, self-employment, having multiple jobs, and canton code. No exclusion restrictions are perfect, but we believe that in the context of Costa Rica, these variables would affect the dependent health variables only through their impact on affiliation with the Caja.

FIGURE 5.1
Age structure of the insured and uninsured, 2006

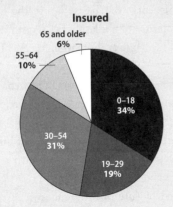
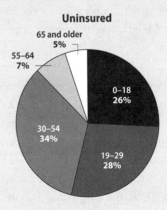

Source: ENSA 2006.

often do not pay taxes for them. The authorities have few tools to detect and prevent self-exclusion and to collect premiums for or from independent or itinerant workers.

Insured people tend to have a higher burden of disease (a metric that summarizes mortality and morbidity conditions in a determined population) and higher prevalence of specific diagnosed diseases, such as diabetes, hypertension, and asthma than uninsured people (table 5.3). This does not imply a negative impact of insurance on health status (a causal relationship cannot be inferred), but it can be considered that if a person feels healthy, they are more inclined to believe that the benefits of paying insurance premiums outweigh the financial cost. Of course, it is also consistent with underdiagnosis in the uninsured population. But there is no statistically significant difference between the two groups' self-perceived health status.

There is no statistically significant difference between the insured and uninsured for general utilization statistics (see table 5.3). For outpatient services, 65% of the insured and the uninsured report having a visit during the last year. For hospital services, 5% in both groups report a hospital admission for at least one night in the last year. There is only one significant difference in use, but it is important: while 49% of insured women ages 40 and older report having received a mammogram, fewer than 40% of uninsured women report having received one. Given the need for a patient to be referred to a high technology diagnostic imaging appointment, it is logical this would be an area where the uninsured are at a disadvantage.

According to the database of hospital discharges in 2006, 16% of people discharged were uninsured, compared with 19% according to household survey data (table 5.4). With childbirth as a leading cause of admissions, substantially more women than men are in the hospital discharge database than in the ENSA household data. But differences in insurance status are not large. ENSA shows that 85.3% of men and 79.7% of women are insured, while at discharge, 81.2% of men and 85.4% of women were insured.

As with the survey data, the discharge data show that the uninsured were more likely to be unmarried, but there is a significant difference between the percentage of survey respondents and discharges who declare they are "cohabitating." Only 6% of insured survey respondents state they are cohabitating, while 19% of insured discharges say they are. There is an incentive to claim cohabitation with a Caja member because it qualifies the patient for dependent benefits.

The discharge data paint a more nuanced picture of differences in behavior between the insured and uninsured. The first is how they are admitted. Some 87% of the uninsured were admitted to hospitals through the emergency room, compared with 58% of the insured. While 39% of the insured are referred to the

TABLE 5.3

Health status and use of insured and uninsured people, 2006

Variable	Definition	Insured N=3,988 (81.30%)		Uninsured N=917 (18.70%)		Difference insured– uninsured	Signifi- cance
		Mean	Standard deviation	Mean	Standard deviation		
Chronic disease	More than one diag- nosed disease	0.269	0.444	0.147	0.354	0.122	***
Hypertension	Diagnosed arterial hypertension	0.095	0.293	0.039	0.195	0.056	***
Diabetes	Diagnosed diabetes	0.032	0.177	0.018	0.132	0.014	**
Asthma	Diagnosed asthma or bronchitis	0.041	0.198	0.009	0.095	0.032	***
Diagnosed disease status	Index, 0, lowest burden of disease, to 100, highest burden of disease	4.565	10.665	2.671	7.955	1.894	***
Self-reported health	Scale, 1, very good, to 5, very bad	2.085	0.707	2.124	0.813	–0.039	
Visit	1 = person visited doctor at least once during last year	0.647	0.478	0.655	0.476	–0.009	
Hospitalization	1 = person hospital- ized at least one night in last year	0.052	0.221	0.050	0.219	0.001	
Emergency	1 = person used emergency services at least once during last year	0.117	0.321	0.102	0.303	0.015	
Mammogram	Woman ages 40 and older received mam- mogram	0.490	0.500	0.397	0.491	0.094	**
Cytology	Woman ages 18 and older received pap smear	0.934	0.248	0.921	0.271	0.014	
Vaccines	Person under age 18 completed vaccinations	0.826	0.379	0.812	0.392	0.015	
Diabetes medicine	Diabetics took diabetes medicines in the two weeks prior to the study	0.733	0.443	0.706	0.462	0.027	
Hypertension medicine	Hypertensives took hypertension medicines in the two weeks prior to the study	0.734	0.442	0.765	0.427	–0.031	

*** significant at $p < 0.01$; ** significant at $p < 0.05$.

Source: ENSA 2006.

TABLE 5.4

Comparison of insured and uninsured people who have been discharged from a hospital, 2006

Variable	Definition	Insured N=224,800 (84.1%)		Uninsured N=42,525 (15.9%)		Difference insured-uninsured	Signifi-cance
		Mean	Standard deviation	Mean	Standard deviation		
Age	Years	28.48	18.567	28.23	19.662	0.253	**
Sex	Female	0.700	0.458	0.634	0.482	0.066	***
Civil status	Married	0.358	0.479	0.186	0.389	0.172	***
Nationality	Costa Rican	0.930	0.254	0.771	0.420	0.159	
Death	Discharged dead	0.0097	0.0978	0.0296	0.170	0.0199	***
Average length of stay	Days	3.758	5.026	5.238	6.951	-1.480	***
Number of previous admissions		0.047	0.246	0.026	0.177	0.022	***
Number of medical visits		1.339	2.892	1.062	2.456	0.277	***
Admission source	Outpatient care	0.387	0.487	0.082	0.274	0.305	
	Emergency room	0.584	0.493	0.874	0.332	-0.290	***
	Childbirth	0.029	0.168	0.044	0.206	-0.015	***
Admission service	Medicine	0.098	0.298	0.136	0.343	-0.038	***
	Surgery	0.167	0.373	0.209	0.407	-0.043	***
	Gyno-obstetrics	0.407	0.491	0.399	0.490	0.008	***
	Pediatrics	0.162	0.368	0.168	0.373	-0.006	***
	Major ambulatory surgery	0.156	0.363	0.017	0.130	0.139	***
	Psychiatry	0.008	0.087	0.040	0.197	-0.033	***
	Intensive care unit	0.002	0.048	0.029	0.167	-0.027	***

*** significant at $p < 0.01$; ** significant at $p < 0.05$.
Source: Hospital discharges database.

hospital through an outpatient provider, only 8% of the uninsured follow this route. What happens to them in the hospital is also different. About 17% of the insured and 21% of the uninsured have minor surgery, but 16% of the insured undergo major ambulatory surgery, compared with only 2% of the uninsured. The uninsured experience considerably longer stays (5.2 days, compared with 3.8 days) and are far more likely to end up in the intensive care unit (3% of uninsured admissions, compared with less than 0.3% of insured). The ENSA data show that the insured appear to be in worse health status than the uninsured (only 14% of the uninsured report having more than one diagnosed chronic condition, compared with 29% of the insured). Finally, the uninsured have a statistically significant higher chance of inpatient death (3%, compared with only 1% for the insured).

In short, despite being healthier, the uninsured enter hospitals directly in more apparent trauma and with less previous attention and planning than the insured. They are significantly more likely to die. These results have implications for patient health outcomes and for health care costs, as hospitals are by far the most expensive places to receive care.

What are the determinants of insurance status?

Probit analysis indicates that insurance status depends primarily on age, employment, nationality, education, and marital status (table 5.5). Not being married significantly decreases the chances of being insured (being married increases an individual's chance by 12 percentage points). Being an immigrant decreases the likelihood of being insured by 19 percentage points relative to being a native Costa Rican, and having less than a secondary education also decreases the probability.

Another large contributor is self-employment. Compared with being unemployed (individuals employed by the government and pensioners are excluded from the analysis because they have no choice whether to be covered), the likelihood of being insured if an individual is self-employed is 12 percentage points lower, again pointing to the independent worker's decision to self-select out of the insurance plan to avoid paying the tax—a problem in all payroll tax–financed systems, made worse as tax rates rise.

Impacts of health insurance

This section discusses the impact of insurance coverage on a number of outcome variables, based on the estimation strategy shown in the appendix.

Does health insurance affect access and use?

Using the ENSA 2006 data, we explored the impact of insurance for the full sample and for subsamples of the household data. There is no evidence of a statistically significant difference between the insured and uninsured in the use of outpatient care, hospitalizations, or emergency services. The lack of a difference extends to insured and uninsured individuals from subsamples of the poorest 40% and the wealthiest 40%. This result reinforces the descriptive data, which show few differences between the insured and the uninsured.[3]

TABLE 5.5

Probit analysis of the determinants of participation—dependent variable: insurance status, 2006

Variable	Partial effect	Standard error	Significance
Sociodemographic			
Age	−0.004	0.002	*
Sex (women=1)	0.013	0.013	
Log of the household monthly income per capita	0.018	0.008	**
Civil status (reference = single)			
Married (married=1)	0.122	0.022	***
Relationship to household head			
Head of household (head of household=1)	−0.017	0.015	
Education (reference = without formal education, primary incomplete and primary complete)			
Secondary	0.027	0.015	*
University	0.033	0.017	*
Employment category (reference = not employed)			
Patron	−0.077	0.062	
Self-employed	−0.125	0.060	**
Private	0.017	0.041	
Nationality			
Costa Rican (Costa Rican=1)	0.192	0.042	***
Urban zone (urban=1)	−0.007	0.013	
Quality of health care services (self-reported)	−0.022	0.006	***
Reference population in the EBAIS to attend	0.000	0.000	
Number of observations		3,070	
Pseudo R^2		0.0668	
Lod pseudo log likelihood		−1,428.41	
Pred. P.		0.871	

*** significant at $p < 0.01$; ** significant at $p < 0.05$; * significant at $p < 0.10$.
Source: ENSA 2006.

We also analyzed subsamples with chronic conditions—one group diagnosed with at least one disease, one group diagnosed with hypertension, and a third diagnosed with diabetes. There is a statistically significant impact only for diabetes: health insurance reduces the probability of both inpatient care and emergency room care for diabetics. Uninsured diabetics (all other things being equal) are more likely to end up in an inpatient bed or the emergency room. In addition, insurance reduces the use of medicines for the diabetic population. These findings suggest that insurance coverage in Costa Rica results in better and safer management of diabetes, probably associated with primary care.

Health insurance does not appear to have any impact on access to diagnostic tests like pap smears in women ages 18 and older and mammograms in women ages 40 and older. The mammography result is different from the descriptive analysis, indicating that controlling for other factors (such as education) eliminated the disparity between the insured and uninsured. In contrast, health insurance improves the likelihood of completing the full series of vaccinations for children age 18 and younger.

From the 2006 hospital discharge data analysis, the insured were significantly less likely to access the hospital through the emergency room, consistent with the descriptive data. The likelihood of having an avoidable hospitalization for a condition that could be managed in an outpatient setting was significantly less for the insured. This result, consistent with the household data result for diabetes, again points to the importance of quality of health care services over quantity. Because no one is denied care in Costa Rica, uninsured people who are sick are generally able to receive treatment, but apparently often later than they should and in a less than optimal setting. For health outcomes and cost-effectiveness, the uninsured are in a position inferior to the insured, who are enrolled with a primary care provider through their EBAIS, and therefore receive appropriate preventive and maintenance care. That, in turn, reduces chronic disease complications and expensive hospitalizations for those diseases.

Does health insurance affect health status?

ENSA includes the variable "self-reported health status," which reflects whether individuals describe their health as very good, good, okay, bad, or very bad. Overall, health insurance significantly improves an individual's self-perception of health status. But it reduces the self-perceived health status for diabetics, interesting because insured diabetics are less likely to need hospital services. Perhaps insured diabetics are more educated about the serious complications associated with their disease and thus consider themselves to be in a worse state of health.

From the hospital discharge data analysis, we have more objective information on health status. Insured mothers are less likely to have babies with low birthweight, which would be consistent with better access to prenatal care through EBAIS. In addition, if we measure severity of illness by the number of days of hospitalization, insured people experience substantially shorter hospital stays. When insured and uninsured people are hospitalized, the insured are healthier by this measure.

Does health insurance affect out-of-pocket expenditures?

The impact of health insurance on financial protection of insured people was estimated using a third data source, the nationally representative Income and

Expenditure Survey of 2004. We estimated per capita out-of-pocket spending on health as a proportion of per capita expenditures and as a proportion of payment capacity, defined as total household expenditures minus household food expenditures.

The average monthly out-of-pocket health expenditure by Costa Ricans in 2004 was US$8.50, but with a high degree of variability (coefficient of variation was estimated at 321%). Per capita out-of-pocket health expenditures represent nearly 3% of per capita expenditure and 3.5% of the payment capacity of individuals. Out-of-pocket health expenditures represent only 2% of the poorest third of the population's per capita expenditures but 4% of the wealthiest third's, the reverse of the usual tendency in the absence of effective financial protection.

Our analysis found no significant impact of health insurance on a Costa Rican's out-of-pocket health expenditures. It is likely this result is due largely to the fact that no person can be denied care in Costa Rica. An individual who arrives at an emergency room needing to be admitted to hospital is admitted, regardless of the ability to pay. So there is no difference in out-of-pocket health expenditures between insured and uninsured individuals.

Conclusions

The main distinguishing characteristic of health insurance in Costa Rica relative to other countries of Latin America and many other middle-income countries is that approximately 81% of the population is affiliated with the Caja and thus covered, but even those who are not covered are guaranteed access to emergency and hospital care provided by the Caja when they are sick or need care. They are not shunted into a separate lower quality system. Therefore everyone is covered by catastrophic insurance; the major difference is that the 19% not affiliated with the Caja do not benefit from assignment to a primary care provider and must seek and pay for those services in the market.

The uninsured are somewhat less educated and more likely to be immigrants, have lower income, be self-employed, and come from healthier age groups than the insured, but in their overall use of health care resources they are similar. If we had only the household data, we would have concluded that the insured gained no advantage over the uninsured except for a higher probability of children receiving all immunizations and better care for diabetics.

However, the hospital discharge data raise concerns. The uninsured are far more likely to enter the hospital through the emergency room. They are likely to have surgery but not to have a planned major surgery; even so, they experience a 36% longer stay. We estimate that simply reducing their length of stay to that of the insured would save about US$8.5 million, or about US$100 per uninsured—probably enough to finance a reasonable level of access to primary care for them.

The uninsured are more likely to be hospitalized for a condition that can be managed in an ambulatory care setting, to end up in the intensive care unit, and to be discharged dead. The hospital data analysis confirms a higher probability of emergency room and inpatient care for uninsured diabetics.

We expected to find few differences between the insured and uninsured in Costa Rica because of the equal access rule. For measures of financial protection and use of services, our expectations were met. Yet in significant ways the uninsured are disadvantaged from a health standpoint. They use medical care resources more haphazardly than the insured. We hypothesize that this happens principally because the insured enter the pyramidal Caja system at the bottom, or primary care level, while the uninsured tend to enter closer to the top. Perhaps, in light of these findings, it would be possible for the Caja to reallocate resources to cover the uninsured in a more health-friendly manner.

Appendix: Details of the Estimations

The estimated models when we use the ENSA 2006 database are the following:

First stage:

$\hat{I}_i(insured_i) = a_0 + a_1 sex_i + a_2 age_i + a_3 linc_i + a_4 married_i + a_5 hoh_i + a_6 secondary_i + a_7 univ_i + a_8 costarican_i + a_9 employed_i + a_{10} zone_i + \sum_{r=11}^{15} a_r region_{ri} + a_{16} iv_i + a_{17} disease\_status_i + a_{18} ebaisxh_i + e_i$

Second stage:

$H_i = b_0 + b_1 sex_i + b_2 age_i + b_3 linc_i + b_4 married_i + b_5 hoh_i + b_6 secondary_i + b_7 univ_i + b_8 costarican_i + b_9 employed_i + b_{10} zone_i + \sum_{r=11}^{15} b_r region_{ri} + b_{16} \hat{I}_i(insured_i) + b_{17} disease\_status_i + b_{18} ebaisxh_i + m_i$

where H_i is the result variable, *sex* is a dummy variable that takes the value 1 if the individual is a woman and 0 if the individual is a man, *age* is the age of the individual, *linc* is the logarithm of per capita household income, *married* is a dummy variable that takes the value 1 if the individual is married and 0 otherwise, *hoh* is a dummy variable that takes the value 1 if the individual is the head of the household and 0 otherwise, *secondary (univ)* is a dummy variable that takes the value 1 if the individual has secondary (university) completed as his highest education level, *costarican* is a dummy variable that takes the value 1 if the individual is a citizen and 0 otherwise, *employed* is a dummy variable that takes the value 1 if the person works and 0 otherwise, *region_r* are regional dummy variables, *insured* is a dummy variable that indicates the coverage of the health insurance system ($\hat{I}_i(insured_i)$ is the estimated value of this variable from the first stage), *disease_status* is an index that shows health status, and *ebaisxh* is the number of people in each health area. For self-reported health status models we add other independent variables: *consult* (a dummy variable that takes the value 1 if if the individual has visited a clinic or hospital during the last year and 0 otherwise), *hospital* (a dummy variable that takes the value 1 if the individual has been hospitalized at least one night during the last year and 0 otherwise), and *emergency* (a dummy variable that takes the value 1 if the person used emergency services at least once during the last year and 0 otherwise).

The estimated models when we use the 2006 hospital discharge database are detailed as follows:

First stage:

$$\hat{I}_i(insured_i) = a_0 + a_1 sex_i + a_2 age_i + a_3 married_i + a_4 costarican_i + a_5 los_i + a_6 previous_i + \sum_{r=11}^{13} a_p prov_{pi} + a_{16} iv_i + e_i$$

Second stage:

$$H_i = b_0 + b_1 sex_i + b_2 age_i + b_3 married_i + b_4 costarican_i + b_5 los_i + b_6 previous_i + \sum_{p=7}^{13} b_p prov_{pi} + b_{14} \hat{I}_i(insured_i) + m_i$$

where H_i is the result variable, *sex* is a dummy variable that takes the value 1 if the individual is a woman and 0 if the individual is a man, *age* is the age of the individual, *married* is a dummy variable that takes the value 1 if the individual is married and 0 otherwise, *costarican* is a dummy variable that takes the value 1 if the individual is a citizen and 0 otherwise, *los* is the number of days an individual remained in a hospital, *previous* indicates the number of earlier entrances to the clinic or hospital, $prov_p$ are province dummy variables, and *insured* is a dummy variable that takes the value 1 if the individual is covered by the health insurance system and 0 otherwise (with $\hat{I}_i(insured_i)$ being the estimated value from the first stage).

Notes

1. The market is to be opened in 2009 and 2012, depending on the type of insurance plan.

2. The Free Trade Agreement breaks this monopoly so international insurance companies can now arrive in Costa Rica, operate their offices there, and offer the public not only health insurance but life and automobile insurance.

3. Insurance has a puzzlingly significant negative impact on use of outpatient care for non–Costa Ricans, but that is for a tiny subsample of only 175.

Health Insurance and Access to Health Services, Health Services Use, and Health Status in Peru

Ricardo Bitrán, Rodrigo Muñoz, and Lorena Prieto

This chapter examines how Peru's eight-year-old Integral Health Insurance (Seguro Integral de Salud, or SIS) has affected access to health services and out-of-pocket spending by its beneficiaries. We use data from the Demographic and Health Survey (DHS), which contains two cross-sectional samples, one for 2000 and another for 2004–07, with a sample spread over five years. We also use data from the National Household Survey (ENAHO), a panel collected over 2002–06.

Classified by the World Bank as a lower middle-income country in 2008, Peru had per capita gross national income of US$7,950 annually in purchasing power parity terms. Life expectancy at birth is 73 years, under-five mortality is 24 per 1,000 in 2008, and 99% of children receive the full course of three doses for their DPT vaccinations by their 23rd month. Total health spending is about 4.3% of gross domestic product (GDP), about 58% of it public and 42% private. Nearly 75% of private spending is out of pocket (World Bank 2010).

The Peruvian health sector

Peru's mixed health system includes a social security–financed sector (EsSalud), a tax-financed public sector (the Ministry of Health, or MINSA), a private sector, and a national police and armed forces sector. The private sector offers health plans with different copayments, deductibles, and ceilings. The main insurers in the system are EsSalud, SIS, and private insurance companies. EsSalud covers about 17% of the population; SIS, 15%; the national police and armed forces, about 1.6%; and the private sector, 1.7% (Portocarrero, Margarita, and Vallejo 2007). Health service providers in the system are MINSA, which is the largest provider network; the parallel EsSalud system; private providers; and the national police and armed forces. Each of these systems provides comprehensive services from the primary level up to complex hospital care. The Health Providing Institutions (Entidades Prestadoras de Salud, or EPS) providers, explained below, deliver mainly low complexity services to supplement EsSalud.

Health social security

EsSalud is the typical social security health insurance system in Latin America. It is financed with a 9% income-based contribution paid by employers and directly provides health services to its beneficiaries through its own network of clinics and hospitals. Beneficiaries are mainly formal sector workers and their families—called regular insurees—which account for 75% of all beneficiaries. EsSalud also has three other types of insurees: retired (17%), subsidized (5%), and elective (3%). Retirees contribute 4% of their pensions. Subsidized insurees include fishers, agrarian workers, and home workers.[1] Voluntary insurees are those who purchase an EsSalud health plan and pay a premium based on the health plan they choose—in competition with private health insurance plans. Voluntary insurees are typically self-employed.

EsSalud has an explicit benefit package (Plan Mínimo de Atención) of 752 diagnoses, which makes it comprehensive rather than minimal. The package includes preventive, promotional, and curative care; welfare and social promotion services; subsidies for temporary disability and maternity; and burial services. It is the same for all but voluntary beneficiaries, who are entitled to a reduced benefits package. EsSalud provides services that cover at least this package through its own provider network or through contracts with other health service providers.

Integral Health Insurance

SIS began in 2001 by merging two health insurance programs: free health insurance for children in public schools (Seguro Escolar Gratuito, or SEG), which was launched in 1997, and the maternal and child health insurance (Seguro Materno Infantil, or SMI), which was launched in 1998 and gradually expanded from two provinces to the whole country. Both programs were targeted to specific populations: SEG to children ages 3–17 in public schools, excluding private school children, and SMI to all pregnant women and children up to age 4 if they were not covered by another insurance system. These programs created for the first time a demand side subsidy that was paid to MINSA providers when services were provided in lieu of simply increasing MINSA's budget to try to reach these groups more effectively.

SIS is an agency under MINSA with its own allocation of resources from the Ministry of Economics and Finance. It has five plans: Plan A for children ages 0–4; Plan B for children and adolescents ages 5–17; Plan C for women before, during, and after childbirth; Plan D for adults in emergencies; and Plan E for poor adults. A new partially subsidized or contribution plan has been added to extend the program to households with some capability to pay. Nevertheless, SIS remained fundamentally a maternal and child health insurance program during the period of our analysis, with 93% of its resources going to Plans A, B, and C in 2004 (Cotlear 2006; Jaramillo and Parodi 2004). Its beneficiaries seek care from MINSA's provider network and make no copayments, because SIS offers full financial coverage. In turn, SIS pays MINSA providers for these interventions—based on a price list previously agreed with MINSA—through a fee-for-service mechanism that covers only the variable costs of care. SIS administrative data show that the number of members increased from 3.6 million in January 2007 to 7.3 million in January 2008 to 12.7 million in the first half of 2010 (see www.sis.gob.pe). In June 2007 SIS covered approximately 33.1% of its target population (based on ENAHO 2004 incidence of poverty).

Eligibility to become beneficiaries is explicitly defined and targeted to the poor and uninsured. Individuals must go to the nearest MINSA health facility and request affiliation by presenting their national identification card. SIS representatives then apply the socioeconomic evaluation form (Ficha de Evaluación Socio Económica) to determine whether they are extremely poor, poor, or nonpoor. Membership is automatic for those who are categorized as poor or extremely poor and who sign a contract with a SIS representative. With the partially subsidized plan, SIS expanded its target population to include all poor families with the same benefits package (preventive and ambulatory care are emphasized, but it also includes an array of priority hospital services), but with a monthly premium that varies between S/.10 ($3.50) and S/.30 ($10.00), depending on income and whether it is for an individual or a family.

It is important to keep in mind, especially when the results of the analysis are presented, what a limited program SIS is. The covered population already has access to MINSA facilities, which they are required to use to benefit from SIS. Little has changed in the operation of MINSA facilities. Employees are civil servants whose salaries are paid as usual. Basically the only difference from regular operations is that for the covered services, the facility receives an extra payment from SIS when it can show it delivered the service to an eligible member of SIS, creating an incentive to provide the covered services to SIS beneficiaries.

Health insurance population coverage in the household surveys

EsSalud and SIS are the health insurers with the highest population coverage, together covering 34.8% of the population (table 6.1). An additional 4% of the population is covered by other types of health insurance, including the national police and armed forces, private insurance plans, and university and private school insurance. Overlapping coverage between EsSalud and SIS and between SIS and other health insurances is negligible; however, about 5% of EsSalud beneficiaries overlap with other types of health insurance. SIS beneficiaries are concentrated in areas with higher informal labor and poverty, like the mountains and jungle. The presence of SIS in these areas helps close the gap in EsSalud population coverage in these regions, yet 62% of the population is still not covered by any type of insurance.

EsSalud beneficiaries are concentrated in the coastal region, with more than half living in Metropolitan Lima. The percentage of the population covered by EsSalud is highest in Metropolitan Lima, reflecting the higher formal employment rate in this region. Regions with less formal labor, like the mountains and the jungle, have lower EsSalud coverage rates. Coverage of EsSalud has remained relatively constant over 2000–07. Although not presented here, coverage estimates based on DHS data are almost identical.

Descriptive information

SIS beneficiaries are mainly poor families. Survey data show that most beneficiaries are children, because the SIS benefit package is focused on maternal-child interventions. In contrast, EsSalud beneficiaries are mainly formal sector workers and their families. They have a slightly older age structure than the general population and the uninsured. They are concentrated in the richer quintiles of per capita expenditure. The uninsured are distributed more homogeneously (except for the richest quintile, which has a lower percentage of uninsured than the rest).

TABLE 6.1
Health insurance population coverage by region, 2006 (%)

Region	EsSalud	SIS	Any health insurance
Metropolitan Lima	27.5	6.1	41.1
Coast	22.4	13.4	37.8
Mountains	11.5	22.7	35.2
Jungle	10.0	27.5	38.4
Total	18.4	16.4	37.9

Source: ENAHO.

Table 6.2 presents descriptive data for several health service demand indicators. Since we are not controlling for the variables used in the regression analyses, the differences between indicators do not necessarily reflect causality by insurance

TABLE 6.2

Use of health services, by type of health insurance, 2005 and 2006 (%)

Indicator	Uninsured	EsSalud only	SIS only	Other	Total
ENAHO 2006					
Presence of chronic disease	22.7	32.7	10.1	25.9	22.5
Population with health problem in the four weeks prior to the survey	52.3	53.0	51.3	43.4	51.9
Hospitalized in the 12 months prior to the survey	3.4	6.7	2.6	6.7	4.0
Sought formal care (with health professional) in the four weeks prior to the survey	19.5	45.3	46.8	46.9	29.4
Use of child growth monitoring in the three months prior to the survey	1.5	3.1	18.5	2.8	4.6
Use of family planning in the three months prior to the survey	4.3	3.4	0.5	1.5	3.4
Use of vaccines in the three months prior to the survey	17.8	16.4	38.0	18.6	20.8
Use of child iron supplements in the three months prior to the survey	0.4	0.7	4.1	0.7	1.1
Use of disease prevention in the three months prior to the survey	1.2	2.3	1.6	2.6	1.5
DHS 2005					
Women's health					
Pap-smear exam in the five years prior to the survey	38.7	62.6	29.3	66.4	43.9
Breast exam in the five years prior to the survey	16.1	42.3	11.0	43.9	21.4
Number of prenatal visits					
None	8.3	2.1	11.5	0.6	7.2
1–4	36.7	19.6	34.8	9.0	32.9
5 or more	55.0	78.4	53.7	90.5	59.8
Person providing assistance at delivery (among women with births)					
No assistance	0.3	0.0	1.3	0.0	0.3
Doctor	35.5	69.5	20.9	92.8	42.1
Midwife	30.1	25.2	29.9	7.2	28.5
Nurse, promoter, or fieldworker	2.7	0.5	8.8	0.0	2.6
Comadrona or partera	16.2	2.5	21.8	0.0	13.8
Other	15.2	2.4	17.3	0.0	12.8
Immunization					
Children ages 18–59 months fully immunized	47.5	64.7	64.7	70.7	58.8

(continued)

TABLE 6.2 (continued)

Use of health services, by type of health insurance, 2005 and 2006 (%)

Indicator	Uninsured	EsSalud only	SIS only	Other	Total
Children with diarrhea					
Children under age 5 with diarrhea in the four weeks prior to the survey	16.3	9.5	18.1	9.8	15.9
Sought formal treatment for diarrhea	27.5	44.2	46.1	37.4	39.2
Place of treatment					
Traditional healer, pharmacy, at home, or with friend	37.4	2.6	15.8	29.9	21.8
Community health worker	0.7	0.0	0.8	0.0	0.7
MINSA facility	48.9	13.1	78.4	0.0	62.1
EsSalud facility	0.0	44.4	0.0	0.0	3.5
Army or private facility	0.0	0.0	0.0	0.0	0.0
Other type of health facility	13.0	37.0	1.4	70.1	9.5
Treated in more than one type of health facility	0.0	2.9	3.6	0.0	2.4
Children with acute respiratory infection					
Children under age 5 with acute respiratory infection in the four weeks prior to the survey	16.7	18.3	20.4	11.9	18.5
Sought formal treatment for acute respiratory infection	54.7	70.4	69.0	90.2	65.4
Place of treatment					
Traditional healer, pharmacy, at home, or with friend	21.6	11.8	8.9	10.5	13.1
Community health worker	0.0	0.0	0.7	0.0	0.4
MINSA facility	45.0	23.4	88.0	7.1	62.7
EsSalud facility	0.0	34.2	0.0	0.0	5.3
Army or private facility	3.8	0.0	0.0	0.0	1.1
Other type of health facility	20.5	21.8	2.2	49.7	12.2
Treated in more than one type of health facility	9.1	8.9	0.3	32.6	5.3
Family planning					
Current use of modern family planning methods	30.4	40.1	5.3	39.5	31.1
Number of growth monitoring visits (children ages 1–4)					
0	10.0	2.8	5.7	0.0	6.4
1	8.3	2.8	4.8	2.2	5.6
2	5.1	4.4	5.3	2.1	4.9
3	6.7	3.8	8.0	3.0	6.7
4	29.6	33.3	31.5	14.9	30.4
5	40.4	52.9	44.7	77.9	45.9

Source: ENAHO and DHS.

affiliation. For example, the higher use of child growth monitoring among SIS beneficiaries probably appears because SIS beneficiaries are much younger than those of EsSalud and the general population. Another indicator—the probability of seeking formal care in the four weeks prior to the survey—is less affected by demographic variables and shows practically no difference between SIS and EsSalud.

It is interesting to note, however, that SIS immunization rates for children are much higher than those for the uninsured and that nearly half of SIS children with diarrhea were taken for treatment, almost exclusively at MINSA facilities. The same is true for children with acute respiratory infections. SIS mothers match or exceed all others in using prenatal care and growth monitoring for their children. As we will see, there are interesting wrinkles in each of these findings when other variables are controlled.

The effects of Seguro Escolar Gratuito/Seguro Materno Infantil and Seguro Integral de Salud health insurance coverage on health care results using Demographic and Health Survey data

We were able to use the 2000 and 2004–07 DHS. Because of limitations, only a cross-sectional regression could be done for 2000 and for 2004–07. In 2000 the SEG/SMI programs were in place; in 2004–07 they had been merged to create SIS. Moreover, the 2004–07 surveys did not report child insurance status, so that was imputed based on the mother's status and rules governing which children would be covered. The full specification is shown in table A6.1 in the appendix; only the key results are discussed in this section.

We know that SIS is targeted, but we do not know the algorithm for the test. To limit the analysis to women who would be eligible for SIS under a perfect targeting regime, we removed the upper two quintiles from the analysis. In the DHS wealth variables are used to create these quintiles. In DHS-based regressions we cannot control for the endogeneity, if it existed for participation in SIS, so we ran univariate regressions where participation in SIS is simply included as a dummy variable.

Probability of being fully immunized (children ages 18–59 months)

Health insurance has a positive association with being fully immunized for children aged 18–59 months. Table 6.3 shows both descriptive statistics and results of a logit regression. The descriptive statistics show that the insured population has higher coverage of full immunization among children than the uninsured but eligible population. The logit regression, which controls for other factors that affect the immunization coverage besides health insurance, confirms that the effect of health insurance is positive: SEG/SMI health insurance increases the probability

TABLE 6.3

Seguro Escolar Gratuito/Seguro Materno Infantil and Seguro Integral de Salud and the probability of being fully immunized (children ages 18–59 months, %)

| Subpopulation | SEG/SMI Health Insurance, 2000 | | | | SIS Health Insurance, 2004-07 | | | |
	All	Quintile 1	Quintile 2	Quintile 3	All	Quintile 1	Quintile 2	Quintile 3
Observed mean of dependent variable								
Among population with health insurance	67	67	68	64	65	62	68	66
Among uninsured but eligible population	62	60	62	65	50	51	50	49
Among total population	63	61	63	65	60	59	62	57
Logit model (predicted mean of dependent variable)								
Simulation with health insurance = 1	64	65	65	63	65	62	67	71
Simulation with health insurance = 0	60	57	61	64	51	52	52	49
Effect of health insurance on dependent variable (percentage points)	+4***	+7***	+4	-1	+14***	+10***	+14***	+22***

*** significant at $p < 0.01$.

Source: Authors' calculations based on DHS 2000 and 2004 datasets.

of being fully immunized by 4 percentage points in 2000, and SIS does so by 14 percentage points in 2004.

The effect of SEG/SMI decreases gradually with income and is statistically significant only in quintile 1. In contrast, the effect of SIS increases steadily with income, yet the effect of SIS is larger than the effect of SEG/SMI even in quintile 1.

Probability of receiving pap-smear exam in last five years (women ages 15–49)
The percentage of women receiving pap smears in the last five years is lower among the insured SIS population (29%) than among the uninsured but eligible population (39%). When we control for other factors such as age, education, and marital status in a logit regression, we show that the effect of health insurance is positive: SIS is associated with a 3 percentage point increase in the probability of receiving a pap-smear exam.

We found a statistically significant interaction effect between SIS and age. The probability of receiving a pap smear exam always increases with age, but does so faster with SIS health insurance. Thus, there is a positive effect of SIS, which is lower among young women and higher among older women; in other words, SIS is associated with an increase in the probability of a pap smear when it is needed more.

Probability of delivery attended by a skilled health professional (women ages 15–49)

Results show no association between SEG/SMI or SIS and the probability of having a delivery attended by a skilled health professional. Although the insured population shows lower rates of assisted deliveries than the uninsured, these are caused by other factors: income, location, education, gender of the household head, marital status, and the number of children living in the household. When these factors are controlled, we find no statistically significant effect of health insurance.

Mean percentage of growth monitoring visits attended (children under age 5)

On average, SIS children attended 54% of their regular child growth monitoring visits, compared with 44% for similar uninsured children (table 6.4). The difference in favor of SIS children is observed across the three bottom quintiles. When controlling for other variables, SIS is associated with a 9 percentage point increase in child growth monitoring visits, with a much higher effect on the bottom quintile. We find a similar result for SEG/SMI in 2000.

We found a statistically significant interaction effect between SIS and the education of the mother. For all levels of mother's education, the predicted number of growth monitoring visits is higher for SIS children, reflecting the effect of the health insurance variable. SIS also attenuates the impact of education. The result is that a child born to a woman with no education, if covered by SIS, is more likely to have a complete cycle of growth monitoring or well-baby visits than if the mother has 15 years of education but is not covered by SIS.

Probability of being formally treated for diarrhea (children under age 5)

SIS is associated with a probability of receiving formal treatment for diarrhea that is 20 percentage points higher relative to the uninsured, with the effect statistically significant in the two bottom quintiles only. We sought possible interaction effects between the health insurance variable and the child's gender and age, the mother's age and education, and the household's urban/rural location, but none of the interaction terms was significant. The effect is similar for SEG/SMI in 2000.

Probability of being formally treated for acute respiratory infection (children under age 5)

SIS is associated with a 23 percentage point increase in the probability of receiving formal treatment for acute respiratory infection, with the effect statistically significant in all quintiles. We found no significant interaction effects.

TABLE 6.4

SEG/SMI and SIS and the mean percentage of growth monitoring visits attended (children under age 5)

Subpopulation	SEG/SMI Health Insurance, 2000				SIS Health Insurance, 2004–07			
	All	Quintile 1	Quintile 2	Quintile 3	All	Quintile 1	Quintile 2	Quintile 3
Observed mean of dependent variable								
Among population with health insurance	41	40	44	41	54	50	55	60
Among uninsured but eligible population	39	33	41	45	44	38	43	50
Among total population	39	34	42	44	50	47	51	56
Ordinary least squares model								
Number of observations	8,060	3,762	2,640	1,658	3,140	1,405	1,066	669
Adjusted R^2	0.11	0.09	0.06	0.11	0.12	0.15	0.10	0.08
Predicted mean of dependent variable								
Simulation with health insurance = 1	44	41	45	50	54	50	54	59
Simulation with health insurance = 0	37	32	40	43	45	37	46	52
Effect of health insurance on dependent variable (percentage points)	+7***	+9***	+6***	+7***	+9***	+13***	+8***	+6***

*** significant at $p < 0.01$.

Source: Authors' calculations based on DHS 2000 and 2004 datasets.

Impact of Seguro Integral de Salud health insurance coverage on health care results using ENAHO data

We were able to use the ENAHO data for 2002–06, which contain less information about health than the DHS but more information on economic variables. We use a 30% panel subsample for which we have five years of data. Because SIS members tend to join when they present themselves for care, we found that we could use double-lagged health insurance status (two years prior to the survey) as an identifying variable to control for endogeneity, leaving us with three years of the panel for analysis (2004–06). As in the previous analysis, the sample is restricted to the bottom three quintiles to reduce the possibility that we are comparing SIS affiliates to individuals who would not qualify for SIS.

Probability of seeking curative health care for symptoms, illnesses, or relapses in the four weeks prior to the survey

The probability of seeking curative health care, with a doctor or other qualified health professional, for symptoms, illnesses, or chronic disease relapses in the four weeks prior to the survey, excluding accidents. Even though there is a large discrepancy between the insured and uninsured in likelihood of seeking care, we find that much of the difference is explained by variables other than insurance. While insurance coverage has a significant, positive effect on the probability of seeking care, its independent effect ranges from 19 percentage points in 2004 to 6 percentage points in 2005 and 2006 (table 6.5).

Probability of spending a positive amount among those receiving formal care in last four weeks, how much is spent, and catastrophic spending (more than 30% of household spending)

The negative impact of SIS on the probability of spending any amount for those receiving care is high. With SIS coverage, the predicted probability of spending anything in 2004 is 13%, for example, compared with 86% for those without coverage. As a result, SIS coverage reduces the probability of spending anything,

TABLE 6.5

Impact of Seguro Integral de Salud on probability of seeking curative health care for symptoms, illnesses, or relapses in last four weeks (all ages)

	2004	2005	2006
Observed mean of dependent variable			
Among population with health insurance	50	42	44
Among uninsured but eligible population	16	16	16
Among total population	24	22	21
Endogeneity tests			
Value of rho in bivariate probit	-0.204	-0.143	-0.312**
Significance of predicted health insurance in primary equation	0.196	0.424	0.114
Model results			
Type of model	probit	probit	biprobit
Number of observations	2,174	1,912	2,008
Pseudo R2	0.13	0.08	na
Predicted mean of dependent variable			
Simulation with health insurance = 1	33	21	7
Simulation with health insurance = 0	14	15	1
Effect of health insurance on dependent variable (percentage points)	19***	6***	6***

*** significant at $p < 0.01$; ** significant at $p < 0.05$.

na not applicable.

Source: Authors' calculations based on ENAHO 2002–2006 panel dataset.

reducing the sample sizes so much for those with any spending that further analysis is not possible.

Summary and conclusions

SIS reduces in an important way the likelihood that those insured will have to spend money out of pocket for health care. At the same time, SEG/SMI and SIS are associated with increased use for a variety of services, both preventive and curative (table 6.6). The biggest effect occurs in the case of formal treatment for diarrhea and acute respiratory infections for children under age 5. Yet it also increases use of ambulatory care for all members when they are sick. Among preventive services, the biggest positive effect of SIS is for immunizations, followed by growth monitoring.

It is clear that SIS has achieved important gains for its beneficiaries, in lower out-of-pocket spending and higher use of services, but we were surprised to find

TABLE 6.6
Summary effects of SIS health insurance (%)

Indicator	SEG/SMI			SIS		
	Baseline	Value	Pro-poor effect	Baseline	Value	Pro-poor effect
Probability of being fully immunized (children ages 18–59 months)	62	+4***	Yes	50	+14***	No
Probability of receiving pap-smear exam in the five years prior to the survey (women ages 15–49)	44	+7***	No	38	+3*	No
Probability of having delivery attended by a skilled health personnel (women ages 15–49)	41	+4	No	56	+3	No
Mean percentage of growth monitoring schedule completed (children under age 5)	39	+7***	No	44	+9***	Yes
Probability of being formally treated for diarrhea (children under age 5)	34	+16***	No	29	+20***	Yes
Probability of being formally treated for acute respiratory infection (children under age 5)	50	+15***	No	52	+23***	No
Probability of seeking curative health care for symptoms, illnesses or relapses in the four weeks prior to the survey				16	+6~+19***	
Probability of spending a positive amount among those receiving formal care in the four weeks prior to the survey				86~92	−67~−81***	

*** significant at $p < 0.01$; ** significant at $p < 0.10$.
Source: Authors' calculations based on DHS and Encuesta Demográfica y de Salud Familiar.

that SIS coverage does not have an effect on institutional deliveries, which is a goal of the program. The reasons will have to be understood better and addressed in future policy changes. Assessing the causes of this partial failure should be a priority for SIS strategists.

Finally, we consider the effect of SIS to be pro-poor when its effect is greatest in quintile 1 and lowest in quintile 3, and not pro-poor otherwise. For example, the effect of SIS on the probability of being fully immunized is greater in quintile 3 than in quintile 1 and thus not considered pro-poor. The effect on the probability of seeking care for acute respiratory infection is constant in every quintile and also not considered pro-poor. The effect on growth monitoring visits, however, is highest in quintile 1 and lowest in quintile 3 and thus considered pro-poor. Although all three bottom quintiles are considered poor and eligible for SIS, it is desirable that the benefits of SIS reach the poor progressively, or at least proportionally, with their income. Cases where most of the effect reaches the less poor instead of the extreme poor (as for immunizations) reflect coverage inequalities that should be addressed.

Appendix: Model specifications

Table A6.1 shows the model specification for each dependent variable, indicating which control variables were included in the regressions. To explore whether the effects of health insurance vary between certain population groups, we included interactions terms between the health insurance dummy variable and the following variables: gender, age, years of education (of patient or patient's mother, depending on the age of the patient), and location.

TABLE A6.1

Dependent variables and control variables

	DHS						ENAHO			
	Probability of being fully immunized (children aged 18–59 months)	Probability of receiving pap-smear exam in last 5 years (women 15–49)	Probability of having delivery assisted by a doctor (women 15–49)	Percentage of child growth monitoring schedule completed (children under 5)	Probability of being formally treated for diarrhea (children under 5)	Probability of being formally treated for ARI (children under 5)	Probability of seeking curative health care for symptoms, illnesses or relapses in last 4 weeks (all ages)	Probability of spending a positive amount among those receiving formal care in last 4 weeks (all ages)	Amount spent by those with positive spending (all ages)	Probability of spending on health more than 30% of total household expenditure, excluding subsistence needs (extreme poverty line)
Quintile 1					Omitted					
Quintile 2	✓	✓	✓	✓	✓	✓	✓	✓	✓	✓
Quintile 3	✓	✓	✓	✓	✓	✓	✓	✓	✓	✓
Quintile 4	✓	✓	✓	✓	✓	✓	✓	✓	✓	✓
Quintile 5	✓	✓	✓	✓	✓	✓	✓	✓	✓	✓
Sex (Female = 1)	✓✓			✓✓	✓✓	✓✓	✓✓	✓✓	✓✓	✓✓
Age		✓✓	✓✓	✓✓	✓✓	✓✓	✓✓	✓✓	✓✓	✓✓
Age squared (×100)							✓	✓	✓	✓
Years of education		✓✓	✓✓				✓✓	✓✓	✓✓	✓✓
Married/concubinate		✓	✓				✓	✓	✓	✓
Female household head	✓	✓	✓	✓	✓	✓	✓	✓	✓	✓
Age of mother	✓✓			✓✓	✓✓	✓✓				
Years of education of mother	✓✓			✓✓	✓✓	✓✓				
Mother is married/concubinate	✓			✓	✓	✓				
Number of children under age 5	✓	✓	✓	✓	✓	✓	✓	✓	✓	✓
Owner of dwelling			Omitted				✓	✓	✓	✓
Lives in urban area	✓✓	✓✓	✓✓	✓✓	✓✓	✓✓	✓✓	✓✓	✓✓	✓✓
Lives in coast region	✓	✓	✓	✓	✓	✓	✓	✓	✓	✓
Lives in mountains region	✓	✓	✓	✓	✓	✓	✓	✓	✓	✓
Lives in Lima region			Omitted				✓	✓	✓	✓
Lives in higher jungle	✓	✓	✓	✓	✓	✓			Omitted	
Lives in lower jungle	✓	✓	✓	✓	✓	✓				
Health post in community			Not available				✓			

✓: indicates variable included in the regression.

✓✓: indicates variable included in the regression, plus a term to capture its interaction with the health insurance dummy.

Source: Authors.

Note

1. The subsidized scheme was implemented in phases: for fishers it began in 1997, for agrarian workers in 2002, and for home workers in 2005.

References

Cotlear, D. (ed.). 2006. *A New Social Contract for Peru: An Agenda for Improving Education, Health Care, and the Social Safety Net*. Washington, DC: World Bank.

Jaramillo, M., and S. Parodi. 2004. "El Seguro Escolar Gratuito y el Seguro Materno Infantil: Análisis de su incidencia e impacto sobre el acceso a los servicios de salud y sobre la equidad en el acceso." Documento de Trabajo 46Lima: Grupo de Análisis para el Desarrollo.

Portocarrero, J., P. Margarita, and C. Vallejo. 2007. "Cuentas Nacionales de Salud: Perú, 1995–2005" Oficina General de Planeamiento y Presupuesto del Ministerio de Salud (MINSA) y Observatorio de la Salud del Consorcio de Investigación Económica y Social, Lima.

World Bank. 2010. *World Development Indicators 2010*. Washington DC: The World Bank. Available at http://data.worldbank.org/sites/default/files/wdi/complete.pdf.

The Impact of Health Insurance on Use, Spending, and Health in Indonesia

Facundo Cuevas and Susan W. Parker

Classified by the World Bank as a lower middle-income country, Indonesia had per capita gross national income of US$3,600 in purchasing power parity terms in 2008. With about half the population residing in rural areas, life expectancy remains fairly low—at 69 years for men and 73 years for women—and under-five mortality high—at 41 per 1,000 in 2008. Child vaccination remains far from universal: in 2008, 77% of children had received the full course DPT vaccination (three doses) by their 23rd month, a good metric for the performance of immunization programs. Total health spending was about 2.2% of gross domestic product (GDP) in 2008, about 55% of it public and 45% private (World Bank 2010).

In this chapter, we study health insurance coverage and its relationship to health, health care use, access to services, and financial protection in Indonesia. For the empirical analysis, we use the 1993, 1997, and 2000 waves of the Indonesian Family Life Survey (IFLS), a multipurpose longitudinal household survey. (A more recent wave was collected in 2008 but was not available at the time of this analysis.) Observing outcomes and decisions of the same individuals over almost a decade provides a unique opportunity to understand the impact of insurance coverage and yields estimates that are purged of some of the most concerning sources of bias.

The Indonesian health system

The Indonesian constitution stipulates that every citizen has the right to social security and emphasizes the role of the state in providing universal social security coverage. But coverage remains far from universal. The social security systems include Askes, a mandatory social health insurance program for civil servants, and Asabri, for police, military, and their dependents. Jamsostek insurance for private sector workers is theoretically mandatory, but firms can opt out if they provide similar health services.

Askes covers an estimated 13.8 million people (plus 1.4 million commercial members), and Jamsostek 2.7 million (1.5 million of them workers). So formal health insurance schemes cover about 18 million people. Adding those covered by private or employer-funded health insurance, about 30 million individuals, or 15% of the population, are estimated to have health insurance.

In September 2004 the Indonesian House of Representatives endorsed a law on the National Social Security System mandating several social security schemes for citizens: old-age pension, old-age savings, national health insurance, work injury insurance, and death benefits for survivors of deceased workers. The new scheme aims to cover all Indonesian citizens—whether formal or informal workers or self-employed (World Bank 2010). The main program is Askes, which provides basic health benefits to poor individuals.[1]

The proportion covered by health insurance is remarkably constant over time, at about 15%, with a majority receiving coverage through the workplace in all three survey years. In 1993 we cannot disaggregate by type of coverage, but data from 1997 and 2000 show that most insurance is through Askes, then Jamostek. Nearly all insurance plans cover outpatient care and some hospitalization as well as some types of surgery.

Usually there is an assumption of fairly static coverage of formal sector and government workers, that they get and retain insurance coverage upon entering a covered job. We discovered the opposite; in fact, our empirical strategy uses changes in insurance status among the same people to analyze the impact of insurance. Of those insured in 1993 (about 15% of the sample), only about two-thirds remained insured in 1997. Similarly, of individuals with insurance in 1997, only about two-thirds remained insured in 2000. Of the uninsured population in 1993 (86%), about 5% gained insurance by 1997, and of the uninsured population in 1997, about 5% gained insurance by 2000. In sum, whereas about 15% of the population is covered by health insurance in any round of the IFLS, only about two-thirds of them retain insurance coverage in the next wave of data collection.

About 23% of the population is covered by insurance in at least one of the rounds. Only about 8% of the population are constantly insured. Overall, then, about 15% of the population have changes in insurance status—that is, are "sometimes insured." This population is the source of variation for the econometric analysis.

Most of those leaving the insured state were previously covered by Askes or Jamostek. But it is more probable that uninsured individuals lost Askes insurance than insured individuals gained Askes insurance between 1997 and 2000. The same is true for "reimbursement" insurance.[2] For Jamsostek the proportion of those losing insurance is about the same as the proportion of those gaining it. There is also movement between the covered population in the type of health insurance. For instance, of the 63% reporting Askes coverage in 1997, 88% remained with Askes, and the rest reported different coverage in 2000.

Descriptive statistics: the insured and the uninsured

Overall, the insured have higher rates of outpatient care use during the four weeks prior to the survey and in each of the three IFLS rounds. In 1993, 27% of the insured adult population received outpatient care, compared with 19% of the uncovered population.[3] For inpatient care for individuals ages 15 and older, those with insurance report higher use of inpatient care during the four weeks prior to the survey than do those without insurance over the three rounds. Also in all three rounds, the proportion of households incurring positive health expenditures is less for insured individuals than for uninsured individuals. Insured individuals have a higher body mass index than the uninsured, weighing on average about five kilograms more. About 22% of the insured population is overweight or obese, compared with about 13% of the uninsured population. Other health indicators do not show worse health for the insured than the uninsured.

In 1993, 27% of insured children reported using outpatient care in the four weeks prior to the survey, compared with 20% of uninsured children. The overall proportion of children using health care decreases over the panel, as expected because older children are less likely to have illnesses. For health status, insured children tend to be taller than uninsured children. Body mass indexes are slightly higher for insured than uninsured children, and these differences increase over time. Anemia levels for insured children are 4–5 percentage points lower than for uninsured children. For such health symptoms as diarrhea and headache, there are no clear patterns of differences between insured and uninsured children.

We divide the population into four groups between each two successive rounds: those who have insurance in both rounds, those who have insurance in neither round, those who gain insurance over time, and those who lose insurance over time. The use of outpatient care falls between 1993 and 1997 for all of the groups, except that those without insurance in 1993 who gained insurance by 1997 maintained their 1993 level of use across time. In other words, those gaining insurance over time increased use relative to those losing insurance.

The probability of spending money on health care between 1993 and 1997 falls for all four groups, but the group gaining insurance over time shows a greater fall in the probability of health expenditures. For health status, the four groups tend to show the same tendencies over time. The always insured group tends to have higher obesity rates than the other groups, but other health measures (including the prevalence of anemia and hypertension) tend to be similar. In sum, these descriptive statistics are consistent with an impact of insurance on health use and expenditures, but not on health status.

Use increases over time for the group that gains insurance and is reduced for the group that loses insurance. The group with insurance in both periods and those without insurance in both periods do not show changes in overall health care use between 1997 and 2000. The probability of making an expenditure increases for all three groups between 1997 and 2000, but the changes for the group that gains insurance are lower than those for the group that loses insurance. Again, for health status, there is little to differentiate the four groups.

We find similar trends for children. Children who gain insurance increase use relative to those who lose insurance. For instance, between 1997 and 2000 the proportion of children using outpatient care increased slightly for the group gaining insurance, from 12% to 13%, but fell for the group losing insurance, from 20% to 15%. Health status indicators for children show no obvious patterns for gaining or losing insurance.

In sum, individuals switching coverage have similar health status and symptoms during the four weeks prior to the survey. However, those gaining insurance are more likely to use care over time than those losing it, and the probability of those gaining insurance to incur health expenditures rises more slowly than that of those losing insurance.

Impacts of insurance on adults

Overall, having health insurance shows important positive and significant effects on indicators of health care use, both in inpatient and outpatient care (see box 7.1 for information on the methodology behind this study). For instance, for adults, having health insurance increases by about 4 percentage points the probability of having outpatient care in the four weeks prior to the survey and the probability of having inpatient care by about 1 percentage point (top 3 rows in table 7.1). For

BOX 7.1
Methodology

This study uses longitudinal information in the Indonesian Family Life Survey to estimate individual fixed effect models that use changes in insurance status for the same people over time to estimate the impacts of insurance coverage. Cross-sectional analyses are likely to suffer from selection problems in who has insurance at a given time. Individual fixed effect estimators rely on variation in health insurance coverage for the same individual (rather than comparing different individuals) and isolate the impact estimates from unobserved time-invariant individual characteristics that could create spurious correlations among insurance, health status, and the use of services.

For the impacts of health insurance, we focus primarily on the use of services and health spending, as well as some health status indicators that might respond quickly to changes in insurance. Such indicators potentially include symptoms such as cough, diarrhea, the flu, high blood pressure (which can be lowered by appropriate medicine), and anemia (which can be remedied by iron tablets)—but we do not include illnesses such as diabetes. We thus concentrate on variables where changes in insurance coverage might have fairly quick effects.

The descriptive analysis shows sufficient variation in insurance coverage for individual fixed effects models to be estimated. These estimates are of course based only on the individuals experiencing changes in insurance coverage over the seven years of the panel, about 15% of the sample.

health spending, insurance significantly reduces the probability of any household health spending, but the impact on average per capita health spending is insignificant. By gender, the impact of health insurance on men and women is similar for inpatient and outpatient care as well as for household health care expenditures.

Insurance increases the probability of having any outpatient care by 5 percentage points for adults in rural areas, compared with 4 percentage points for urban adults (middle and bottom 3 rows in table 7.1). For inpatient care, rural areas show positive and significant impacts of insurance for the group of all adults, but in urban areas, there are no statistically significant impacts. Also in rural areas, insurance significantly reduces the probability of household health care spending (mostly for female insured adults), and there are significant impacts, albeit smaller, in urban areas. Overall, then, insurance has slightly larger impacts for the rural population, especially for women.

Impacts on use of outpatient care are higher for adults in the bottom 50% of the expenditure distribution (a proxy for relative income), compared with adults in the top 50% of the distribution (table 7.2). For instance, whereas the impact of insurance on the probability of having any outpatient care is 4 percentage points

TABLE 7.1

Effects of health insurance on use, by gender and location

	Individual fixed effects on adults older than age 15 at baseline					
	Had any outpatient care in the four weeks prior to the survey	Number of times that had outpatient care in the four weeks prior to the survey	Had any inpatient care in the 12 months prior to the survey	Number times that had inpatient care in the 12 months prior to the survey	Household health expenditures (> 0)	Monthly per capita expenditure on health (real rupiahs)
Adults	0.04 [0.0111]***	0.10 [0.0219]***	0.01 [0.0057]*	0.01 [0.0061]**	−0.03 [0.0126]**	−349.55 [435.5682]
Female	0.04 [0.0161]**	0.11 [0.0327]***	0.01 [0.0086]	0.01 [0.0093]	−0.04 [0.0143]**	−297.17 [495.9211]
Male	0.05 [0.0142]***	0.09 [0.0278]***	0.01 [0.0071]**	0.01 [0.0075]**	−0.03 [0.0148]*	−374.14 [466.2524]
Adults living in rural areas	0.05 [0.0200]**	0.12 [0.0436]***	0.02 [0.0087]*	0.02 [0.0096]*	−0.04 [0.0218]*	−319.06 [389.1802]
Female	0.05 [0.0294]*	0.14 [0.0669]**	0.02 [0.0134]	0.02 [0.0149]	−0.05 [0.0251]**	−687.37 [448.7407]
Male	0.0474 [0.0268]*	0.0895 [0.0567]	0.0144 [0.0111]	0.0121 [0.0117]	−0.0335 [0.0250]	−44.8885 [452.5782]
Adults living in urban areas	0.04 [0.0133]***	0.09 [0.0251]***	0.01 [0.0072]	0.01 [0.0077]	−0.03 [0.0151]*	−354.04 [574.0108]
Female	0.04 [0.0193]*	0.10 [0.0372]**	0.00 [0.0107]	0.01 [0.0116]	−0.03 [0.0171]	−230.62 [648.6015]
Male	0.04 [0.0166]***	0.09 [0.0311]***	0.01 [0.0090]	0.02 [0.0095]*	−0.03 [0.0180]	−505.88 [616.9774]

*** significant at $p < 0.01$; ** significant at $p < 0.05$; * significant at $p < 0.10$.

Note: Numbers in brackets are standard errors.

Source: Authors' calculations based on 1993, 1997, and 2000 Indonesian Family Life Surveys.

for adults in the top 50% of the distribution, it is 6 percentage points for those in the bottom 50% of the distribution. For outpatient care during the four weeks prior to the survey, insurance increases the number of visits by 0.07 for adults in the top 50% of the distribution, compared with 0.17 for those in the bottom 50%. Surprisingly, however, the impact of health insurance on reducing household health spending is negative and significant only for women in the lower income groups, whereas for upper income groups the impact is negative and significant only for men.

We now turn to potential impacts of insurance on indicators more closely associated with health status, including weight, body mass index, high blood pressure,

TABLE 7.2

Effects of health insurance on use, by expenditure distribution

	Individual fixed effects on adults older than age 15 at baseline					
	Had any outpatient care in the four weeks prior to the survey	Number of times that had outpatient care in the four weeks prior to the survey	Had any inpatient care in the 12 months prior to the survey	Number times that had inpatient care in the 12 months prior to the survey	Household health expenditures (>0)	Monthly per capita expenditure on health (real rupiahs)
Adults in top 50% of expenditure distribution	0.04 [0.0136]***	0.07 [0.0249]***	0.01 [0.0073]	0.01 [0.0075]	−0.03 [0.0144]**	−562.42 [601.7865]
Female	0.04 [0.0196]*	0.09 [0.0375]**	0.01 [0.0108]	0.01 [0.0113]	−0.03 [0.0169]	−516.71 [675.4978]
Male	0.04 [0.0167]**	0.04 [0.0303]	0.01 [0.0091]	0.01 [0.0093]	−0.04 [0.0167]**	−599.81 [650.0818]
Adults in bottom 50% of expenditure distribution	0.0547 [0.0190]***	0.1733 [0.0437]***	0.0087 [0.0084]	0.0165 [0.0103]	−0.02 [0.0252]	398.5821 [226.5667]*
Female	0.04 [0.0279]	0.15 [0.0655]**	0.00 [0.0131]	0.01 [0.0162]	−0.05 [0.0267]*	485.23 [361.6902]
Male	0.0634 [0.0268]**	0.1949 [0.0587]***	0.0212 [0.0103]**	0.0254 [0.0126]**	0.0088 [0.0307]	285.6729 [219.4914]

*** significant at $p < 0.01$; ** significant at $p < 0.05$; * significant at $p < 0.10$.

Note: Numbers in brackets are standard errors.

Source: Authors' calculations based on 1993, 1997, and 2000 Indonesian Family Life Surveys.

hemoglobin levels and anemia, and activities of daily living, including ability to carry a heavy load, walk 5 kilometers, and kneel (table 7.3). Among these indicators, we have tried to choose some, among those available, where it is feasible that health insurance might have an impact fairly quickly. Even so, the health status variables chosen are likely to take longer to react to having insurance than such variables as health clinic visits or health care expenditures.

Overall, there are few consistent findings of significant and positive impacts of health insurance. There are no significant coefficients on the impact of insurance on obesity, hemoglobin levels, or high blood pressure, except for insurance reducing the prevalence of hypertension stage 1 for women in rural areas. There are a couple modest impacts of insurance on some activities of daily living. In particular,

TABLE 7.3

Effects of health status, by gender and location

	Individual fixed effects on adults older than 15 years at baseline										
	Body mass index (BMI)	Overweight (BMI between 25–29.9 kg/m2)	Obesity (BMI ≥ 30 kg/m2)	Hemoglobin (g/dl)	Low hemoglobin (iron deficit: hb ≤ 12 women, hb ≤ 13.5 men, hb ≤ 11 child)	High blood pressure	Hypertension stage 1 (systolic 140-159 or diastolic 90-99)	Hypertension stage 2 (systolic ≥ 160 or diastolic ≥ 100)	Difficulty/ unable to carry heavy load	Difficulty/ unable to walk 5 kilometers	Difficulty/ unable to kneel
Adults	0.03 [0.0458]	0.01 [0.0079]	0.00 [0.0039]	-0.04 [0.0535]	0.01 [0.0173]	-0.01 [0.0174]	0.00 [0.0149]	0.01 [0.0086]	0.00 [0.0083]	0.01 [0.0104]	-0.01 [0.0051]
Female	-0.02 [0.0650]	0.00 [0.0119]	-0.01 [0.0062]	-0.01 [0.0679]	0.02 [0.0234]	0.01 [0.0230]	0.01 [0.0189]	0.02 [0.0115]	0.01 [0.0129]	0.01 [0.0161]	0.00 [0.0074]
Male	0.09 [0.0608]	0.01 [0.0104]	0.00 [0.0042]	-0.06 [0.0797]	0.00 [0.0239]	-0.02 [0.0256]	0.00 [0.0226]	0.00 [0.0130]	-0.02 [0.0088]*	0.00 [0.0112]	-0.01 [0.0067]*
Adults living in rural areas	0.09 [0.0792]	0.01 [0.0125]	0.00 [0.0048]	0.02 [0.0980]	0.01 [0.0322]	0.00 [0.0341]	-0.03 [0.0285]	0.00 [0.0175]	0.01 [0.0141]	0.01 [0.0190]	-0.02 [0.0090]*
Female	0.09 [0.1167]	0.01 [0.0203]	0.00 [0.0086]	0.06 [0.1326]	0.03 [0.0419]	-0.03 [0.0474]	-0.06 [0.0350]*	0.02 [0.0238]	0.02 [0.0215]	0.03 [0.0312]	-0.03 [0.0134]**
Male	0.11 [0.0945]	0.02 [0.0126]	0.00 [0.0031]	-0.01 [0.1435]	-0.02 [0.0456]	0.02 [0.0459]	0.00 [0.0422]	-0.01 [0.0258]	0.00 [0.0161]	0.00 [0.0190]	0.00 [0.0127]
Adults living in urban areas	0.02 [0.0562]	0.01 [0.0100]	-0.01 [0.0052]	-0.06 [0.0638]	0.02 [0.0205]	-0.01 [0.0202]	0.01 [0.0174]	0.01 [0.0098]	-0.01 [0.0101]	0.01 [0.0125]	0.00 [0.0061]
Female	-0.06 [0.0790]	0.00 [0.0146]	-0.01 [0.0079]	-0.03 [0.0790]	0.02 [0.0281]	0.01 [0.0262]	0.03 [0.0225]	0.02 [0.0132]	0.00 [0.0159]	0.01 [0.0188]	0.01 [0.0089]
Male	0.10 [0.0773]	0.01 [0.0140]	0.00 [0.0060]	-0.07 [0.0962]	0.01 [0.0278]	-0.05 [0.0306]	-0.01 [0.0268]	0.00 [0.0148]	-0.02 [0.0105]**	0.00 [0.0138]	-0.02 [0.0079]*

** significant at p < 0.05; * significant at p < 0.10.

Note: Numbers in brackets are standard errors.

Source: Authors' calculations based on 1993, 1997, and 2000 Indonesian Family Life Surveys.

health insurance reduces the probability of difficulties in kneeling (for women in rural areas and men in urban areas) and in carrying heavy objects for men.

Disaggregating by spending category, the results show no significant impacts of insurance on the health status indicators for adults in wealthier households (table 7.4). But for adults in poorer households, there is an unexpected significant increase in the probability of having anemia for females and a significant reduction in blood pressure associated with health insurance for adult males. Overall, then, the impacts on health status are much less widespread than those on use by adults and do not provide convincing evidence of a strong effect of insurance on health status.

Before turning to estimates of the impact of insurance on children, it is worth noting that, because our sample includes all adults ages 15 and older, some of the transitions from having health insurance to not having health insurance are related to young individuals entering the labor market for the first time and retirement decisions of older individuals. To ensure that such transitions are not driving the results, we re-estimate the previous tables for adults using the population of adults ages 35–50. Overall, results (available upon request) of the impact of insurance on health care use are quite similar to previous results. For health status indicators, as with the entire adult population, there are few significant impacts of insurance in this population. There continues to be an impact of insurance on reducing problems associated with kneeling for adults in rural areas. We conclude that transitions associated with entering the labor market for the first time or exiting due to retirement are not driving the reported results.

Impacts of insurance on children

We now turn to insurance impacts on children. Overall, insurance significantly increases the use of outpatient care for children, but curiously only for female children in both rural and urban areas, with a 4 percentage point increase in the probability of using outpatient care in the four weeks prior to the survey (table 7.5). Insurance significantly increases the use of inpatient care but notably again only for girls, both in rural and urban areas. Insurance reduces the probability of making positive household health expenditures for male children, although there is no overall effect on household health expenditures. Table 7.5 also includes the impacts of insurance on body mass index, obesity, and hemoglobin levels for children, but there do not appear to be any significant impacts of health insurance on these variables, with the exception of a surprising positive impact of insurance on increasing obesity of girls living in rural areas.

There are some significant impacts of insurance on children from both upper income and lower income households (table 7.6), but again mainly for girls. In

TABLE 7.4

Effects of health status, by expenditure distribution

	Body mass index (BMI)	Overweight (BMI between 25–29.9 kg/m2)	Obesity (BMI ≥ 30 kg/m2)	Hemoglobin (g/dl)	Low hemoglobin (iron deficit: hb ≤ 12 women, hb ≤ 13.5 men, hb ≤ 11 child)	High blood pressure	Hypertension stage 1 (systolic 140–159 or diastolic 90–99)	Hypertension stage 2 (systolic ≥ 160 or diastolic ≥ 100)	Difficulty/ unable to carry heavy load	Difficulty/ unable to walk 5 kilometers	Difficulty/ unable to kneel
					Individual fixed effects on adults older than 15 years at baseline						
Adults in top 50% of expenditure distribution	0.0265 [0.0568]	0.0075 [0.0097]	-0.0041 [0.0050]	-0.0452 [0.0635]	-0.0101 [0.0206]	0.0109 [0.0208]	0.0112 [0.0179]	0.0037 [0.0102]	-0.0041 [0.0101]	0.0028 [0.0123]	-0.0041 [0.0062]
Female	-0.0504 [0.0781]	-0.0022 [0.0141]	-0.0071 [0.0077]	-0.0322 [0.0783]	-0.0132 [0.0277]	0.0128 [0.0284]	0.0237 [0.0230]	0.0076 [0.0141]	0.0057 [0.0156]	0.0007 [0.0192]	0.0005 [0.0090]
Male	0.1155 [0.0772]	0.0196 [0.0139]	-0.0011 [0.0057]	-0.0468 [0.0947]	-0.0087 [0.0281]	0.0038 [0.0305]	-0.0032 [0.0272]	0.0006 [0.0152]	-0.0165 [0.0107]	0.0034 [0.0130]	-0.0096 [0.0084]
Adults in bottom 50% of expenditure distribution	0.0651 [0.0772]	0.0106 [0.0137]	-0.0053 [0.0058]	-0.0117 [0.0983]	0.058 [0.0317]*	-0.0479 [0.0318]	-0.0241 [0.0264]	0.0147 [0.0163]	-0.0042 [0.0146]	0.0194 [0.0194]	-0.0146 [0.0086]*
Female	0.0755 [0.1202]	0.018 [0.0219]	-0.0089 [0.0098]	0.0511 [0.1325]	0.0877 [0.0433]**	-0.0176 [0.0390]	-0.0355 [0.0334]	0.0405 [0.0201]**	0.0095 [0.0228]	0.0473 [0.0295]	-0.013 [0.0132]
Male	0.0663 [0.0936]	0.0028 [0.0134]	-0.0014 [0.0053]	-0.0675 [0.1471]	0.0187 [0.0449]	-0.0832 [0.0469]*	-0.0094 [0.0402]	-0.0129 [0.0249]	-0.0199 [0.0156]	-0.0127 [0.0211]	-0.0173 [0.0111]

** significant at p < 0.05; * significant at p < 0.10.

Note: Numbers in brackets are standard errors.

Source: Authors' calculations based on 1993, 1997, and 2000 Indonesian Family Life Surveys.

TABLE 7.5

Effects of health insurance on youth and health status for children, by gender and location

	Had any outpatient care in the four weeks prior to the survey	Number of times that had outpatient care in the four weeks prior to the survey	Had any inpatient care in the 12 months prior to the survey	Number times that had inpatient care in the 12 months prior to the survey	Household health expenditures (> 0)	Monthly per capita expenditure on health (real rupiahs)	Body mass index (BMI)	Overweight (BMI between 25-29.9 kg/m2)	Obesity (BMI ≥ 30 kg/m2)	Hemoglobin (g/dl)	Low hemoglobin (iron deficit: hb ≤ 12 women, hb < 13.5 men, hb < 11 child)
Children	0.03 [0.0118]***	0.04 [0.0183]*	0.01 [0.0042]**	0.01 [0.0049]**	-0.05 [0.0170]***	300.45 [429.2084]	0.03 [0.0673]	0.01 [0.0065]	0.00 [0.0035]	0.01 [0.0605]	-0.01 [0.0187]
Female	0.05 [0.0169]***	0.05 [0.0260]*	0.01 [0.0058]*	0.01 [0.0075]*	-0.02 [0.0196]	624.68 [738.7300]	0.05 [0.0936]	0.01 [0.0091]	0.00 [0.0043]	0.06 [0.0775]	-0.04 [0.0264]
Male	0.02 [0.0165]	0.02 [0.0262]	0.01 [0.0062]	0.01 [0.0064]	-0.08 [0.0215]***	-80.24 [357.9235]	-0.01 [0.0882]	0.01 [0.0090]	0.00 [0.0054]	-0.04 [0.0846]	0.00 [0.0250]
Children living in rural areas	0.04 [0.0208]*	0.07 [0.0341]**	0.01 [0.0065]*	0.01 [0.0073]**	-0.04 [0.0276]	606.98 [609.8549]	0.05 [0.1066]	0.00 [0.0089]	0.00 [0.0029]	0.02 [0.0938]	-0.01 [0.0311]
Female	0.05 [0.0279]*	0.07 [0.0473]	0.02 [0.0087]**	0.03 [0.0107]**	-0.03 [0.0328]	1071.56 [1,034.9960]	0.06 [0.1477]	0.01 [0.0145]	0.00 [0.0008]**	0.11 [0.1337]	-0.04 [0.0382]
Male	0.03 [0.0310]	0.06 [0.0519]	0.00 [0.0095]	0.00 [0.0095]	-0.06 [0.0340]*	48.24 [411.7411]	0.03 [0.1361]	0.00 [0.0085]	0.00 [0.0063]	-0.07 [0.1296]	0.01 [0.0499]
Children living in urban areas	0.03 [0.0143]**	0.02 [0.0216]	0.01 [0.0054]	0.01 [0.0063]	-0.05 [0.0211]**	148.60 [560.3776]	0.01 [0.0847]	0.01 [0.0087]	0.00 [0.0050]	0.01 [0.0771]	-0.02 [0.0233]
Female	0.05 [0.0212]**	0.04 [0.0312]	0.00 [0.0076]	0.01 [0.0100]	-0.01 [0.0242]	359.76 [979.4172]	0.02 [0.1190]	0.01 [0.0116]	0.00 [0.0064]	0.05 [0.0952]	-0.04 [0.0349]
Male	0.02 [0.0196]	0.01 [0.0303]	0.01 [0.0079]	0.01 [0.0082]	-0.09 [0.0269]***	-121.87 [479.3178]	-0.04 [0.1113]	0.01 [0.0123]	0.00 [0.0072]	-0.02 [0.1072]	0.00 [0.0286]

*** significant at $p < 0.01$; ** significant at $p < 0.05$; * significant at $p < 0.10$.

Note: Numbers in brackets are standard errors.

Source: Authors' calculations based on 1993, 1997, and 2000 Indonesian Family Life Surveys.

TABLE 7.6

Effects of health insurance on use and health status for children, by expenditure distribution

	Had any outpatient care last 4 weeks	Number of times that had outpatient care last 4 weeks	Had any inpatient care last 12 months	Number of times that had inpatient care last 12 months	Household health expenditures (>0)	Monthly per capita expenditure on health (real rupiahs)	Body mass index (BMI)	Overweight (BMI between 25–29.9 kg/m2)	Obesity (BMI>=30 kg/m2)	Hemoglobin (g/dl)	Low hemoglobin (iron deficit: hb ≤ 12 women, hb < 13.5 men, hb < 11 child)
				Individual fixed effects on children ages 15 or younger at baseline							
Children in top 50% of expenditure distribution	0.0305 [0.0146]**	0.0273 [0.0233]	0.0065 [0.0055]	0.0081 [0.0064]	-0.0517 [0.0199]***	-7.9504 [552.6415]	0.0448 [0.0819]	0.0172 [0.0080]**	-0.0007 [0.0045]	0.0661 [0.0747]	-0.0293 [0.0226]
Female	0.0489 [0.0204]**	0.0505 [0.0314]	0.0101 [0.0077]	0.0123 [0.0099]	-0.0158 [0.0227]	-15.2164 [930.6213]	0.0856 [0.1123]	0.0246 [0.0114]**	0.0044 [0.0057]	0.105 [0.0916]	-0.0565 [0.0316]*
Male	0.0139 [0.0209]	0.0062 [0.0344]	0.0035 [0.0078]	0.0046 [0.0081]	-0.0886 [0.0253]***	-57.3121 [502.5411]	-0.0115 [0.1099]	0.0075 [0.0110]	-0.0049 [0.0071]	0.032 [0.1070]	-0.0053 [0.0299]
Children in bottom 50% of expenditure distribution	0.0407 [0.0197]**	0.0523 [0.0279]*	0.0113 [0.0054]**	0.0137 [0.0064]**	-0.035 [0.0323]	1,135.11 [627.3474]*	0.0109 [0.1153]	-0.0078 [0.0110]	0.0005 [0.0053]	-0.1189 [0.1021]	0.0199 [0.0333]
Female	0.0536 [0.0303]*	0.0555 [0.0475]	0.0101 [0.0075]	0.0157 [0.0102]	-0.0165 [0.0384]	2,235.08 [1,187.3908]*	-0.0277 [0.1687]	-0.0252 [0.0145]*	0.0009 [0.0056]	-0.0487 [0.1451]	0.0094 [0.0478]
Male	0.0312 [0.0255]	0.0552 [0.0339]	0.0109 [0.0097]	0.0103 [0.0097]	-0.0546 [0.0404]	28.3983 [269.1923]	0.0206 [0.1386]	0.0111 [0.0154]	0.0006 [0.0068]	-0.2303 [0.1344]*	0.0312 [0.0464]

*** significant at $p < 0.01$; ** significant at $p < 0.05$; * significant at $p < 0.10$.

Note: Numbers in brackets are standard errors.

Source: Authors' calculations based on 1993, 1997, and 2000 Indonesian Family Life Surveys.

particular, girls in both lower and higher income households show significant impacts of health insurance on the use of outpatient care. Insurance also increases the use of inpatient care for children in lower income households. Yet it decreases the likelihood of having any health expenditures among the rich by about 5 percentage points, with no impact on poorer households. For poorer insured households there is an increase in per capita spending for girls. For health status variables there are some significant impacts, with some inconsistencies. Health insurance is associated with higher proportions of overweight children in upper income households and a lower proportion of overweight female children in lower income groups. Health insurance is also significantly associated with lower rates of anemia for girls in upper income groups.

The results are for all children younger than age 15. But health insurance might be more important for health outcomes for younger children than older children, particularly in the first few years of life. So we repeat our analysis of the impacts of insurance for three groups of children, those ages 3 and younger in 1993, those ages 5 and younger, and those ages 8 and younger. We might expect that any impacts of health insurance would be stronger for the younger age groups, but concentrating on these age groups significantly reduces the sample size. We also include child height as an extra outcome variable.

While the coefficient on the impact of insurance on health care use continues to be positive, the results generally lose significance, consistent with the smaller sample size or suggesting that insurance might have less impact on health use for younger age groups. For health status measures, for younger children, the results show an overall significant reduction in obesity for children under age 3 and children under age 5 at baseline and a slight increase for young girls in the proportion of those overweight for those insured. But for female children in rural areas, there is a positive impact of insurance on increasing both body mass index and the probability of being overweight (but not obese). Young male children under age 3 show a significant reduction in the proportion obese of about 3 percentage points. There are no significant impacts of insurance on child height.

Conclusion

Our findings show consistently that health insurance increases the use of both inpatient and outpatient care over the length of the panel, for both adults and children. There is also evidence that health insurance reduces the probability of any health care spending; nevertheless, while the effect on the overall amount of per capita spending is consistently negative, it is not statistically significant. It is important to note some differences by subgroup in the impacts of insurance. In particular, lower income groups tend to show higher impacts of use with insurance, and there is some evidence of higher impacts of insurance in rural areas than in urban areas.

For health status, the evidence is less uniform, with many indicators of health status for both adults and children showing little relationship with insurance coverage. There are, however, a few exceptions—particularly some small positive effects of insurance on reducing problems associated with activities of daily living for adults and a potential impact of reducing high blood pressure for adults in lower income groups. But for children there appear to be few impacts of health insurance on health status indicators. There are some suggestions that insurance reduces child obesity for some age groups but increases it for others, so there are no obvious conclusions here. Child height is unaffected by insurance status in all of the groups studied.

How can insurance increase overall use of services without increasing, at least in clearly measurable ways, health status? One possibility might be that those without insurance find ways of coping when faced with health issues that might affect their health status. For example, they see free or low cost public providers, use savings, and ask friends or pharmacists for assistance. Alternatively, illnesses that substantially affect health status might be infrequent enough that impacts on these rare events are difficult to observe. It may be that—compared with other factors affecting health, such as genetic, behavioral, or random components—insurance could at best have very small impacts. Finally, some aspects of health are likely difficult to alter no matter how much attention is received—for instance, obesity, an important indicator of health but notoriously difficult to overcome.

In chapter 2 of this volume Giedion and Diaz argue that future studies of the impact of health insurance should focus on health outcomes more likely to be alterable and measurable. We agree that this should form the basis for future research. It seems unlikely that health insurance might directly affect many standard self-reported measures such as days ill or getting a fever or headache. It seems equally unlikely that insurance would affect the probability of certain types of illness, such as breast cancer. Insurance might, however, promote earlier diagnoses of chronic illnesses, though for this study we did not have information on such variables. Finally, there may be contexts where increased use does not necessarily lead to an improvement in health because the client was either not particularly ill or the ailment does not respond well to treatment, such as the common cold. In these circumstances, use might mitigate symptoms but not necessarily measured physical health.

Notes

1. See Setiana (2005) for a short but comprehensive history of the health financing policy in Indonesia as well as the reform program.

2. Instead of Jamsostek, firms may opt for a system where the firm reimburses the employee for medical expenditures.

3. We also carried out descriptive analysis comparing the groups of those always having insurance to those never having insurance. But these results were qualitatively similar to those presented here, so we omit them to save space.

References

Setiana, Adang. 2005. "Social Health Insurance Development as an Integral Part of the National Health Policy: Recent Reform in Indonesian Health Insurance System." Paper presented at the International Conference on Social Health Insurance in Developing Countries, December 5–7, Berlin. [www.socialhealthprotection.org/pdf/SHI-ConfReader_Druckkomprimiert.pdf].

———. 2008. *Investing in Indonesia's Health: Challenges and Opportunities for Future Public Spending.* Health Public Expenditure Review. Washington, DC: World Bank.

World Bank. 2010. *World Development Indicators 2010.* Washington, DC: World Bank.

The Impact of a Social Experiment—Rural Mutual Health Care—on Health Care Use, Financial Risk Protection, and Health Status in Rural China

Winnie Yip and William Hsiao

In 2002 the Chinese government announced a new national policy for rural health care—the New Cooperative Medical Scheme (NCMS). First rolled out in a small number of pilot counties in 2003 and targeted to cover the entire rural population by 2010, the goals are to improve access to health care and reduce inequality and medical impoverishment. The government has allocated new resources to the scheme, targeting the poor western and central regions. The national policy guidelines for the scheme have only two requirements: voluntary enrollment and priority to cover catastrophic health expenditures. Apart from this, local governments are free to design their own programs, turning China into a laboratory for experimentation.

To assist China in developing a rural health care system tailored to conditions in poorer regions and designed to be sustainable in the long run, we conducted a social experiment of a community-based prepayment scheme—Rural Mutual Health Care (RMHC)—following the national guidelines but augmented with other interventions to improve quality and efficiency.

The primary objective of this chapter is to empirically evaluate the RMHC's impact on access to care, financial risk protection, and health status. Using a pre-post treatment-control study design and longitudinal household/individual surveys one year before the interventions and annually for three years after the interventions, we estimate the impact effects of the RMHC, combining difference-in-difference estimation with propensity score matching to control for observable and unobservable time-invariant differences between the treatment and control groups.

Rural health care in China

Key challenges confronting the rural health care system
From the early 1950s to 1980 China's strategy for rural health care emphasized prevention and basic health care. It developed a three-tiered organization for delivery of health care. In rural areas this consisted of village health posts, township health centers, and county hospitals, which together provided a structure for efficient patient referrals to treat health problems. The Cooperative Medical System provided nearly universal insurance coverage in rural areas. Financed primarily by the welfare fund of the communes (collective farms), the system organized health stations, paid village doctors to deliver primary care, and provided drugs. It also partially reimbursed patients for services received at township and county facilities. At its peak in 1978 it covered 90% of China's rural population, making basic health care accessible and affordable and offering peasants financial protection against large medical expenses.

When China reformed its rural economy in 1979 and introduced the Household Responsibility System, the communes disappeared, and without this funding base, the Cooperative Medical System collapsed, leaving 90% of all peasants uninsured. Village doctors became private practitioners with little government oversight, earning their income from patients on a fee-for-service basis. Further, like all transition economies, China experienced a drastic reduction in the government's capacity to fund health care as government revenue shrank. Government subsidies as a share of public health facilities' total revenues fell to a mere 10% by the early 1990s. To keep health care affordable, the government maintained strict price controls by setting prices for basic health care below cost. At the same time, the government wanted facilities to survive financially, so it set prices for new and high-tech diagnostic services above cost and allowed a 15% profit margin on drugs.

These policies created perverse incentives for providers who had to generate 90% of their budget from revenue-producing activities, turning hospitals, township health centers, and village doctors alike into profit-seeking entities. Providers overprescribe drugs and tests while hospitals race to introduce high-tech services and expensive imported drugs that give them higher profit margins (Liu and Mills 1999). To increase their profits village doctors often buy cheap counterfeit or expired drugs and sell them to patients at the higher official price (Blumenthal and Hsiao 2005). Referrals within the three-tiered delivery system also collapsed, as each level of provider competed with the other for patients, duplicating tests and services. Health care spending soared, growing 16% a year—7 percentage points faster than gross domestic product (GDP) growth—and patient out-of-pocket health spending also grew at an average of 16% from 1978 to 2003 (Blumenthal and Hsiao 2005; Smith, Wong, and Zhao 2005).

In less than two decades China had transformed its rural health care system from one that provided prevention and affordable basic health care for all to one in which people could not afford basic health care, driving many families into poverty (Hesketh and Zhu 1997a, 1997b; Hsiao 1984; Lindelow and Wagstaff 2005; Watts 2006, 2007). The 2003 National Health Survey found that 46% of the rural Chinese who were ill did not seek health care, and among them, 40% cited cost as the main reason (Center for Health Statistics and Information 2004). Another 22% of those advised by physicians to be hospitalized refused to do so because they could not afford it. Of those who did become hospitalized, about 35% discharged themselves against their doctor's advice because of cost. Studies have found that 30%–40% of those below the poverty line attributed their poverty to medical expenditures (Center for Health Statistics and Information 2004; Watts 2006).

China's national policy for rural health care

In 2002 the Chinese government announced the NCMS, but conspicuously absent from its stated goals are improving health outcomes and reducing inefficiencies in health care delivery. Targeted to cover the entire rural population by 2010, more than 90% of the rural population was covered by the end of 2008.

For the scheme's initial waves the government subsidized each farmer in western and central provinces with 20 RMB (1 RMB = US$0.125), shared equally between the central and local governments, if the farmer pays an annual premium of at least 10 RMB to enroll (Central Committee of CPC 2002; Watts 2006). The subsidy was increased to 40 RMB (US$5) in 2006, then again to 80 RMB in 2007, 100 RMB in 2008, and 120 RMB in 2009, with the individual's contribution rising to 20 RMB (Anonymous 2009). Exactly how such a scheme will address the multiple challenges in rural health care has been left open, and the central government encourages local governments to experiment with different workable schemes.

Rural mutual health care

Beyond the government's limited goals for the NCMS, the RMHC project aimed to improve the efficiency and quality of health care and the health status of people. The project simulated the government subsidy of 20 RMB for each villager who prepaid a premium to enroll. It followed the two government guidelines of voluntary enrollment and coverage of hospitalization. But to improve quality and efficiency, it adopted several features targeted at the village doctors, who, because of their convenient location, provide most of the services.

Design of rural mutual health care

The RMHC has three major design features: financing and benefit packages; organization of service provision, including provider payment method; and the use of community governance in management.

Financing and benefit packages

The RMHC integrated both the (simulated) government subsidies and the villagers' premiums into one single risk-pooled fund to cover primary care as well as hospital services. Coverage of primary care is a cost-effective way to improve health outcomes, providing incentives for the patients to use basic and primary health care rather than to seek care in hospitals. It also makes villagers more willing to prepay into the RMHC and reduces adverse selection. In any voluntary scheme, villagers are more willing to enroll if the expected benefits of enrollment exceed the cost of premiums. Because the distribution of health risks is such that a small proportion of individuals use a large share of total health expenditure, as shown in the contingency table (table 8.1), a scheme that covers only hospitalization would more likely attract the old and the sick, making it financially unsustainable.

We offered three benefit packages with annual premiums ranging from 12 RMB to 18 RMB. All covered primary care, hospital services, and drugs at all levels of facilities with no deductibles. To finance such comprehensive coverage with limited funding (32–38 RMB per person, when health expenditures per person were about 150–180 RMB), coinsurance rates ranged from 55% to 60%, with rates for visits to village clinics lower than those for visits to higher facilities, to encourage use of the village clinic. Ceilings for hospitalizations were also introduced (400 RMB for admissions to township health centers and 8,000 RMB for admissions to county hospitals).

Organization of provision and provider payment

By covering both primary care and hospitalization the RMHC had the financial power to introduce interventions improving the efficiency and quality of the delivery system by changing the organizational and incentive structure on the supply side. The RMHC Fund Office, a single purchaser, selected the best village doctors (often two to three per village) on a competitive basis. Since no clinical performance

TABLE 8.1

Contingency table on the distribution of households' total annual health expenditure in Zhangjai Town, Zhen'an County, 1999

Concentration of households (%)	Accumulated amount spent (RMB)	Accumulated spending as a share of total health expenditure (%)
1	96,040	20.7
5	242,530	42.1
10	330,378	61.0
20	408,967	77.9
30	442,590	85.2
40	458,602	92.6
50	463,577	97.7
60	464,831	99.9
70	465,124	100.0
80	465,124	100.0
90	465,124	100.0
100	465,124	100.0

Note: Population of 9,784.

Source: Authors' compilation of claims data from Zhangjai Town's Cooperative Medical System.

records exist at the village level in China (as in most countries), selection is based on a combination of qualifications and villager voting. The office contracted with these village doctors, compensating them with a salary plus a bonus based on performance measures, including conforming to established protocols of treatment for common diseases such as upper respiratory infection and diarrhea; maintaining patient medical records; delivering public health functions such as immunizations; and receiving high patient satisfaction ratings. This de-linked village doctors' compensation from their drug-dispensing activities and aimed to reduce overprescribing and sales of fraudulent drugs.

The contracts and their annual renewals also allowed the RMHC to screen and regulate village doctors. Provider contracts would explicitly outline provider responsibilities and payment, restricting village doctors to tasks within their level of competency (whereas they previously competed with township and county providers) and to primary care and prevention. In addition, village doctors were not allowed to purchase drugs directly. Instead, township health centers (covering 10,000–15,000 people) purchased drugs in bulk through competitive bidding and distributed them directly to village doctors through a central distribution system, helping to assure drug safety at minimum cost. Doctors not selected saw their patient loads drastically reduced because villagers who enrolled in the RMHC could receive reimbursements only if they consulted the contracted village doctors. In our experiment, in which close to 80% of the villagers enrolled, village doctors had very high incentives to improve their performance to increase their chances of being selected.

Community governance

The RMHC used community governance rather than management by the government alone. Since villagers had an interest in ensuring that they would benefit from the scheme, they were in the best position to see that the funds were properly used and to choose the most attractive benefit package for the community. Each village elected a representative to serve with government officials, township health center directors, and town financial auditors on the Fund Board at the township level, where the risks were pooled. The board decided on the benefit package that best reflected their fellow villagers' preferences; for example, all chose coverage of primary care and drugs at the village level because villagers desired basic health care and drugs at nearby locations. The board also managed and controlled the Fund Office that financed and contracted with service providers. To monitor the daily activities of village doctors, villagers elected five volunteers to form a village management committee to check village clinics' hours of opening, their cleanliness, whether essential drugs are available, and most important the attendance of village doctors at their clinics.

The prevailing New Cooperative Medical Scheme model in the western and central regions

Many counties in the western and central regions adopted a model that combines an individual medical savings account with high-deductible catastrophic insurance. Typically, this scheme collects 10 RMB from the farmer and assigns an average of 8 RMB (US$1) to an individual savings account that can be used by the farmer to pay for outpatient visits. The government's 20 RMB subsidy plus the 2 RMB remaining premium would be used for risk-pooling to cover inpatient hospital expenses that exceeded a deductible (for example, the NCMS site near our RMHC intervention site has a deductible of 800 RMB). Besides the deductible, the patients still have to pay 40%–60% of covered inpatient hospital costs. The benefit package also caps the benefit payment between 10,000–20,000 RMB (US$1,250–US$2,000) (Mao 2005; Ministry of Health 2007). But there is no supply side intervention to deal with the waste caused by unnecessary treatments and drugs.

The key features of the RMHC and NCMS benefit packages commonly found in the western and central regions are compared in table 8.2. In both models, the premium is similar, at about 30 RMB per person.

Study design and data

We chose the study design, data collection, and analytical methods that would allow us to conduct a prospective impact evaluation and draw evidence-based conclusions.

Study design

The RMHC adopted a pre-post, treatment-control study design. RMHC was implemented in three towns, one in Guizhou and two in Shaanxi provinces. We chose these western provinces because our goal is to help China find a rural health care model suitable for poorer regions and because the health officials in these provinces invited us to conduct our experiments there. In these two provinces we first identified towns representative of the socioeconomic conditions in China's low-income regions and randomly selected three as our intervention sites. Together, the three towns encompassed a population of about 60,000 people (15,000 in each of the two towns in Shaanxi and 30,000 in Guizhou). We further selected two control towns (one in each province) that matched the RMHC intervention sites in socioeconomic conditions, availability of health facilities, and distance to city centers, based on available official statistics. These control sites did not experience any intervention in health

TABLE 8.2

Rural Mutual Health Care and New Cooperative Medical Scheme benefit packages

	RMHC	NCMS
Deductible	0	800 RMB
Individual savings account	0	Deposit 8 RMB each year
Reimbursement rate for outpatient visit		
Village health posts	45%	0
Township health centers and above	40%	0
Reimbursement rate and caps for hospitalization		
Township health centers	40%, capped at 400 RMB	40%–60% of the amount exceeding the deductible, capped at 10,000–20,000 RMB
County hospitals and above	40%, capped at 8,000 RMB	40%–60% above deductible, capped at 10,000–20,000 RMB

Source: Authors' design for Rural Mutual Health Care and authors' estimates for New Cooperative Medical Scheme.

care until 2006, when the government introduced its schemes. In 2003 the average annual income per person was about 1,400–1,800 RMB (US$175–US$225) at the study sites and, on average, villagers spent about 8%–10% of their annual income on health care. The RMHC began its initial enrollment in October 2003 and went into full operation immediately thereafter. To reduce adverse selection, enrollment was by household. The experiment was planned for three years and concluded in early 2007.

Data collection

The findings here are based primarily on analyses using data from longitudinal household (and individual) surveys conducted one year prior to the intervention (December 2002) and each of the three years after—2004, 2005, and 2006. The same survey instruments were used for all waves and for both the intervention and control sites. For this chapter we included data only from 2002 (baseline) and 2005 because in 2006, new interventions were introduced in the control sites, and 2004, a year after the interventions, captures only short-term effects.

Within the three intervention and two control towns, we randomly selected 18 villages (the number of villages selected within a town was proportional to its population). In the pre-intervention year we randomly selected one out of every three households in each village, yielding a total sample of 2,329 households (8,582 individuals) in the intervention sites and 752 households (2,865 individuals) in the control sites. We successfully re-interviewed 87% (83%) of these households (individuals) in 2005. Attrition was primarily due to households migrating from the town. Households dropped out in each wave were replaced with households with similar income and household size. Response rates in both rounds were high, close to 98%.

The household/individual questionnaire was designed to collect data measuring three primary outcome variables: access to care, financial risk protection, and health status as well as a set of control variables (table 8.3).

The enrolled and the nonenrolled

The RMHC achieved average enrollment rates of 78%, increasing from 70% in the initial year to almost 85% in the final year as villagers gained trust in the scheme and experienced its benefits.

Table 8.3 shows that our treatment sample, those who enrolled in the RMHC, are different from those who chose to not enroll in the RMHC (since enrollment is voluntary) and from those in the control site. The enrolled-in RMHC sites had worse health, had higher use rates, and were more likely to experience catastrophic expenditure in the baseline than the nonenrolled. The data reflect adverse selection—that is, those who chose to enroll in RMHC are those who are more likely to

TABLE 8.3
Outcome variables at baseline

Variable	RMHC Enrolled	Nonenrolled	Control
Use[a]			
Visit an outpatient provider in the two weeks prior to the survey (1/0)	0.173	0.094	0.132
Visit a village clinic in the two weeks prior to the survey (1/0)	0.141	0.056	0.087
Visit a township health center in the two weeks prior to the survey (1/0)	0.022	0.032	0.028
Visit a county hospital in the two weeks prior to the survey (1/0)	0.010	0.006	0.017
Number of outpatient visits in the two weeks prior to the survey	0.352	0.185	0.220
Self-treat in the two weeks prior to the survey (1/0)	0.056	0.040	0.028
Hospitalized in the 12 months prior to the survey (1/0)	0.033	0.022	0.039
Catastrophic expenditure[b]			
Out-of-pocket health expenditure more than 10% income net of food expenditure	0.296	0.211	0.259
More than 15%	0.245	0.190	0.227
More than 20%	0.212	0.164	0.193
More than 30%	0.171	0.130	0.147
Impoverishment[b]			
Percentage below $1/day: full sample	0.221	0.275	0.183
Percentage below $1/day: lowest 25% income sample	0.626	0.781	0.502
Health status (1=problem, 0=no problem)[c]			
Any of the five dimensions with problem	0.49	0.37	0.375
Mobility	0.08	0.048	0.055
Self-care	0.05	0.030	0.036
Usual activity	0.11	0.058	0.103
Pain/discomfort	0.31	0.148	0.226
Anxiety/depression	0.40	0.180	0.307
Socioeconomics			
Income per capita	1,885	1,700	2,481
Household wealth	−0.65	−0.68	−0.51
Illiterate education	0.27	0.25	0.26
Primary education	0.46	0.44	0.40
Junior high education	0.22	0.25	0.27
Senior high education	0.03	0.04	0.05
Tertiary education	0.01	0.02	0.02
Sociodemographics			
Male	0.50	0.59	0.51

(continued)

TABLE 8.3 (continued)
Outcome variables at baseline

Variable	RMHC		
	Enrolled	Nonenrolled	Control
Age	40	36	42
Single	0.17	0.34	0.09
Married	0.76	0.61	0.86
Divorced/separated	0.01	0.01	0.01
Widowed/other	0.06	0.04	0.04
Migrant	0.07	0.11	0.04
Health status			
Ill in last month	0.26	0.16	0.17
1+ chronic conditions	0.17	0.13	0.14
Current smoker	0.34	0.32	0.41
Current drinker	0.27	0.27	0.19
Very good sexual and reproductive health	0.10	0.14	0.11
Good sexual and reproductive health	0.24	0.31	0.19
Average sexual and reproductive health	0.41	0.38	0.51
Bad/very bad sexual and reproductive health	0.24	0.17	0.18
Household characteristics			
Household size	4.0	4.1	3.8
Distance from village clinic (miles)	2.1	2.1	2.5
Distance from township health center (miles)	14	13	10
Distance from county hospital (miles)	65	74	63

a. Unit of observation is individuals older than age 15 who self-responded and children under age 15 proxied by their parents. Sample sizes for the enrolled, nonenrolled, and controls were 2,998, 1,134, and 1,745, respectively.

b. Unit of observation is households. Sample sizes for the enrolled, nonenrolled, and controls were 1,519, 507, and 692, respectively.

c. Unit of observation is individuals older than age 15 who self-responded (as opposed to using proxies) to the surveys. Sample sizes for the enrolled, nonenrolled, and controls were 1,665, 610, and 1,219, respectively.

Source: Authors.

have higher use and expenditures, including the less healthy and older individuals. This supports our choice of using the control site, rather than the nonenrolled as the comparison group. Comparing the sample that enrolled in the RMHC with those in the control sites, the differences are smaller than those observed with the nonenrolled, but differences still exist.

Table 8.4 shows the balancing properties of the propensity score matching and resulting reductions in observable differences between the treatment and control

TABLE 8.4

Matching balancing properties between the Rural Mutual Health Care and controls

	Prematching		Postmatching Kernel		
	Standardized difference[a]	t-statistic	Standardized difference[a]	t-statistic	Bias reduction[b]
Socioeconomics					
Log (income/capita)	-42.2	-12.86	-1.4	-0.59	96.6
Log (income/capita) squared	-42.8	-13.1	-1.5	-0.62	96.6
Household wealth	-17.3	-5.25	-5.7	-2.34	67
Household wealth squared	-1.6	-0.49	4.1	1.62	-149.9
Primary education	12.7	3.72	6.1	2.32	52
Junior high education	-11.1	-3.32	-2.9	-1.12	74.4
Senior high education	-9.9	-3.05	-6.1	-2.43	38.6
Tertiary education	-7.5	-2.37	-1.8	-0.81	75.6
Sociodemographics					
Male	-0.5	-0.16	-1.9	-0.71	-239.4
Age	-10.4	-2.95	-11.1	-4.04	-7.1
Age squared	-4	-1.15	-9	-3.21	-126
Married	-25	-7.07	-11.8	-4.3	53
Divorced/separated	4	1.12	2.5	0.9	37.9
Widowed/other	6.5	1.86	3.7	1.36	43.9
Migrant	15.4	4.28	-1.5	-0.51	90.1
Health status					
Ill in last month	24.4	6.93	-3.5	-1.24	85.6
1+ chronic conditions	10.5	3.02	1.6	0.58	84.9
Current smoker	-13.1	-3.89	-4.9	-1.9	62.7
Current drinker	17.6	5.06	-4.3	-1.56	75.4
Good sexual and reproductive health	11.8	3.4	0.8	0.29	93.4
Average sexual and reproductive health	-19.7	-5.81	-5.4	-2.08	72.5
Bad/very bad sexual and reproductive health	14.7	4.23	4.4	1.61	70.4
Household characteristics					
Household size	16.3	4.71	1.4	0.52	91.6
Distance from village clinic[c]	-22.6	-6.79	-6.8	-2.85	69.8
Distance from township health center[c]	47.5	14.06	8.2	3.48	82.8
Distance from county hospital[d]	6.0	1.64	18.7	7.33	-209.8
LR-Chi square (27 df)	1,242.52		180.68		

a. The raw differences in intervention/control sample means as a percentage of the square root of the average of the intervention/control sample variances respectively.

b. The percentage reduction in standardized differences.

c. 0–10 or more miles, increments of 1 mile.

d. 0–100 or more miles, increments of 10 miles.

Source: Authors.

groups. Matching has reduced the baseline differences significantly for the majority of observable characteristics between the two groups. In addition, we also controlled for changes in these variables between the baseline and 2005 in the estimation. Standard errors were bootstrapped and clustering at the household level was
accounted for.

Impacts of the Rural Mutual Health Care Scheme
Table 8.5 presents the difference-in-difference plus propensity score matching estimates, or the "impact estimates," and the baseline values for comparison.

Access to care
The estimates show that the RMHC increased the probability of an outpatient
visit by 0.12 ($p < 0.01$), from a baseline of 0.173. The increase primarily represented
visits to village doctors, followed by visits to township health centers. The number
of visits increased by 0.155 ($p < 0.01$) from a baseline of 0.35. The RMHC also
reduced the probability of self-medication by about two-thirds (by 0.038 from a
baseline of 0.056; $p < 0.05$). But we did not find any statistically significant impact
on hospitalization.

The RMHC has, in addition, some distribution effects. The lowest and highest
income individuals experienced the greatest increases in outpatient use of village
doctors, while the middle-income group experienced a substantial increase in the
use of township health center services (results not presented here). A full benefit-
incidence analysis is beyond the scope of this chapter because, in particular, without knowing the content of the services, we cannot assess how much of the increase
in township health center use is health improving (a real benefit) and how much is
waste (with a neutral or negative effect on health).

Financial risk protection
Defining catastrophic health spending as out-of-pocket health spending greater
than 10%, 15%, 20%, and 30% of household income net of food expenditures, the
RMHC reduced the rates of catastrophic health spending by 0.075 (from 0.296;
$p < 0.05$), 0.076 (from 0.245; $p < 0.05$), 0.28 (from 0.212; $p = 0.44$) and 0.050 (from
0.171; $p = 0.14$), respectively. It also reduced medical impoverishment by 0.129
(from a baseline rate of 0.626; $p < 0.05$) for those in the lowest income quartile.

Health status
The RMHC significantly reduced the probability of having a problem in any of
the five self-reported dimensions: mobility, self-care, usual activities (work, study,

TABLE 8.5

Impacts of the Rural Mutual Health Care Scheme

	Baseline	Impact estimates	95% confidence interval	p-value
Use				
Visit an outpatient provider in the last 2 weeks (1/0)	0.173	0.122	0.0701, 0.1748	0.000
Visit a village clinic in the last 2 weeks (1/0)	0.141	0.098	0.059, 0.138	0.000
Visit a township health center in the last 2 weeks (1/0)	0.022	0.020	0.002, 0.039	0.030
Visit a county hospital in the last 2 weeks (1/0)	0.010	0.001	−0.018 0.019	0.926
Number of outpatient visits in the last 2 weeks	0.352	0.155	0.0516, 0.2589	0.003
Self-treat in the last 2 weeks (1/0)	0.056	−0.038	−0.0682, −0.0072	0.016
Hospitalized in the last year (1/0)	0.033	−0.009	−0.0300, 0.0110	0.365
Catastrophic expenditure				
Out-of-pocket health expenditure more than10% income net of food expenditure	0.296	−0.075	−0.1489, −0.0011	0.047
More than 15%	0.245	−0.076	−0.1497, −0.0021	0.044
More than 20%	0.212	−0.028	−0.1003, 0.0439	0.444
More than 30%	0.171	−0.050	−0.1159, 0.0160	0.137
Impoverishment				
% below $1/day: full sample	0.221	−0.024	−0.0822, 0.0344	0.421
% below $1/day: lowest 25% income sample	0.626	−0.129	−0.2370, −0.0204	0.020
Health status (1=problem, 0=no problem)				
Any of the five dimensions with problem	0.49	−0.244	−0.3106, −0.1773	0.000
Mobility	0.08	−0.024	−0.0502, 0.0019	0.069
Self-care	0.05	−0.007	−0.0302, 0.0171	0.587
Usual activity	0.11	−0.018	−0.0540, 0.0178	0.322
Pain/discomfort	0.31	−0.095	−0.1528, −0.0376	0.001
Anxiety/depression	0.40	−0.252	−0.3185, −0.1859	0.000

Note: The impact estimates are based on the differences-in-differences, combined with propensity score matching estimation. The results shown here used the kernel matching algorithm. We also conducted sensitivity analyses using other matching algorithms, such as nearest four neighbor and local linear matching, and the results do not change the conclusions. Changes in income, household wealth, and other household and individual characteristics that occurred between baseline and 2005 were also controlled for in the estimation.

Source: Authors.

housework, family, or leisure), pain/discomfort, and anxiety/depression. The impact estimate is −0.244 ($p < 0.01$)—that is, adjusting for differences between the treatment and comparison groups, the treatment group experienced a greater reduction (by 0.244 percentage points) in the probability of having a problem in any of the five dimensions after the RMHC than did the comparison group. Compared with a baseline value of 0.49, a reduction of about 49%. We also found that the RMHC significantly reduced the probability of pain/discomfort and anxiety/depression by 0.095 ($p < 0.01$) and 0.252 ($p < 0.01$), from baselines of 0.31 and 0.40, respectively.

We did not find statistically significant reduction in usual activity, problems with mobility, or use of self-care. To investigate why the RMHC did not have any significant impact on these dimensions, we examined subgroup differences by age and gender. For those older than 55, the RMHC significantly reduced the probability of having problems in mobility (impact estimate = −0.060; baseline = 0.193; $p < 0.01$) and usual activity (impact estimate = −0.094; baseline = 0.261; $p < 0.01$). Those older than 55 experienced a reduction in probability of 0.096 (baseline = 0.449; $p < 0.01$) for pain/discomfort, whereas those younger than 35 experienced a reduction of only 0.054 (baseline = 0.311; $p < 0.01$). In contrast, for anxiety/depression, the estimates for those older than 55 were not significant, while the estimates were −0.163 ($p < 0.01$) for those younger than 35, and −0.104 ($p < 0.01$) for those between 35 and 55 (Wang and others 2009). We found no statistically different impact on the health dimensions by gender, conditional on the same age group.

Conclusions

The RMHC improved the population's access to basic health care and their health status, while reducing the risk of catastrophic health expenditure and impoverishment. Because the interventions were not phased in, we cannot isolate the independent effect of each on the observed impacts. But because the design of the RMHC was based on generalizable theories and concepts, we can draw some logical conclusions.

By covering primary care in addition to hospitalization, the RMHC reduced financial barriers to accessing primary health care, which in turn improved health status. Our findings that the oldest age group experienced significant improvements in mobility and usual activities and reductions in pain/discomfort provide suggestive evidence for the access hypothesis. Many older people in our sample (as in many rural areas of China) suffer from chronic pain. Making access affordable allows them to seek care to relieve their pain and discomfort and improve their mobility and daily activities.

We did not find any statistically significant impact of RMHC on hospitalization. This could be because RMHC is ineffective in improving access to hospitalization. But it could also be due to a substitution of outpatient use for less serious cases—since the RMHC now provided coverage for outpatient care—or to an improvement in health status as a result of improved access to basic health care. Unfortunately, we were not able to test these hypotheses.

Covering both primary care and hospitalization contributed to the reduction in medical impoverishment and catastrophic expenditure as well. In fact, in a separate analysis, we compared the impact of RMHC on financial risk protection with an alternative scheme commonly found among NCMS models in western China and that covers only hospitalization but with higher caps in reimbursement. To our surprise, we found the RMHC to be more effective in reducing medical impoverishment than this catastrophic insurance scheme. The primary reason is that the NCMS does not address a major cause of medical impoverishment: expensive outpatient services for chronic conditions. By covering only hospitalizations, it does not protect chronic patients with major outpatient health expenditures (Yip and Hsiao 2009).

Another possible explanation for the achievements in access, health status, and financial risk protection was the reduction in inefficiencies and inappropriate treatment brought about by changes in the organization and incentive structure of the delivery system under the RMHC. For example, at the primary care level, spending per visit to the village doctor in RMHC sites dropped from 16 RMB in the baseline to about 10 RMB in 2005, whereas spending per visit in the control site grew to about 18 RMB over the same period. By analyzing prescription records collected by the RMHC Fund Office, we ascertained that the reduction in expenditure per visit was largely attributed to a reduction in drug prices of almost 30%—and to reductions in the number of drugs prescribed, the number of prescriptions for antibiotics and steroids, and the number of intravenous injections for treatment of common cold. After implementation of the drug bulk purchasing policy and audits by the Fund Office, the use of fake and expired drugs was eliminated, whereas the use of counterfeit drugs in the control sites remained at about 30%.

A final important aspect of the RMHC is that it placed some power in the hands of the community, who used it to ensure that the program was organized and managed to yield the most benefits for their community. While we did not evaluate this aspect, we conducted focus groups and interviews with villagers at large and villagers elected to serve on the Board and village management committee. We found that the villagers were willing to monitor the operations of the RMHC and were effective in doing so. Their involvement resulted in a better use of funds, reductions in waste and efficiencies, and a benefit package that reflected villagers' preferences and for which they were willing to prepay.

At the conclusion of the experiment, the government of Guiyang, where one of the intervention sites was located, immediately replicated our scheme to cover around 1.7 million rural Chinese. In 2008 Shaanxi province followed suit and began to replicate the RMHC throughout the province, which has more than

30 million rural inhabitants. When the findings of this social experiment were presented to China's top officials, the government revised its policies for the NCMS. It decided that NCMS benefit packages should cover both primary care and hospitalizations, that bulk purchasing and central distribution of drugs should be established, and that community governance should be greatly encouraged (Ministry of Health and Ministry of Finance 2007, 2008; Zhu 2008). Many provincial health leaders have come to recognize that unless inefficiencies are reduced, the NCMS will not be sustainable in the long run. They are beginning to experiment with ways to reform payment incentives and the organization of the delivery system.

There are several plausible explanations for why our findings influenced both central and local government policies. First, our findings provide evidence for the decisionmakers. Second, we engaged top health and political leaders as partners throughout the social experiments by regularly briefing them on the findings and by incorporating Chinese policy needs and current situations into the design. These leaders felt a sense of ownership of the experiments and were more motivated to incorporate the lessons into their policies and scale up the experiments to a larger population. The fact that the RMHC consistently received high public satisfaction ratings—85% of the enrolled were satisfied with the scheme, with almost 90% wishing to continue their enrollment—also appealed to the policymakers because they knew that there would not be major resistance when they scaled up the RMHC.

Several limitations to our study should be taken into account for future studies and experiments. First, caution should be exercised in extrapolating our findings to settings that have different socioeconomic conditions than our intervention sites. The fact that Guizhou and Shaanxi agreed to be our experimental sites may mean that their local leaders are more progressive and our findings may not generalize to localities lacking such leaders. Second, our health outcome measurements are self-perceived; we do not have objective health measures. This limitation is mitigated somewhat by other studies that have already demonstrated the strong correlation between self-perceived health status and other more objective measurements such as mortality and disability. Third, our study design prevents us from separating the independent effects of the various aspects of interventions. Another possible bias stems from attrition. But this is of little concern since the attrition rate for the treatment group is less than 9%, and although the attrition rate for the control group is higher (about 20%), we did not find any statistically significant differences in the baseline characteristics between the followed-up and the lost samples, except for marital status and whether the person has a chronic condition. To the extent that these characteristics do not change much over the three-year period of study, they are controlled for by a difference-in-difference model.

Although we should be conservative about the conclusions, this chapter demonstrates that a well designed social experiment can inform policy actions and generate knowledge about health system strengthening. While experimentation and prospective evaluation have been used and advocated for evaluating the effectiveness of development programs, especially for education, their use for health systems is still limited and in its infancy (Duflo and Kremer 2005). No single health care system model would suit the needs of the world. As countries continue to search for the models that best match their needs and conditions, well designed social experiments with objective evaluations offer a promising way forward.

References

Anonymous. 2009. The standing conference of State Council of China adopted Guidelines for Furthering the Reform of Health-care System in principle. Ministry of Health of China. http://www.moh.gov.cn/publicfiles/business/htmlfiles/mohbgt/s3582/200901/38889.htm. (in Chinese) (accessed Mar 13, 2009).

Blumenthal, D., and W. Hsiao. 2005. "Privatization and its discontents—the evolving Chinese health care system." *New England Journal of Medicine* 353 (11): 1165–70.

Center for Health Statistics and Information. 2004. *An analysis report of the National Health Survey in 2003.* Beijing, China: Ministry of Health.

Central Committee of CPC (the Communist Part of China). 2002. *Decisions of the central committee of the communist party of China and the State Council on further strengthening rural health work.* Beijing, China.

Duflo, E., and M. Kremer. 2005. "Use of Randomization in the Evaluation of Development Effectiveness." In G. Pitman, O. Feinstein, and G. Ingram, eds., *Evaluating Development Effectiveness.* New Brunswick, NJ: Transaction Publishers.

Hesketh, T., and W. Zhu. 1997a. "Health in China: From Mao to market reform." *BMJ* 314 (7093): 1543.

———. 1997b. "Health in China: The healthcare market." *BMJ* 314 (7094): 1616.

Hsiao, W. C. 1984. "Transformation of health care in China." *New England Journal of Medicine* 310 (14): 932–36.

Lindelow, M., and A. Wagstaff. 2005. *China's health sector—why reform is needed.* Washington, DC: World Bank.

Liu, X., and A. Mills. 1999. "Evaluating payment mechanisms: how can we measure unnecessary care?" *Health Policy and Planning* 14 (4): 409–13.

Mao, Z. 2005. *Pilot program of NCMS in China: System design and progress.* Washington, DC: World Bank.

Ministry of Health. 2007. *China's New Cooperative Medical Scheme: Report on Development and Results.* In Chinese. Beijing, China: Peking Union Medical College Press.

Ministry of Health and Ministry of Finance. 2007. "Directions for Improving Risk Pooling and Reimbursement Policies for New Cooperative Medical Scheme." In Chinese. Document no. 253. Beijing, China.

———. 2008. "Announcement on New Cooperative Medical Scheme." In Chinese. Document no. 17. Beijing, China.

Smith, P., C. Wong, and Y. Zhao. 2005. *Public expenditure and the role of government in the Chinese health sector.* Washington, DC: World Bank.

Wang, H., W. Yip, L. Zhang, and W. Hsiao. 2009. "The impact of rural mutual health care on health status: evaluation of a social experiment in rural China." *Health Economics* 18 (2): 65–82.

Watts, J. 2006. "China's rural health reforms tackle entrenched inequalities." *Lancet* 367 (9522): 1564–65.

———. 2007. "Protests in China over suspicions of a pay-or-die policy." *Lancet* 369 (9556): 93–4.

Yip, W., and W. C. Hsiao. 2009. "Non-evidence-based policy: how effective is China's new cooperative medical scheme in reducing medical impoverishment?" *Social Science & Medicine* 68 (2): 201–9.

Zhu, C. 2008. "Directions for Health Reform and Its Companion Policies." Beijing, China: News Office of the Ministry of Health.

Colombia's Big Bang Health Insurance Reform

Ursula Giedion, Carmen Elisa Flórez, Beatriz Yadira Díaz,
Eduardo Alfonso, Renata Pardo, and Manuela Villar

Colombia is one of the few developing countries that have introduced government-subsidized universal health insurance by drastically changing social security schemes and breaking the public sector monopoly. The reforms began in 1993, when approximately 28% of the population was covered by insurance through the traditional Latin American approach of a social security system delivering services directly to the covered population. By 2005 health insurance (with choice of provider) reached more than 70% of the total population and close to 60% of the lowest two income quintiles.

Recent estimates suggest that insurance coverage reached 86% of the population by the end of 2006, with another 2% covered by military and other programs. The population is covered through two regimes: the contributory regime for the employed and self-employed (covering 40% of the population in 2006) and the subsidized regime for the poor (covering 46% of the population in 2006; Clavijo 2009). By 2009 coverage had expanded to 89% (Tsai 2010).

For this chapter the gradual implementation of the subsidized health insurance regime for the poor provides a unique opportunity to apply semiparametric methods (propensity score matching, double difference, and matched double difference) to identify differences in health-related outcomes between those with insurance and those without (see box 9.1 for details on the data and methodology of this study). The impact of the contributory regime on similar variables is analyzed using an

BOX 9.1
Data and methodology

No single household survey in Colombia synthesizes data on access, use, health status, and financial protection for the population. Whereas recent Colombian Demographic and Health Surveys (DHS) (1995, 2000, and 2005) offer household data on access, use, and health status for small children and women of child-bearing age, the Living Standards Measurement Survey 2003 (LSMS) provides information on general use of health care and out-of-pocket spending as well as a wealth of socioeconomic data (including information on employment).

We used DHS data to evaluate the subsidized regime on access, use, and health status. In contrast to the contributory regime, the gradual implementation and still incomplete coverage of the subsidized regime among the poor allowed us to apply semiparametric methods to identify differences in health outcomes between those with insurance and those without.

We used LSMS data to evaluate the impact of the contributory regime on health-related outcome variables. LSMS data do not, however, include any health status variables that can be expected to change as a consequence of benefits provided under the contributory regime. The analysis of the contributory regime therefore did not try to look at the impact of health insurance on health status. Further, we had to resort to either propensity score matching or instrumental variables to evaluate the impact of the contributory regime, as we had only one cross-sectional data set (LSMS 2003). Given that almost all of those working as formal workers participate, matching affiliates (through propensity score matching) to similar nonaffiliates was impossible, so we used instrumental variables. The table below summarizes the data used in the analysis.

Summary of data sources for evaluation

	Subsidized regime		Contributory regime	
	Access, utilization, and health status	Financial protection	Access and utilization	Financial protection
LSMS 2003 (cross-sectional data)	✓		✓	✓
DHS 1995, 2000, and 2005 (cross-sectional and repeated cross-sectional data)	✓			
Administrative data at the municipal and state level	✓	✓	✓	✓
Census data at the block level	✓	✓	✓	✓

Source: Authors.

instrumental variable approach. Those without insurance nevertheless remain eligible for services provided directly by the government through public facilities, so those without insurance in this analysis retain access to traditional public providers.

The main goal of this chapter is to analyze existing household data to provide information on the impact of the Colombian health insurance scheme on key performance indicators of the health system. Specifically, it seeks answers to the following questions: Has insurance improved access to and use of health services for individuals in case of an adverse health event? Has insurance reduced the risk of having to confront an out-of-pocket health payment that destabilizes the financial welfare of the household or causes the household to fall below a poverty line? Has insurance improved health outcomes?

Main features of the Colombian health sector reform

Colombia is a lower middle-income Andean country of 45 million inhabitants, more than 70% in urban areas. The country is divided into 32 departments, 1,099 municipalities, and 3 special districts—Bogotá, Cartagena, and Santa Marta (Ministry of Planning 2008). Per capita gross national income was US$8,430 in 2008, in purchasing power parity terms. Adult literacy was 93% in 2008, and basic service coverage is good, with 99% of urban households having access to improved water sources (77% rural) and 78% of all households having access to improved sanitation facilities. About 45% of the population was below the national poverty line, and about 28% lived on US$2 or less per day in 2006. The infant mortality rate is 16 per 1,000 live births, and average life expectancy is above 70 years. About 6.1% of GDP is spent on health, with 84% of that amount financed through taxes. Of the 16% coming from private funds, only about half is out of pocket. About US$284 per capita is spent on health (World Bank 2010).

Before the health reform in the early 1990s, Colombia had a health system similar to others in Latin America. A vertically integrated social insurance system, based on payroll taxes for formal workers, basically covered only the employed worker.[1] A tax-financed system of public providers served the poor and the not so poor, the latter especially for hospital and surgical services. A private provider system operated for all those with the ability to pay or for those dissatisfied with the services provided in the traditional social insurance and the public system.[2]

With Law 100 in 1993 Colombia introduced universal health insurance, a policy implemented in only a few Latin American countries. For those with sufficient income (above one minimum wage, about US$170), a payroll tax of 12.5% is collected and a comprehensive insurance plan (*plan obligatorio de salud,* or mandatory health plan) is provided within the *régimen contributivo* (contributory regime). For the poor whose eligibility to subsidies is determined by a proxy means test called *sistema de identificación de beneficiarios,* or beneficiary identification system, the government purchases, with a mixture of tax revenue and a solidarity contribution from payroll taxes,[3] insurance coverage in the *régimen subsidiado* (subsidized regime).

In both cases the affiliated family or individual chooses a health insurance company—*entidad promotora de salud,* or EPS (health-promoting entity)—whose ownership may be public, private, or mixed, and which may be for profit or non-profit. The insurance company, in turn, contracts health services with a network of public, private, or own service providers.

The government establishes the benefits package and sets the premium to be paid to each insurance company for each individual, with a risk adjustment by age, sex, and location. The premium is about US$252 per person annually in the contributory regime and US$146 per person in the subsidized regime.[4] Those insured through the contributory regime have access to a benefits package more comprehensive than that provided by the subsidized regime (figure 9.1, which shows clearly the "cut-out" method of managing the cost of the benefits package). Services not included in the subsidized regime package are the responsibility of the public hospital network, as are all services for the uninsured. Insurable benefits for the subsidized regime were to expand progressively to converge with those covered by the contributory regime. According to Law 100/1993, the two plans were supposed to converge by 2000, a promise still unfulfilled. However, Constitutional Court ruling T-760 on 31 July 2008, mandated the immediate unification of benefits plans for children and concrete steps to move toward equal benefits for all (Tsai 2010; Yamin and Parra-Vera 2009).

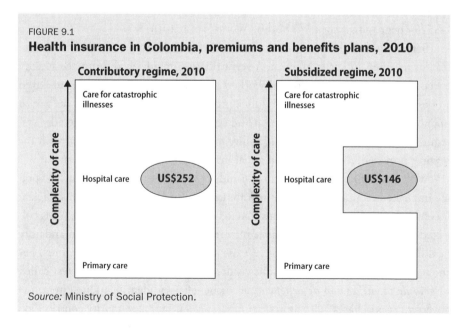

FIGURE 9.1
Health insurance in Colombia, premiums and benefits plans, 2010

Source: Ministry of Social Protection.

In each regime benefits are unrelated to the financial contribution of the affiliate. The financial contribution is established as a percentage of income and is thus independent of the risk of the insured. The government has established a mechanism for channeling resources from individuals whose payroll contributions are greater than the premiums for themselves and their families toward individuals whose contributions are less. The solidarity fund (*fondo de solidaridad y garantía*) receives the "excess" contributions and reassigns funds toward those whose contributions fall short of the capitation rate of the subsidized regime. This equalization fund, through a complex process, makes sure that payroll contributions based on income are transformed into risk-adjusted premiums for all insured, both for contributor and dependents in the contributory regime and on a solidarity contribution for the poor. In this integrated risk-pooling scheme individuals at high risk of disease subsidize those at low risk, those with higher ability to pay subsidize those without, and those in productive ages subsidize the young and the elderly. Figure 9.2 presents a simplified version of the flows of funds and affiliations within the current Colombian health system.

Conceptual framework

Health insurance in Colombia serves the dual purpose of promoting health by making routine health care services more accessible and protecting individuals and families against large financial losses in case of an adverse health event.

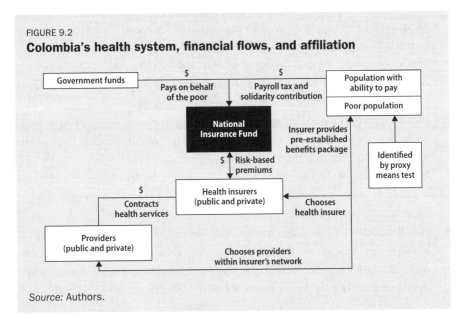

FIGURE 9.2
Colombia's health system, financial flows, and affiliation

Source: Authors.

We hypothesize that when services in Colombia become more affordable through health insurance, patients will use them more often, will seek care with less delay, and may be more likely to have a regular source of care. This reasoning follows standard economic theory, which says that health insurance coverage induces greater medical care use by reducing the cost of care to patients (Phelps 2009), as well as evidence in developed countries (Institute of Medicine 2009).

We speculate that, all other things being equal, those insured by the subsidized regime and contributory regime experience fewer financial barriers to access and use more health care than the uninsured do. We further speculate that health status improves as a result of increased access to health care and that health insurance provides financial protection to individuals by reducing catastrophic out-of-pocket health spending.

Several comments are relevant to this framework.

- Health insurance is not a homogeneous good. It varies in both extent (benefits, level of copayment, and conditions of access) and duration. In this study the benefits package provided under the contributory regime is much larger than that offered by the subsidized regime, so we decided to evaluate the impact of each regime separately. Further, health insurance does not improve access to all health services. We cannot expect changes in access, use, and outcome variables that are not related to the benefits offered under the insurance plan we are evaluating.

- The effect of health insurance may vary across population groups. Geographic variation in the supply of care to insured and uninsured individuals is one potentially important source of heterogeneity.

- Health outcomes depend on many more variables than just health insurance coverage, and people who have health insurance and those who do not differ in many ways other than in their health insurance coverage.

- Health outcomes partially determine health insurance coverage, and vice versa. So health status will most probably differ systematically among individuals grouped by health insurance categories.

- Health insurance does not have a direct impact on health. Instead, it changes individuals' and households' decisions related to the use of health care services by reducing financial barriers to access.

- Health status is a complex concept, and the impact of health insurance on health status depends on the health status variable we choose. If better access is the means by which health status may improve due to health insurance, we should concentrate on the measures of health status that can be reasonably well connected to access to health services.

Health insurance coverage

The increase of health insurance coverage among Colombians is the one successful outcome on which most observers—foes or friends of the reform—would probably agree. Household survey data from 2003 presented by Escobar (2005) indicate that overall health insurance (subsidized regime and contributory regime) increased from less than a quarter of the population before the reform (1993) to almost two-thirds a decade later (table 9.1). The most recent administrative data from the Ministry of Social Protection indicate that health insurance reached more than 90% of the population by 2007. Growth has been especially fast among the poorest 20% of the population, with an almost eightfold increase in one decade.[5]

No major differences are detected in coverage of the target population (in the lower quintiles) by gender. Small children (ages 0–5) in the poorest SISBEN level are least protected by the subsidized regime. This result is worrisome, both because this group is especially vulnerable to adverse health events and because the coverage policy of the subsidized regime officially gives priority to this vulnerable group.

Substantial differences can be observed at the municipal level: in 2004 more than 40% of all municipalities had coverage of more than 80%, but close to 20% had coverage still below the 20% level.[6] This is explained mainly by the inequity in the public per capita health resources available locally to finance the subsidized regime.

Though less dramatic, growth in the coverage of the contributory regime has also been important. In 1993 the contributory mandatory social insurance scheme covered around 9.4 million people (about 26% of the population). A decade later, the number of affiliates had grown to 17 million (39% of the population), increasing coverage by close to 80% in one decade. Before the reform, mostly formal

TABLE 9.1
Health insurance coverage, 1993–2003 (%)

Quintile	1993	1997	2003
1 (poorest)	6.1	43.4	46.5
2	16.5	48.7	52.5
3	27.5	59.0	58.2
4	35.3	65.7	69.3
5 (richest)	43.1	76.7	82.7
Total	23.8	57.1	61.8

Source: Escobar 2005, based on Casen survey (1993) and LSMS (1997, 2003) household surveys.

sector workers of the private and public sector had access to a full benefit plan, and family coverage was limited. Under the Social Security Institute (Instituto de Seguros Sociales, or ISS), which covered formal private sector workers, only pregnant and dependent wives and their small children (younger than age 1) had access to a few birth-related services, leaving the remaining services and all other dependent family members uncovered.[7,8]

With reform the number of beneficiaries (dependent, nonpaying family members) more than doubled between 1993 and 2003 (+129%), and the number of contributing affiliates increased 36%, rising from 4.9 million contributing affiliates to 6.8 million a decade later. Independent workers, fewer than 10% of affiliates before the reform, represented more than 18% a decade later, and their number had increased more than threefold. Family coverage was nationwide and unrelated to type of employment. Under the reform, eligibility started to be based on income: all workers declaring a monthly income equal to or above one official minimum salary as a basis for payroll taxes were required to affiliate with the contributory regime. From then on, the whole family was to be insured (spouses, partners, dependents, and parents in some cases).

Because of these modifications, most contributory regime affiliates were in urban areas (more than 90%) in 2005, compared with 78% of the general population (CEPAL 2006). Coverage of affiliates older than age 57 increased more than did any other group in the last decade. These adults, either retired or close to retirement, represented 9% of affiliates in 1993 and about 13% a decade later, larger than their share in the population.

Access and use of services

We hypothesize that both the subsidized and the contributory health insurance regimes introduced in Colombia in 1993 have improved the health status of the insured by making access more affordable. As a result, we are speculating that, all other things being equal, affiliates of the subsidized regime and contributory regime experience fewer financial barriers to access, use more health care, and get health care earlier than the uninsured.

Subsidized regime

Propensity score matching estimates confirm that the subsidized health insurance scheme increases access for the poor (table 9.2).[9] Those affiliated with the subsidized regime are 40% more likely to have used outpatient health services in the month prior to the survey than the uninsured and less than half as likely to have experienced barriers to access when needing care (−38%).

TABLE 9.2

Propensity score matching results-estimated treatment effect for the subsidized regime on access and use, national level, radius (bandwidth 0.0001), 2005

Outcome variable	Enrolled in the subsidized regime (treatment group)	Not insured (control group)	Difference (%)	Significance
Used ambulatory services in the 12 months prior to the survey	0.686	0.492	40	***
Birth attended by a doctor	0.819	0.757	8	***
Birth attended by a skilled professional	0.862	0.808	7	***
Birth in a health facility	0.869	0.812	7	***
Immunization child complete	0.395	0.365	8	*
Not receiving medical care when needed	0.259	0.420	-38	***
Not receiving medical care when needed due to supply reasons	0.289	0.131	120	***
Number of prenatal visits	5.560	5.261	6	***
Child taken to a health care facility when coughing	0.451	0.378	20	***
Child taken to a health care facility when having diarrhea	0.329	0.235	40	*

*** significant at $p < 0.01$; * significant at $p < 0.10$.

Note: Other matching methods (double difference and matched double difference) were implemented with similar results. Results from these methods can be obtained from the authors on request.

Source: Authors' calculations based on DHS 2005 data.

Barriers to access may lie on the demand side with the household (such as income, knowledge, and the like) or on the supply side, as a distant health facility, bad service, delayed appointments, excessive procedures and formalities to get an appointment, asking for service but not getting it, or consulting without results. Insurance in Colombia reduces demand side financial barriers and creates an affiliation with service providers, so it should reduce demand side barriers considerably, and this is borne out by the data. For the insured, barriers to access are more related to supply of health services (+120%) when compared with the uninsured.

There is a clear benefit for insured pregnant women in accessing prenatal and post-partum care: insured women have more prenatal visits (+6%), are more likely to give birth in a health facility (+7%), and have a higher probability of being assisted either by a doctor (+8%) or by skilled personnel during childbirth (+7%).

The benefits extend to their children as well. Parents of insured children in the subsidized regime have a greater probability of taking children to a health care facility when they are coughing (+20%) or suffering from diarrhea (+40%). Affiliated children are more likely to have their immunization series completed for their age (+8%), even though immunizations are widely available, free for all, and heavily promoted.

Urban-rural differences
Insurance seems to have been important in bringing about improvements for the rural population often greater than for the urban population (table 9.3). In many cases the difference between the treatment and the control groups in rural areas is twice that in urban areas. For a child receiving health services when he or she has a cough, there is a 15% difference between the insured and uninsured in urban areas, compared with 33% in rural areas.

Contributory regime

Self-employed and their families
Health insurance under the contributory regime improves access and use indicators of independent workers for most variables, and the results are statistically significant for almost all coefficients (table 9.4).[10] Looking at the self-employed[11] separately from the rest of the insured in the contributory regime (the left side of table 9.4), on average 20% of them face financial barriers to access when in need of health services. According to our instrumental variable estimates, the contributory regime reduces the incidence of financial barriers by 47 percentage points for the self-employed, a large improvement in access. In contrast to the subsidized regime, there is no statistically significant impact of the contributory regime on the probability of suffering from supply side access barriers for this group.

In the descriptive statistics we also find that only 26% of all self-employed—whether affiliated with the insurance program or not—receive all medicines prescribed. Health insurance provided by the contributory regime increases by 52 percentage points the probability of receiving all prescribed medicines (see table 9.4). Even so, there is still much to do, as only 53% of the insured in the contributory regime reported receiving all prescribed medicines at the time of the survey.

Sample means indicate that, on average, the self-employed without insurance use at least some (39%) dentist or physician preventive care during the year, or both (16%). In contrast, 42% of those affiliated with the contributory regime went

TABLE 9.3

Propensity score matching results-estimated treatment effect for the subsidized regime for access, use, and health status, by rural-urban status, kernel Epanechnikov, 2005 (bandwidth 0.001)

	Urban				Rela-tive impact	Rural			
	Enrolled in the subsidized regime (treatment group)	Not insured (control group)	Difference (percent)	Signifi-cance		Enrolled in the subsidized regime (treatment group)	Not insured (control group)	Difference (percent)	Signifi-cance
Used ambulatory services in the 12 months prior to the survey	0.702	0.530	33	***	<	0.657	0.440	49	***
Birth attended by a doctor	0.901	0.875	3	***	<	0.678	0.637	6	**
Birth attended by a skilled professional	0.933	0.914	2	**	<	0.740	0.698	6	**
Birth in a health facility	0.942	0.927	2	*	<	0.747	0.684	9	***
Immunization child complete	0.450	0.421	7	*	≈	0.329	0.311	6	–
Not receiving medical care when needed	0.208	0.352	-41	***	>	0.324	0.498	-35	***
Not receiving medical care when needed due to supply reasons	0.267	0.133	101	***	≈	0.348	0.172	102	***
Number of prenatal visits	5.767	5.805	-1	***	<	5.167	4.549	14	***
Child taken to a health care facility when coughing	0.477	0.414	15	***	<	0.404	0.303	33	***
Child taken to a health care facility when having diarrhea	0.362	0.326	11	–	–	0.324	0.235	38	–

*** significant at $p < 0.01$; ** significant at $p < 0.05$; * significant at $p < 0.10$.

Note: Other matching methods (double difference and matched double difference) were implemented with similar results. Results from these methods can be obtained from the authors on request.

Source: Authors' calculations based on DHS 2005 data.

TABLE 9.4

Instrumental variable results-estimated treatment effect for access and use in the contributory regime, 2003

Outcomes	Self-employed, or independent, workers and their families		Relative impact	Formally employed, or dependent, workers and their families	
	Difference	p		Difference	p
Preventive health care use (physician or dentist visit at least once per year)	0.459	***	>	0.342	***
Preventive health care use (physician and dentist at least once a year)	0.152	[0.0138]***	<	0.272	**
Formal health care services use	0.256	[0.0328]***	<	0.567	***
Informal health care services use	−0.052	[0.0136]***	>	−0.027	*
Self-medication when having a health problem	−0.148	[0.0266]***	<	−0.276	[0.0392]***
No health care use when having a health problem	−0.021	[0.0064]**	≈	−0.020	[0.0083]*
Supply side barrier to access	0.090			−0.045	*
Demand side barrier to access	−0.353	[0.1766]*	>	−0.210	[0.0506]***
Financial barrier of access	−0.473	[0.1524]**	>	−0.144	[0.0337]***
Access to medications (patients given at least some of the prescribed medicines)	0.755	[0.0325]***	≈	0.760	[0.0248]***
Access to medications (patient was given all of the prescribed medicines)	0.516	[0.0390]***	<	0.568	[0.0268]***
Timeliness of service for general physician and dentist	1.525	[1.0454]		−0.910	[0.4151]*
Timeliness of service for visit to specialist	−1.948	[1.5022]		0.322	[0.6083]

*** significant at $p < 0.01$; ** significant at $p < 0.05$; * significant at $p < 0.10$.

Note: "Relative" impact indicates for which population group (independent or dependent) the impact has been more important in case both variables are found to be statistically significant. Numbers in brackets are standard errors.

Source: Authors.

to a general physician or dentist at least once during the year prior to the survey. Isolating the effect of insurance from other variables using either a dentist or a physician at least once a year for checkups or preventive care improves by 46 percentage points for the self-employed, and the use of both improves by 15 percentage points (see table 9.4). Furthermore, health insurance under the contributory regime increases the probability of using formal care (+26 percentage points) rather than informal care[12] (–5 percentage points) and reduces self-medication when having a health problem (–15 percentage points).

The formally employed and their families

Results for the formally employed and their families are similar to those for the self-employed. The contributory regime has improved access to and use of preventive, curative, and formal health care services and reduced access barriers and self-medication. It reduces the incidence of supply side barriers by 5 percentage points and the number of days waiting for an appointment to the general physician or dentist by about one day (–0.91), considerable given that waiting times for the uninsured are on average six days. Note that for supply side barriers and waiting times the results are statistically significant only for dependent workers.

Comparing self-employed and formally employed workers

Using the instrumental variable approach we find that for access barriers, the impact of the contributory regime seems to be more important for the self-employed than the formally employed (see table 9.4), especially for the probability of suffering from financial barriers to access. For example, the probability of encountering a financial barrier drops 14 percentage points among the formally employed due to insurance coverage, whereas it drops almost 50 percentage points among the self-employed insured. The self-employed face, on average, worse basic access conditions than the rest of the sample, so insurance might have a more important marginal impact for them because diminishing marginal returns set in for these basic access variables for the formally employed.

The formally employed and their families benefited more than the self-employed for several other variables—including the probability of using formal health care services (general physician, specialist and dentist visit, services provided in a health facility by a nurse or medical caretaker), the probability of using preventive dental and general physician visits at least once a year, and reduction in the use of self-medication to confront medical problems. On the use of preventive care we might hypothesize that the opportunity cost of time is lower for the formally employed (they can take off from work for a preventive care visit without losing income) than for the self-employed (they have to pay themselves for the time lost for a preventive visit).

Financial protection

According to our calculations, 14% of Colombian households that use health services devote on average more than 30% of their monthly nonsubsistence income to health-related out-of-pocket spending. This percentage drops to 5% for the total population.[13] It is difficult to tell whether this incidence is high or low because no universal benchmark exists and because comparisons across countries can be misleading and are therefore not advisable due to the differences in contexts and methods. As expected, vulnerability to catastrophic spending increases for the poorest individuals. Of the richest 20% who use health services, 6.6% have out-of-pocket spending greater than 30% of their monthly nonsubsistence income, compared with 16.9% for those in the poorest quintile and 31.7% in the next poorest quintile (table 9.5).

If we raise the threshold from 10% to 40% of nonsubsistence income, the incidence of catastrophic expenditure drops from 32% to 11%, a consequence of the well known skewed distribution of health spending (figure 9.3) Most households using health services spend less than 20,000 Colombian pesos (US$10 in 2003) when using health services, or between 0% and 15% of their available income. The frequency of spending more drops rapidly thereafter, and only a fraction of households spend more than 200,000 pesos (US$100). This has important consequences for the sample size available to estimate the impact of health insurance on financial protection: the higher the threshold beyond which an out-of-pocket expenditure is considered catastrophic, the smaller the sample size and therefore the less the information available to generate significant results.

Only 4% of households that used health services in 2003 fell below the endogenous poverty line when incurring out-of-pocket expenditures. Comparing results by insurance status, we find that, with a threshold of 30%, the incidence of catastrophic expenditure is highest among those lacking insurance (34%) followed by

TABLE 9.5

Incidence of catastrophic and impoverishing expenditure by income quintile and insurance status (simple means), population that has used health services, 2003 (percent)

Insurance status and income quintile	Capacity to pay (percentage of nonsubsistence income defining a catastrophic expense)			
	10%	20%	30%	40%
Total	32.0	21.0	14.0	11.0
Uninsured	63.9	45.4	34.0	23.9
Subsidized regime	37.9	27.6	20.8	17.5
Contributory regime	16.9	8.5	4.4	3.4
Quintile 1 (poorest)	37.6	25.0	16.4	11.5
Quintile 2	51.2	40.5	31.7	26.2
Quintile 3	29.7	19.0	11.6	6.6
Quintile 4	20.5	10.0	6.2	5.0
Quintile 5 (richest)	20.4	9.3	6.6	5.4

Source: Flórez, Giedion, and Pardo 2010.

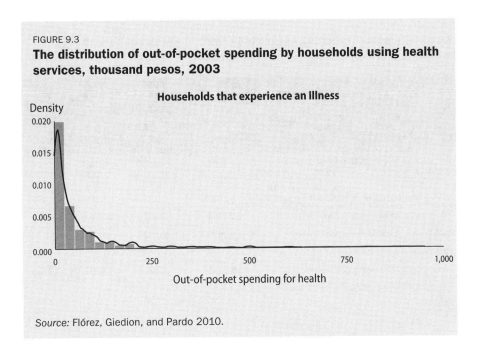

FIGURE 9.3

The distribution of out-of-pocket spending by households using health services, thousand pesos, 2003

Source: Flórez, Giedion, and Pardo 2010.

those affiliated with the subsidized regime (20.8%), and finally those affiliated with the contributory regime (4.4%) (see table 9.5).

These differences by insurance status are important, but to know whether they are due to insurance or other characteristics that might systematically differ across groups, we used propensity score matching in the subsidized regime and instrumental variables to correct for selection bias.

Subsidized regime

The average monthly income of households in the subsidized regime is US$180, and their capacity to pay roughly US$98 (Flórez, Giedion, and Pardo 2010). Compared with uninsured households, households insured with the subsidized regime have a smaller probability (−21 percentage points) of having an out-of-pocket payment that is greater than 10% of their capacity to pay (table 9.6). By the same token, insured households in the subsidized regime have a lower probability of facing an out-of-pocket health expenditure greater than 20% or 30% of their non-subsistence income (−14 and −11 percentage points respectively), compared with uninsured households. When households face out-of-pocket health expenditures more than 40% of their ability to pay, the positive impact of the subsidized regime is lower—but a difference in favor of the insured households can still be observed (−4 percentage points).

TABLE 9.6

Propensity score matching estimated effect of catastrophic and impoverishing health spending in the subsidized regime

	Propensity score matching (probit includes proxy for household health status)			
	Enrolled in the subsidized regime (treatment group)	Not insured (control group)	Difference	Significance
Catastrophic spending (10% capacity to pay)	0.3942	0.6080	-0.21	***
Catastrophic spending (20% capacity to pay)	0.2783	0.4202	-0.14	***
Catastrophic spending (30% capacity to pay)	0.2029	0.3136	-0.11	***
Catastrophic spending (40% capacity to pay)	0.1594	0.1956	-0.04	*
Falls below the endogenous poverty line	0.0609	0.0513	0.01	
Falls below the national poverty line	0.0638	0.1003	-0.04	*
Falls below the national indigence line	0.0435	0.0414	0.00	
Falls below the endogenous or the national poverty line[a]	0.0986	0.1407	-0.04	*

*** significant at $p < 0.01$; * significant at $p < 0.10$.

a. Endogenous (to the household) poverty line = basic household basket of goods and services.

Source: Authors.

The results show that as the cost of the catastrophic event increases, the protective effect of insurance decreases, probably a reflection of the level of coverage of the benefits package for the poor, because the plan covers ambulatory and catastrophic care (low frequency, high cost) and coverage is limited for standard hospital care except some frequent surgeries such as appendectomies and hysterectomies. So, with a threshold of 40% any out-of-pocket spending more than US$40 would be catastrophic. Given that coverage for hospital services is limited it is not surprising that differences between those insured under the subsidized regime and their comparable counterparts tend to be small.

No solid evidence emerges for the impact of the subsidized regime on impoverishment due to health-related out-of-pocket spending. Results are barely or not statistically significant for two of the four poverty lines. It is difficult to identify the mitigating impact of the subsidized regime on impoverishing health spending due to its low incidence and the similarity of incidence between insured and uninsured households.

Contributory regime

The mitigating effect of the contributory regime for insured households facing catastrophic health spending follows a similar pattern to that of the subsidized regime.[14] As out-of-pocket expenditures for health increase as a percentage of the household's nonsubsistence income, the mitigating effect of insurance decreases.[15] The contributory regime has an explicit benefits plan that requires copayments at the time of the use of services. For adverse health events treatable with technologies that are part of the insurance plan, the contributory regime has the capacity to mitigate the financial impact. But for technologies outside of the plan, there is no protection for individuals.

Health insurance under the contributory regime improves financial protection for the formally employed as well as for the self-employed and their families (table 9.7). The impact of health insurance on financial protection is greater, and results tend to be more significant, among the self-employed than other insured workers. For instance, for a catastrophic threshold of 30%, health insurance under the contributory regime reduces the probability of suffering from a catastrophic out-of-pocket health expenditure by 27% among the self-employed but only 4% (and without statistical significance) among other workers. For impoverishing adverse health events, results were not statistically significant.

Health status

Subsidized regime

Evaluating the impact of health insurance on health status is extremely complex. Possibly the most challenging issue is to find health status variables subtle enough to capture changes underlying the quality of life that can be related to improved access to services covered under the benefits packages. In addition, without any real panel data, we will never know whether observed differences are the result of health insurance or whether health insurance is partly the result of observed health status. If we observe that those affiliated have, on average, a worse perception of their health status, is that because health insurance worsens health or because those ill are more prominent among those seeking affiliation? It comes therefore as no surprise that no conclusive evidence emerges on the impact of health insurance on the health status variables that are available in the DHS. For the impact of the subsidized regime on health status, the results of the analysis based on the simple comparison of means provide mixed evidence. No significant differences are observed for the survival of small children. Affiliates have a higher incidence of low birthweight (+43%) and complications after delivery (+5%) but a less favorable perception of their health status (−3%) and a lower incidence of extremely low birthweight (−77%). After controlling for other variables, insurance does not appear to have a significant impact in explaining differences in health status, except low birthwweight, which is worse for the uninsured (table 9.8).

TABLE 9.7

Estimates of the impact of the contributory regime on the incidence of catastrophic expenditure by type of employment, 2003

	Formally employed workers				Self-employed workers			
	Simple difference	Probit control	Ivprobit	Biprobitiv	Simple difference	Probit control	Ivprobit	Biprobitiv
Catastrophic spending (10% capacity to pay)	-0.3281 [0.0747]***	-0.2712 [0.0775]***	-0.2408 [0.0826]**	-0.3143 [0.1567]*	-0.4685 [0.0539]***	-0.5212 [0.0699]***	-0.6278 [0.2064]***	-0.6227 [0.1565]***
Number of observations	1,117	1,117	1,117	1,117	1,031	1,031	1,031	1,031
Hausmann			-0.1226				-0.1785	
rho-wald test				0.118				0.6952*
Catastrophic spending (20% capacity to pay)	-0.2165 [0.0529]***	-0.131 [0.0376]***	-0.0716 [0.0275]**	-0.0786 [0.0633]	-0.3685 [0.0436]***	-0.3274 [0.0440]***	-0.5644 [0.1827]***	-0.6127 [0.0870]***
Number of observations	1,117	1,117	1,117	1,117	1,031	1,031	1,031	1,031
Hausmann			0.3579				-0.8916	
rho-wald test				-0.2479				0.8032*
Catastrophic spending (30% capacity to pay)	-0.141 [0.0371]***	-0.0419 [0.0228]	-0.0186 [0.0128]	-0.0174 [0.0221]	-0.292 [0.0396]***	-0.2727 [0.0350]***	-0.4283 [0.1153]***	-0.5174 [0.1070]***
Number of observations	1,117	1,117	1,117	1,117	1,031	1,031	1,031	1,031
Hausmann			0.4097				-0.7733	
rho-wald test				-0.3551				0.2356
Catastrophic spending (40% capacity to pay)	-0.1091 [0.0326]**	-0.0392 [0.0254]	-0.0185 [0.0116]	-0.0213 [0.0355]	-0.1861 [0.0410]***	-0.1394 [0.0303]***	-0.1467 [0.1041]	-0.2029 [0.1326]
Number of observations	1,117	1,117	1,117	1,117	1,031	1,031	1,031	1,031
Hausmann			0.124				0.1077	
rho-wald test				-0.2528				0.2094

*** significant at $p < 0.01$; ** significant at $p < 0.05$; * significant at $p < 0.10$.

Note: Results for each variable are presented with two rows below the coefficient. The first row corresponds to the Hausmann test and the second to rho-wald. These are two tests for exogeneity of the affiliation variable. The first test corresponds to the two stage probit model (probit instrumental variable) and the second corresponds to the bivariate probit model. Rejection of this test means that affiliation is not exogenous in the original model and that it is necessary to use the instrumental variable approach. On the other hand, when the Ho is accepted, one continues to use the probit model with controls because the test indicates that the affiliation is not endogenous. If affiliation is not endogenous, selection bias in this result variable is due only to observable variables that are included in the model. For this case only the probit model is necessary. The most robust coefficients are marked in bold.

Source: Authors.

TABLE 9.8

Propensity score matching results-estimated treatment effect on subsidized regime participants for health status, national level, radius (bandwidth 0.0001), 2005

Health status outcome variable	Enrolled in the subsidized regime (treatment group)	Not insured (control group)	Difference (percent)	p
Complication after delivery	0.313	0.322	-3	
Extremely low birthweight	0.006	0.006	-2	
Extremely low birthweight from card	0.000	0.010	-100	
Low birthweight	0.085	0.052	63	***
Low birthweight from card	0.077	0.038	100	

*** significant at $p < 0.01$.

Note: Other matching methods (double difference and matched double difference) were implemented with similar results. Results from these methods can be obtained from the authors on request.

Source: Authors' calculations based on DHS 2005 data.

Conclusion

Insurance coverage has increased greatly not only for the general population but also for the poor. Both the subsidized regime and the contributory regime have increased access to and use of health services among their beneficiaries and made positive changes in financial protection in the case of an adverse health event. But, to estimate the impact of insurance on health outcomes, we need data different from those available. Our results are inconclusive for those in the subsidized regime, and the LSMS data do not support such an analysis for those in the contributory regime.

Insured individuals are much less likely to experience barriers to access when needing care, and when facing such barriers they are less likely to be financial and more likely to be supply reasons such as excessive waiting times, low quality, and unfriendly personnel. This result shows that the improvement in access through insurance coverage could now be further enhanced by emphasizing policy measures to improve quality of care.

The insured also use ambulatory health services more often than the uninsured. Poor and insured children suffering from diarrhea or respiratory infections, still among the main causes of premature death among small children in Colombia, are more likely to visit a health care facility than their uninsured counterparts.

Despite the fact that immunizations are provided directly by the local health authorities for free and irrespective of the individual's insurance status, insurance increases immunization coverage. This shows that the benefits of health insurance are not limited to reduced financial barriers and may provide other more indirect paybacks. This effect might be related to increased knowledge connected to an affiliated mother's greater exposure to preventive health information and prodding by providers. Similarly, affiliated women benefit from improved access to delivery-related care. They receive more prenatal visits, and they are more likely to give birth in a health facility and to be attended by a doctor or a skilled professional.

The self-employed and their families in the contributory regime, who were uninsured under the social security system operating until 1993, seem to have benefited most. Nevertheless, descriptive data indicate that much remains to be done on some key health indicators, as close to a third of the self-employed insured still do not use any preventive health care services and 45% do not receive all medicine prescribed for them.

The financial protection effects of insurance, for both schemes, are greater when the household faces low health-related expenses. This means that the protective effects of insurance fall as the cost of the adverse health effect rises, exactly the opposite of what should happen. Within the contributory regime, the self-employed benefit more from insurance during financially catastrophic health events than do other workers. In any case, health insurance in Colombia does provide financial protection to households, mitigating the financial effects of an adverse health event, but surely the design could be improved to provide more protection when households face greater risks.

The evidence on the impact of the subsidized regime on health status seems less convincing. This result is related primarily to the quantity, characteristics, and quality of the health status variables in the DHS. Those surveys concentrate mainly on health status variables related to women of child-bearing age and small children (child survival, complications after delivery, and birthweight, for example). Health insurance definitely increases use of professional care for all aspects of child delivery and care; the challenge is the contribution of those services to improving the outcomes measured in the survey. As argued in chapter 2, connecting outcome variables in surveys more directly to what insurance can do would help sort this out.

Despite popular belief in Colombia, our results indicate that insurance matters for the rural population and has improved access to and use of care, particularly for the rural poor. Moreover, although social health insurance schemes are criticized for the difficulty of attracting the self-employed, our results show that the benefits of insurance are even more important among this group than for others insured in the contributory regime.

Colombians need to address several important challenges if they want to further improve the benefits from the health insurance scheme and make their system more sustainable. Now that access has substantially improved and financial barriers have been reduced, improving service quality becomes a key issue for researchers and policymakers to consider and a key incentive issue in the design of reimbursement policies. Similarly, the goal of the current administration to affiliate more than 50% of the population with the subsidized regime will require careful consideration of the financial sustainability of this subsidy expansion. Most important, eligibility for the subsidized regime should be a transient feature conditioned on financial need, not a permanent and rigid right. Incentives must be created to foster mobility from the subsidized regime to the contributory regime for those escaping poverty. The limits of the financial protection offered by the insurance system are often amenable to relatively inexpensive fixes by the insurer that can provide tremendous benefits to those incurring catastrophic expenses.

Notes

1. Before the reform, mostly only formal sector workers of the private and public sector had access to a full benefit plan, and family coverage was limited. Under the Social Security Institute (Instituto de Seguros Sociales, or ISS), which covered formal private sector workers, only pregnant and dependent wives and their small children (under age 1) had access to a limited array of birth-related services, leaving the remaining services and all other dependent family members uncovered.

2. See Harvard Master Plan of Health Reform Implementation, 1997, for a synthesis of the situation prior to the reform.

3. 1.5 percentage points of the 12.5% payroll tax contribution is channeled to the subsidized regime.

4. Since 2005 those not poor enough to qualify for the subsidized regime but not wealthy enough to be affiliated with the contributory regime are affiliated with a partial subsidy system. Benefits covered under the system are limited to coverage for catastrophic illnesses (such as cancer, AIDS, and diabetes). Given that the data used in this study stem from 2005 (when the affiliation under the system just started), the impact of the partial subsidy system is not analyzed here.

5. Detailed information on coverage by SISBEN levels and by income is in Giedion, Díaz, and Alfonso (2007).

6. Coverage has since increased but no updated information is available at the municipal level.

7. This section is based on a conversation with Gilberto Barón, director of the Planning Division of the ISS prior to the reform.

8. In the late 1970s the ISS introduced family coverage in some small towns and villages. In the early 1990s coverage was extended to some special economic groups, such as priests, self-employed, and independent workers, and domestic helpers, prior to the major reform of 1993.

9. Although results presented here are for analysis done using propensity score matching, analysis was also done using double difference and matched double difference producing similar results to propensity score matching.

10. Information for the contributory regime refers to 2003, and the household dataset come from LSMS 2003.

11. Excludes the population affiliated and qualifying for the subsidized regime.

12. Informal care includes consulting a druggist, apothecary, quack, and the like when facing a health problem.

13. Detailed statistics for the incidence of catastrophic and impoverishing expenditure in the total (not just the user) population can be requested from the authors and are presented in detail in Flórez, Giedion, and Pardo (2010).

14. Note that the use of different methods to evaluate the impact of the subsidized regime (propensity score matching) and contributory regime (instrumental variables) on financial protection does not allow a straightforward comparison of the coefficients. The sign and statistical significance of results can, however, be compared.

15. As measured by the household's nonsubsistence income, as indicated earlier.

References

Barón, G. 2006. *Cuentas de Salud de Colombia 1993-2003: El gasto nacional en salud y su financiamiento.* Bogota: Colombian Ministry of Social Protection.

Clavijo, S. 2009. "Social Security Reforms in Colombia: Striking Demographic and Fiscal Balances." Working Paper WP/09/58. International Monetary Fund, Washington, D.C.

Buchmueller, T., R. Kronick, K. Grumbach, and J. G. Kahn. 2005. "The Effect of Health Insurance on Medical Care Utilization and Implications for Insurance Expansion: A Review of the Literature." *Medical Care Research and Review* 62 (1): 3–30.

CEPAL (Economic Commission for Latin America and the Caribbean). 2006. *Anuario Estadístico 2006.* Santiago: Economic Commission for Latin America and the Caribbean.

Escobar, M. L. 2005. "Health Sector Reform in Colombia." Washington, DC: World Bank, Development Outreach.

Flórez, C., U. Giedion, and R. Pardo. 2010. "The Impact of Health Insurance in Colombia on Financial Protection." In A. Glassman, A. Giuffrida, M. Escobar and U. Giedion, eds., *From Few to Many: Ten Years of Health Insurance Expansion in Colombia Latin America*, Washington DC: Brookings Institution Press.

Gaviria, A., C. Medina, and C. Mejía. 2006. "Assessing Health Reform in Colombia: From Theory to Practice." *Economía* (7)1: 29–72.

Institute of Medicine. 2009. *America's Uninsured Crisis: Consequences for Health and Health Care.* Washington, DC: The National Academies Press.

Khan, A. A., and S. M. Bhardwaj. 1994. "Access to Health Care: A Conceptual Framework and its Relevance to Health Care Planning." *Evaluation & the Health Professions* 17 (1): 60–76.

Levy, H., and D. Meltzer. 2001. "What Do We Really Know about Whether Health Insurance Affects Health?" ERIU Working Paper 6. University of Michigan, Economic Research Initiative on the Uninsured, Ann Arbor, MI.

McLaughlin, C. G., and L. Wyszewianski. 2002. "Access to Care: Remembering Old Lessons." *Health Services Research* 37 (6): 1441–43.

Penchansky, R., and J. W. Thomas. 1981. "The Concept of Access: Definition and Relationship to Consumer Satisfaction." *Medical Care* 19 (2): 127–40.

Phelps, C. 2009. *Health Economics (4th Edition).* Boston, MA: Addison Wesley Higher Education

Trujillo, A., J. Portillo, and J. Vernon. "The Impact of Subsidized Health Insurance for the Poor: Evaluating the Colombian Experience Using Propensity Score Matching." *International Journal of Health Care Finance and Economics* 5 (3): 211–39.

Tsai, T. 2010. "Second Chance for Health Reform in Colombia." *The Lancet* 375 (9709): 109–10.

World Bank. 2007. *Healthy Development: The World Bank Strategy for Health, Nutrition, and Population Results.* Washington, DC: International Bank for Reconstruction and Development.

———. 2010. *World Development Indicators 2010.* Washington, DC: World Bank.

Yamin, A. and O. Parra-Vera. 2009. "How Do Courts Set Health Policy? The Case of the Colombian Constitutional Court," PLoS Medicine 6(2):147-150. Available at http://www.ncbi.nlm.nih.gov/pmc/articles/PMC2642877/pdf/pmed.1000032.pdf.

Chapter 10

Main Findings, Research Issues, and Policy Implications

Maria-Luisa Escobar, Charles C. Griffin, and R. Paul Shaw

This book contains rich and varied analyses of the impact of health insurance in different socioeconomic and organizational settings. It begins with a comprehensive literature review that distills findings on prior studies that examine causal effects between health insurance and health outcomes. This is followed by seven country case studies, most of which use advanced statistical techniques and new data sources to shed light on how health insurance improves health outputs and outcomes. This chapter summarizes the main findings, the methodological issues that can understate or diminish the estimated impact of health insurance on health, and the country scenarios that illustrate the art of the possible for policymakers interested in scaling up well designed health insurance programs.

To a large extent, selecting the countries was opportunistic, as explained in chapter 1. In view of pressing policy concerns in many low-income countries, as well as major gaps in our knowledge of the impacts of health insurance, we chose countries where scaling up health insurance aims to be more inclusive of the poor and where available data permit explorations of the impact on health status. No pretense is made, therefore, that findings reported here come from a uniform dataset or research methodology applied to all countries or that all studies satisfy the "gold standard" for empirical robustness as described in chapter 2. Instead, several caveats and qualifiers should be kept in mind.

Above all, we have learned that health insurance is not a homogeneous product (like an approved oral medicine or vaccine). It tends to be heterogeneous in the entitlements to medical goods and services created for health insurance members; the quantity, quality, and distribution of providers where members can access services; the extent that copayments and deductibles affect out-of-pocket spending by members; and so on. This heterogeneity cannot be controlled or made uniform. It shapes the impact that health insurance has on outputs and outcome measures in one country versus another, so that the measured effects of health insurance on access, service uptake, and out-of-pocket spending vary widely across countries. The temptation to generalize findings across countries must be tempered accordingly.

We have also learned that the extent to which health insurance succeeds in being pro-poor has more to do with a purposive effort to design health insurance in a way that benefits the poor than with any presumption that health insurance is automatically and intrinsically pro-poor or anti-poor. Health insurance has important design features that can benefit low-income households, such as pooling contributions by rich and poor households, then paying for treatment of illnesses that disproportionately fall on the poor. But if health insurance fails to enroll the poor or extend services to them, the distributional impacts of health insurance on equity will likely be muted. Accordingly, to generalize that health insurance does, indeed, contribute to greater equity in health care consumption will be conditional on successful pro-poor design features. This caveat also applies to generalizations we might be inclined to make about distributional impacts of health insurance on women and children. Pooling risks is equity improving within the risk pool, but who benefits depends on who is in the risk pool and how it is designed to function.

Finally, we have learned that the robustness of empirical analysis varies across case studies. Robustness depends on the comprehensiveness and quality of datasets, availability of appropriate measures of impact, success in controlling for endogeneity, and appropriate application of statistical models. This caveat forms the backbone of chapter 2, where checklists of key methodological concerns are used to score the quality of a wide variety of studies and the robustness of the empirical estimates they have reported. Managing these problems well is critical if empirical findings are to be taken seriously.

With these caveats in mind, the collective findings in this book do lend themselves to some conservative generalizations that advance not only the evidence base but also contribute information to current policy debates on the desirability of scaling up health insurance. The next section considers the accumulation of evidence in six areas.

Six general findings

In this volume the estimated benefits of health insurance among the insured are measured relative to conditions affecting the uninsured. In this sense, the uninsured represent a baseline for determining the value added of health insurance. This prompts the questions: What does it mean to be uninsured? What is health insurance trying to improve on? The first case study, on Namibia, provides useful insights into these questions in an African context. First, it reveals that even though uninsured households (about half) presumably have access to a reasonably well functioning public health system, they are less likely to report an illness than those with public or private insurance. And when they do report illness, they are less likely to seek care. Moreover, the health shocks experienced by those without insurance lead to higher medical expenses, reduced food and nonfood consumption, and fewer assets than among insured households. Consequences of being without insurance are likely to be particularly dire for Namibian households in the bottom income quintile: they are three times more likely to have a hospitalization (three or more days) than those in the top quintile and one and a half times more likely to have HIV/AIDS or die. The data point to substantial differences among population groups even in the presence of a relatively well financed and functioning public system of direct service delivery.

Findings from the other case studies, while not explicitly designed to profile households without health insurance, deepen the foregoing perspective by conveying that those without insurance are more prone to:

- Go without treatment.
- Self-treat and self-medicate.
- Benefit less from preventive services.
- Have much higher shares of out-of-pocket spending as a percentage of their disposable income.
- Incur catastrophic financial loss, borrowing, or indebtedness.
- Have poorer self-perceptions of their health status.

Although young single people tend to be more prevalent among the uninsured, especially if health insurance requires voluntary enrollment, a large share of the uninsured in the low- and middle-income countries covered in this book tend to be relatively poor families with low levels of education, self-employed workers, migrants, and people living in rural and remote areas.

Turning now to the impact of health insurance in the countries examined in this book, table 10.1 distills the main findings. They are based on empirical estimates that for the most part have attempted to purge the effects of endogeneity and quantify impacts of health insurance on the insured relative to the uninsured. We conclude that the evidence reasonably supports six generalizations, all of which provide further support for—and extend—the findings from the global literature review in chapter 2.

Health insurance can produce significant positive impacts on access and use

In Colombia low-income health insurance members are 41% more likely to have had an outpatient visit in the 12 months prior to the survey than low-income non-members even though the latter have access to public clinics and hospitals. Insured Ghanaians had 72% lower outlays than the uninsured but were twice as likely to use formal care and half as likely to self-treat or use informal practitioners. Insured mothers paid 90% less for prenatal and delivery care. Only 13% paid anything, compared with 81% of the uninsured. While the magnitude of impacts varies by study and country, these findings are consistent with the hypothesis that insurance removes barriers to access. All studies found an increase in use of services (see table 10.1).

Increased access is the first step toward increased uptake of cost-effective outpatient services known to affect preventable communicable diseases, such as immunizations, as reported in Peru. This is a major appeal of health insurance in countries where health services are underused, especially by women and children. The complement of increased access and use is reduced prevalence of no treatment, self-treatment, and informal care. Ghana and China both reported self-treatment among the insured around 30% lower than among the uninsured; in Colombia bringing the self-employed into the contributory scheme caused substantial improvements in their use of preventive and dental services as well as medicines, and it lowered their use of self-medication and informal care.

Health insurance can and does benefit poorer households as much as better off households, if not more

To a large extent, this finding is associated with well designed health insurance programs that target low-income households, as in Peru, Colombia, and Costa Rica. The voluntary scheme in Ghana has few contributors, and the targeting of subsidies except by age needs improvement. China's experiment is targeted to poorer rural provinces, but because it is voluntary, the poorest households are the last to enroll. Integral Health Insurance (SIS) in Peru, the subsidized regime in Colombia, and the noncontributory regime in Costa Rica use means tests to achieve this goal. The poor in Peru and Colombia gain substantial benefits from insurance coverage. The case study on Indonesia demonstrates that health insurance can exert positive

TABLE 10.1

Observed impacts of health insurance on selected indicators

Country	Increases use	Reduces self-treatment	Reduces out-of-pocket spending	Benefits relatively poor households	Improves self-assessed health status and/or uptake of cost-effective preventive services
Namibia	na	na	na	No, voluntary insurance taken up first by the rich	na
Ghana	Yes	Yes	Yes, a large reduction in having any spending for acute care and deliveries	No, voluntary insurance taken up first by the rich; exemptions not well targeted	No effects found in pre-post analysis, but propensity score matching suggests a large insurance impact on prenatal care, facility delivery, and Caesarean section. Insurance substantially reduced expenditures on these services despite higher use.
Costa Rica	No effect because all needing care may receive it by paying or for free if indigent, even if not insured	na	No impact on out-of-pocket health spending because emergency care is free to all; nonemergency care free to indigents	No difference among quintiles as 81% of the sample have health insurance and indigents receive free care even if not insured	+ impact on vaccinations for children under age 18. Reduced use of inpatient and emergency care for those with diabetes, more appropriate dosages for insured diabetics. Uninsured are younger, healthier but more likely to enter hospital through emergency room, to have a longer stay, and to die. + effect on perceived health status (except diabetics). Reduces hospital length of stay and low birthweight newborns.
Peru	Yes	na	Yes, out-of-pocket and catastrophic spending; large reduction in probability of any spending	Yes, explicitly targeted health insurance for low-income households but some effects more pro-poor than others	Strong + change for having full immunization series complete for children. + formal treatment of child diarrhea and acute respiratory infection, especially poorer households. + effect on growth monitoring visits for children under age 5. Small + effect on attended deliveries and on probability of receiving a Pap smear, but only for older women (appropriately). No effect on institutional deliveries.

(continued)

TABLE 10.1 (continued)

Observed impacts of health insurance on selected indicators

Country	Increases use	Reduces self-treatment	Reduces out-of-pocket spending	Benefits relatively poor households	Improves self-assessed health status and/or uptake of cost-effective preventive services
Indonesia	Yes	na	Yes, reduces probability of any spending but not overall amount spent	Yes, larger use impacts for rural and poor households, but does not apply to out-of-pocket spending	+ effect for outpatient care and spending for female children. Small effect to reduce problems with activities of daily life and reduction in high blood pressure for adults in lower income group.
China	Yes, increased outpatient but not inpatient	Yes, self-medication	Yes, out-of-pocket and catastrophic spending	Yes, explicit targeting of the poor by design (poor geographical area); within sample richer households enrolled in voluntary scheme	Improved self-assessed health status and mobility among oldest age group. Vastly improved prescribing behavior of providers and eliminated fake and expired drugs. Significantly reduced the probability of pain/discomfort and anxiety/depression.
Colombia	Yes	Yes, contributory regime reduces informal care use, self-treatment, no health care	Yes, out-of-pocket and catastrophic spending; but still unnecessarily high due to design	Yes, through the subsidized regime, larger impacts for low-income rural households	+ impacts of subsidized regime on receiving care when needed, skilled birth attendance, birth in health facility, number of prenatal visits, child getting treatment for cough or diarrhea, and full immunization of child. + impacts of contributory regime on making preventive doctor/dental visits and getting full course of medicines.

Note: na=no account or not explicitly evaluated.

distributional effects on rural versus urban women and children, even in a fairly short timeframe, and in that case it appears that poorer households gained the most from insurance coverage in gaining access.

The impact of health insurance on measures of health status is weak and irregular—but strong for self-perceptions

This finding is interesting but far less important than the impact on actual behavior. Two studies examine the impacts on self-reported health status. Using a standardized measure of self-reported health status—EQ-5D dimensions—the China study reports the probability of having a problem in any of the EQ-5D dimensions among the insured was 49% less than among the uninsured. In the Costa Rica study health insurance improves an individual's self-perception of health status, with the insured having a higher probability of perceiving their health status to be good or very good. Moreover, the probability of declaring good or very good health status was 10 percentage points higher for a subsample of insured people with at least one diagnosed chronic disease than for those who are uninsured. Yet for diabetics, insurance reduced their self-perceived health even though it improved their treatment significantly over uninsured diabetics.

Health insurance reduces out-of-pocket payments, thus reducing vulnerability to having to pay at times of illness or injury

In Ghana uninsured patients had out-of-pocket spending three times that of the insured for formal care, three times that for informal care, and twice that for hospital care. In Indonesia health insurance has a significant negative effect on the likelihood of out-of-pocket spending, showing larger effects for rural over urban adults and the largest effects for rural women. It also appears to have a greater impact on reducing expenditures for those who are poor, more isolated, and with lower availability of health services—all variables correlated with residence in rural areas. In Peru the probability of any spending on health services among those receiving formal care in the four weeks prior to the survey was only 13% for those covered by SIS but 86% for those without it. SIS almost eliminated spending for its affiliates. And in Costa Rica health insurance had a significant impact on reducing per capita spending on health both as a proportion of total per capita spending and as a proportion of capacity for payment. As expected, however, the quantitative impact of health insurance on out-of-pocket spending varies considerably depending on the health goods and services covered and the schedule of copayments or deductibles. Consistently across the studies, insurance tends to increase the probability of no expenditures, while those incurring costs tend to spend as much as before or more.

Health insurance reduces the incidence of catastrophic financial loss due to high costs associated with serious illness or injury

Studies examining the relationship between health insurance and catastrophic financial loss tend to rely on proxies rather than on measures that actually gauge whether a financial catastrophe occurred at times of serious illness or injury. From the Namibia case, for example, it is clear that families with a health problem may rely on coping mechanisms such as borrowing from family, selling assets, and changing consumption patterns, which most surveys cannot account for. Four of the studies in this volume proxied catastrophic financial loss as a rising share of household nonsubsistence expenditures on health. The China case study defines catastrophic health spending as out-of-pocket spending greater than 10%, 20%, 30%, and 40% of household income (net of food expenditures). It found that having health insurance reduced rates of catastrophic spending by significant margins and reduced medical impoverishment by about one-fifth for those in the lowest income quartile. In Colombia both the subsidized and contributory regimes reduce catastrophic expenditures, but their protection decreases, and out-of-pocket expenditures increase for the most serious, costly illnesses—so while there is catastrophic protection, its impact drops off just when it is most needed. In both plans costs for uncovered or partially covered services cause the problem. Costa Rica's program provides a significant margin of financial protection to everyone, whether insured or not. Out-of-pocket health expenditures represent only 2% of total expenditures for the poorest third of households and 4% for the richest third. In the absence of financial protection, this pattern is typically reversed, with much higher percentages for all households, but especially for the poor.

Research issues

Chapter 2 concludes that methodological problems undermine the robustness of more than half of past health insurance studies, such that causality cannot reliably be established. Accordingly, chapter 2 provides guidelines to detect and correct such problems. Nine issues cropped up to varying degrees in the case studies in this volume (figure 10.1). Without appropriate adjustments, especially in retrospective analysis, one or more of these issues can diminish the measured impact of health insurance, as explained below.

Endogeneity

Because health insurance tends to be plagued by adverse selection, failure to fully control for endogeneity means that people with poor health self-select to join health insurance. Thus we might infer empirically that insurance causes poor health because of self-selection of the sick into insurance pools. In Ghana, for example,

FIGURE 10.1

Factors diminishing the measured impact of health insurance

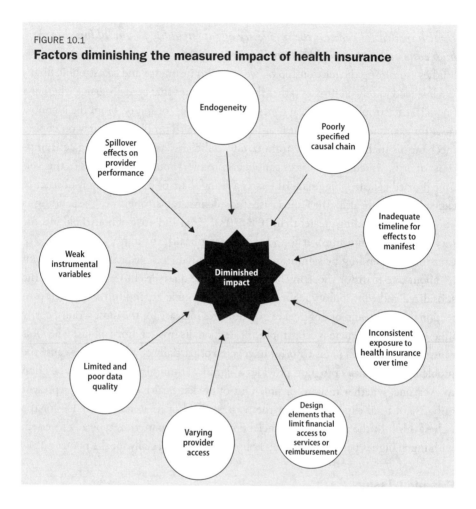

people reporting chronic conditions were more likely to enroll in voluntary insurance, and among richer households pregnant women were more likely to enroll. The positive impact of health insurance on health would be underestimated as a result. Alternatively, perceived health status could appear to worsen with health insurance, whereas in fact, health insurance may make people more knowledgeable through more contacts with professionals, resulting in better health outcomes. This certainly seems to be the case for diabetics in Costa Rica, who clearly get much better care if insured but consider themselves sicker than uninsured diabetics do.

Poorly specified causal chain
Health insurance does not act directly on mortality-based measures (such as child or adult mortality or life expectancy) or measures of stock or stature (such as

height-for-age or weight-for-age)—it acts on improving health through access to clinically proven medical services known to improve health. An attempt to connect health insurance causally to more general health outcome measures that are slow to change or rarely observed and are affected by many other factors will likely understate or diminish its impact. Thus, researchers should concentrate on measures of health status that can be reasonably well connected to access to health services offered under the health insurance arrangement being analyzed.

Inadequate timeline for effects to manifest

Scaling up health insurance requires advances on many fronts before significant and consistent effects emerge. Enrollments may well double in a short period, but this does not mean provider networks are fully functioning, that quality issues have been resolved, that patient entitlements are clear, or that insured households have built trust in new medical schemes. Chapter 2 suggests that at least 12–18 months may be required to detect effects. Anything shorter than that may underestimate the longer term effects of health insurance. Thus the study of the social experiment in China is instructive, but it may understate impacts that accumulate over time or start to show up after providers and patients gain additional years of experience with the plan.

Inconsistent exposure to health insurance over time

In medical terms, when people are enrolled in health insurance as part of an experiment to determine how they fare against those not enrolled, the enrollees are regarded as the treatment group. Further, we know from in-depth studies of compliance from the pharmaceutical industry that a major problem in studies of drug effectiveness is that many people in the treatment group do not comply with prescription instructions or drop out of treatment. Without appropriate controls, this results in inconsistencies in exposure to drug treatments that can understate estimated drug impacts. In health insurance studies, the term we use to describe such individuals can be adopted from the Indonesia study in chapter 7, called switchers. The less they are controlled for, the more effects of health insurance may be underestimated. Switching is an even more significant problem if it is driven by self-selection—in when sick, out when well.

Design elements that limit financial access to services or reimbursement

Policies on copayments, deductibles, and coinsurance by health insurance plans tend to vary widely across countries and even within countries. Insurance may induce households to use more medical services as financial barriers fall, or the insurance plan may have a benefit cut-out, as in Colombia, or limits may reduce catastrophic protections, as in China. Failure to appreciate such features may lead to the superficial conclusion that health insurance has far less impact on access and out-of-pocket spending among poor households than expected. Without appreciating the nature of the design issue, researchers may unintentionally understate or diminish the effect that health insurance could have on financial access and financial risk protection, because they typically cannot incorporate specific plan attributes in their analysis.

Varying provider access

Increasingly, health insurance funds act as purchasers of services for their members by contracting with networks of providers—public, private, nongovernmental organizations, or a mix. In some countries, contracted networks of providers may be fairly extensive, providing medical entitlements to health insurance members in both urban and rural areas. But in many rural and remote areas provider networks are likely to be much thinner. The more that provider networks are uneven, the less the estimated effects of health insurance are likely to be. This consideration may diminish the measured impact of health insurance more than expected, because of inadequate recognition of key organizational features of delivery.

Limited and poor quality data

When data limitations prevent disaggregating the insured and uninsured into different subgroups, the possible impact of health insurance on groups of particular interest, such as women and children in rural areas, will be obscured. Moreover, small impacts of health insurance based on highly aggregated data may obscure large impacts among subgroups—which tend to cancel out when aggregated. In such cases impacts of health insurance would be underestimated for such groups.

Weak instrumental variables

Confronted by unobservable variables that may be distorting the estimated relationship between the dependent variable (health outcomes) and the independent variable (health insurance), researchers often resort to replacing health insurance with an instrumental variable. The strength of this approach is based on the plausibility of the instruments, which in turn must comply with three assumptions (Wooldridge 2001). First, the instrument must substantially explain affiliation with the insurance plan. Second, it should not have any direct effect on the outcome variable of interest. Third, it should not have an indirect effect on the outcome through other variables left out of the outcome equation. At the simplest level, in most datasets it is difficult to find instrumental variables that affect insurance status but not the variable of interest, such as use of health services or health status. Judgments and tradeoffs are always made in trying to solve this problem.

Spillover effects on provider performance

Scaling up a well designed health insurance program will have wide ranging impacts on the finance, organization, regulation, and behavior of the health system as a whole. Typically the policy change involves partial or full separation of public finance and provision with increased efficiencies through contracting, improved targeting of public subsidies for health care to the poor, and a better demarcation between public spending for acute care and public spending for population-based health care. In other words, health insurance may have positive spillover effects that also improve the lot of the uninsured relative to the insured. When this happens, the impact of health insurance would tend to be underestimated as the rising tide of greater efficiency and equity of public subsidies "lifts all boats."

Policy implications

Policymakers hope that in introducing or scaling up health insurance, the health and well-being of citizens will be enhanced. Yet the uneven evidence in the past has exposed policymakers in some countries to far-ranging debate, if not cynicism, about the intended effects of health insurance. China is a case in point, with some studies showing little or no consistent effects on important health outcome parameters and others showing positive effects on access, use, and financial risk protection.

Realistically, this is a matter of designing the intervention to address the problem. Scaling up health insurance in low- and middle-income countries can, indeed, deliver the kinds of effects that appeal to policymakers but only if the design of health insurance explicitly embodies features that can yield those effects, an adequate provider network is in place to serve the insured (or the intervention works on providers too), and the details of implementation and execution of the policy are managed well so the reform performs as designed. Five of the case studies—Ghana, China, Peru, Colombia, and Costa Rica—help illustrate the art of the possible in these dimensions.

Ghana—saving nearly 1.5 million disability-adjusted life years

The toll of mortality and morbidity in Ghana was about 12 million disability-adjusted life years in 2004. About 71% of this toll was attributable to communicable diseases, maternal and perinatal conditions, and nutritional deficiencies.

Four major killers—including infectious/parasitic diseases, respiratory diseases, and maternal and prenatal conditions—are responsible for 68% of the country's disease burden. Combating communicable diseases has been a major policy goal of government for the last decade. Obstacles to reducing the disease burden in the country have included a publicly funded health system providing low quality care, financial barriers to care for poor households, a strong propensity for people to self-treat at times of illness or injury, and a lack of knowledge and use of preventive practices among households.

Ghana started to reform its approach to battling disease in 2003 by embarking on an ambitious policy to scale up health insurance and achieve universal coverage by 2015–20. The initial health insurance platform consisted of three district level health mutual organizations in 1999. The number of mutuals spontaneously expanded to 47 in 2000. In anticipation of universal health insurance, the mutuals expanded to 159 in 2002, and to 258 in 2003. Government goals of 40% national enrollment by 2004 were surpassed, and current enrollment is about 60%. Features of Ghana's health insurance program relevant to combating major diseases include:

- Local and community involvement to educate and enroll households in health insurance.
- Emphasis on prevention to combat communicable diseases, such as HIV/AIDS, malaria, and tuberculosis.
- Entitlement to cost-effective quality services locally, attuned to the epidemiological challenges of the populace.
- Cross-subsidizing premiums of the relatively rich with those of the poor and relying on a value-added tax to subsidize premiums of the poorest households.

An estimate of the possible impact of health insurance on the disease burden in Ghana enlists the following assumption: enrollment in health insurance draws people into care at a modern health facility and away from self-treatment and motivates them to use clinically proven interventions known to prevent or cure priority communicable diseases. Based on data for 2007 the empirical analysis in chapter 4 shows that 88% of those enrolled in health insurance sought care at a modern facility at times of illness, against 42% for those not enrolled. The prevalence of self-treatment declined by 29 percentage points, from 62% among nonenrollees to 33% for enrollees. Whether enrollees make best use of cost-effective preventive and curative interventions that reduce the incidence of communicable diseases cannot yet be quantified. It seems reasonable to assume, however, that the motives to do so would be high, fueled by provider reimbursement policies that emphasize prevention as a way of reducing more costly curative cases and by clients now entitled access to demand services for premiums paid.

A crude estimate of the impact of Ghana's health insurance program on priority diseases might therefore be based on the following.

- By 2007, 60% of the population is enrolled in health insurance.
- For the 60% enrolled the propensity to use modern care and not self-treat is about one-third higher than for the nonenrolled, or 18% (60% × 30%).
- The four major communicable disease killers are responsible for 68% of Ghana disability-adjusted life years.
- Effective use of clinically proven interventions to combat the major killers by 18% of health insurance enrollees reduces the disease burden of the four major killers by 12.2% (68% × 18%).
- About 1.46 million disability-adjusted life years would have been saved by health insurance (12.2% × 12 million) in 2007.

To put this estimate of 1.46 million disability-adjusted life years saved into perspective, imagine that a fully successful, vertical disease control program to eliminate malaria was implemented in Ghana. The result would be to reduce the overall burden of disease by 8.2%, or 984,000 disability-adjusted life years. Eliminating both malaria and tuberculosis through vertical disease control programs would reduce the overall burden of disease by 11.1%, or 1.33 million disability-adjusted life years. Such comparisons show that tackling today's disease control priorities through health insurance has promise. Admittedly, these back-of-the-envelope estimates are imprecise and require careful evaluation. The effects on maternal and child health would also need to be incorporated. The point is to illustrate the possible quantitative impact of health insurance relative to other common health interventions.

China—reducing copayments and coinsurance and building trust

Starting in 1979 China transformed the agricultural production system from collective farming to the household responsibility system. Its Cooperative Medical System, which provided community-based insurance to up to 90% of the rural population, collapsed with the end of the communes. Later, it adopted a policy of benign neglect and let market forces take over. Township health centers and county hospitals began to rely on profits from drugs, laboratory tests, and surgeries for their incomes. Close to 60% of China's total health expenditures were soon consumed by drugs, compared with about 20% in other low-income countries. At the same time, the majority of villagers were not covered by any form of organized health care financing, subjecting them to major financial risk.

The 2003 National Health Survey found that 46% of rural Chinese who were ill did not seek health care, and among them 40% cited cost as the main reason.

Another 22% of those advised by physicians to be hospitalized refused to do so because they could not afford it. Of those who became hospitalized, about 35% discharged themselves against their doctor's advice because of cost. When faced with life-threatening conditions, many Chinese were either driven into poverty or had to borrow money at usurious rates, reduce their nutritional intake, and discontinue their children's schooling to pay for care. Studies have found that medical spending accounts for 30%–40% of poverty.

To improve this situation, and to recapture the benefits of the Cooperative Medical System, the government launched the New Cooperative Medical Scheme (NCMS) in 2003, with all rural county-level jurisdictions to be covered by 2008. Under this policy the central government provided a subsidy of 10 RMB per enrollee, to be matched by the local government, with additional premium contributions from the villagers. In 2006 the subsidies were increased to 20 RMB for both the central and local governments. By late 2006 more than 400 million people were enrolled in the scheme, which was functioning in more than half of China's rural counties.

But the NCMS has fallen short of expectations. Although outpatient and inpatient use increased by 20%–30%, enrollment was lower among poor households, there was no impact on out-of-pocket spending among the poor, and increased ownership of expensive equipment among central township health centers was not associated with any impact on the cost per case (Wagstaff and others 2007). Analyzing the design of the NCMS helps explain these impacts (or lack of them). In particular, the NCMS budget was likely too small to reduce households' out-of-pocket spending, and copayments in the scheme were high, reflecting large deductibles, low ceilings, and high coinsurance rates. The high copayments were also likely to have discouraged use of services among poor households, perhaps even discouraging them from enrolling.

Dissatisfaction with several design elements of the NCMS prompted a modified approach. Working with the same rate of central and local government subsidy, the NCMS approach has been recast as an experimental community-based prepayment scheme targeted to rural populations—the Rural Mutual Health Care (RMHC)—and applied in two low-income counties in the western region of the country. The RMHC provided a broader benefit package that included a wide array of outpatient services that enrollees wanted, in addition to more traditional hospital benefits. It also featured cost-effective drugs from a reduced formulary at negotiated and controlled prices. It reduced copayments and coinsurance. It selected doctors competitively and put them on a salary. And it shifted more responsibility and involvement to villagers.

During the 2004–06 piloting stage, the RMHC accomplished the following:

- Increased enrollment rates from 60% in the first year of the study to 90% in the last year.
- Increased monthly outpatient visits by 70%, with the greatest increases in villages (versus townships) and among those with chronic conditions.
- Reduced self-medication by 42%.
- Reduced those not seeking care for financial reasons from 12.7% in the baseline year to 3.3% in 2006; reduced those hospitalized and discharging themselves because of financial difficulties from 57% in the baseline year to 40% in 2006.
- Increased use in villages most for those in the bottom and top income groups.
- Did not increase more costly inpatient use.
- Reduced catastrophic health spending.
- Reduced those who perceive themselves to be in poor or fair health by 37%.
- Encountered high levels of reported satisfaction, with 70%–90% satisfied or very satisfied.

The RMHC now has the potential of contributing to the government's disease control priorities, like tuberculosis. At present, national tuberculosis strategies include faster and more accurate diagnostic tests, fixed-dose combinations to treat cases, case monitoring with mobile phones, new inputs such as laboratory networks, and improved coordination of tuberculosis service delivery to combat multidrug resistance. But analysts warn these necessary inputs may not be sufficient to achieve optimal results. Patient delay in seeking diagnosis for tuberculosis in China has been attributed to lack of ability to pay (actual and perceived), particularly among rural residents (Tang and Squire 2005; Liu and others 2007; Zhang and others 2007). Financial costs also enter as a barrier to compliance since many patients decide to stop treatment due to costs. While the internationally recommended strategy for tuberculosis control (DOTS) treatment is theoretically free in China, providers often supplement DOTS with additional high cost drugs—for example, for liver function—because provider incomes are tied to profits, creating incentives to push high priced drugs the poor cannot always afford (Tang and Squire 2005; Liu and others 2007).

The RMHC can complement national tuberculosis strategies in three ways: by reducing the financial barrier for patients to seek initial diagnosis; by diminishing the propensity of individuals to self-treat or seek no treatment (up to 30% of cases); and by combating perverse incentives among health care providers who deter (or delay) referrals of suspected tuberculosis patients to the appropriate level of care, to capture fees associated with their illness. By contracting village doctors and compensating them with a salary plus a bonus, based on performance measurements, the RMHC increased use of established protocols of treatment for common diseases such as tuberculosis-related upper respiratory infection and diarrhea.

At the conclusion of the RMHC experiment in 2007 the government of Guiyang, one of the intervention sites, immediately replicated the scheme to cover around 1.7 million rural Chinese. In 2008 Shaanxi province followed suit and began to replicate the RMHC throughout the province, which has more than 30 million rural inhabitants. When the findings of this social experiment were presented to China's top officials, the government revised its policies for national health insurance, which emphasized coverage for hospital care. It decided that national health insurance benefit packages should cover both primary care and hospitalizations. Bulk purchasing and central distribution of drugs would be established. And community governance would be greatly encouraged, all substantially the result of the pilot and analytical work summarized in chapter 8.

Peru—rapid inroads into the health of the poor

Health insurance in Peru illustrates the art of the possible because it represents a purposive, strategic intervention to target health insurance to the poorest households (chapter 6). It does so by consolidating two pro-poor schemes initiated in 2001 into a program called Seguro Integral de Salud (SIS) and scaling up enrollment from 3.6 million in 2001 to more than 10 million today. SIS beneficiaries are mainly poor families. Its benefit package focuses on maternal-child interventions, and its membership is largely children.

By no means does SIS match anyone's conventional idea of a health insurance plan. Historically, patients have enrolled at the point of service when they seek care, if they qualify through a means test, and remain enrolled for a year. Affiliates are tied to Ministry of Health service providers, and the same services they consume through SIS have always been free or heavily subsidized. Yet SIS entitles affiliates to a clearly defined package of services, at no cost at the point of service, and providers receive a fee for service covering variable costs when they can show the service was provided. The three major changes are the explicit targeting to the poor (mainly poor mothers and their children), an entitlement to specific benefits, and a financial benefit that provides a pecuniary incentive to a public facility to seek out SIS affiliates and provide services to them.

Perhaps more than any other study in this book, SIS has made rapid inroads on health conditions of the poor in the short timeframe of six years. The program can be credited with improvements that feed directly into Peru's goal of achieving the Millennium Development Goals because preventable communicable diseases among low-income households represent such a large share of the country's disease burden. To this end, SIS is helping put the country on a fast track to:

- *Improve rates of immunization among children ages 18–59 months.* The probability of children ages 18–59 months being immunized is 65% for low-income health insurance members, compared with 50% for low-income nonmembers, an absolute gain of 15 percentage points and a relative increase of 30%.

- *Improve rates of treatment for diarrhea among children under age 5.* The probability of children under age 5 treated for diarrhea is 50% for low-income health insurance members, compared with 29% for low-income nonmembers, an absolute gain of 21 percentage points and a relative increase of 72%.

- *Improve rates of treatment for acute respiratory infection.* The probability of low-income children under age 5 with health insurance being formally treated for acute respiratory infection is 73%, compared with 51% for those without health insurance, an absolute gain of 22 percentage points and a relative increase of 43%.

Colombia—a big bang reform

For those seeking to scale up universal health insurance in record time and to combat age-old inequalities in access to health and other social services, Colombia provides inspiration. Prior to the introduction of an ambitious health reform in the early 1990s, Colombia had a vertically integrated social insurance system based on payroll taxes for formal workers basically covering only the employed contributor. It had a tax-financed system of public providers serving the poor and the not so poor, the latter especially for hospital and surgical services. And it had a private provider system for all those with the ability to pay or those dissatisfied with the services provided in the traditional social insurance and public systems.

Following the reforms, the government pursued universal health insurance, mobilizing the private sector to provide coverage for a publicly determined benefits package, injecting competition among public and private providers and insurers, and designing and implementing an explicit basic benefits package, with client choice of provider. In the process the government established a solidarity fund to channel resources from individuals whose payroll contributions were greater than the premiums for themselves (the contributory regime) toward individuals whose contributions are less (the subsidized regime). This equalization fund made sure that payroll contributions based on income were transformed into risk-adjusted premiums for all insured, rich and poor. Through this integrated risk-pooling, those with low risk of disease subsidize those with high risk, those with the ability to pay subsidize those without the ability to pay, and those in productive ages subsidize the young and the elderly.

With 65% of the population below the national poverty line, between 1993 and 2003, coverage of households in the bottom income quintile rose almost eightfold, from 6.1% to 46.5%. Compare this with a near tripling of coverage among the population as a whole, from 23.8% to 61.8%. By 2005, 70% of the total population was covered, with close to 60% coverage of the bottom two quintiles. By 2007 enrollment was estimated to be about 90%. In just 16 years Colombia did what took many European countries 100 years.

This reform was particularly effective in improving outcomes for the poor, their dependents, and the self-employed, the groups least likely to be covered by insurance prior to the reform. For poor citizens insurance coverage reduces the probability by 21 percentage points that they will incur an out-of-pocket payment greater than 10% of their income (after subsistence expenses are deducted) even though they are 41% more likely to use ambulatory care during the previous 12 months. Insurance fundamentally alters the care of children in poor families as well; relative to the uninsured, if they have a cough or diarrhea, they are 17% and 23%, respectively, more likely to be taken to a health care facility than an uninsured child. Immunization coverage is higher for the insured; births are far more likely to take place in a facility and to be attended by a doctor or skilled professional. The pattern of higher use and greater financial protection prevails for the self-employed who are now insured. As Colombia approaches 100% coverage of the population, these impacts will be extended to those who remain excluded.

Costa Rica—boosting coverage from 15% to 90%

Costa Rica provides another example of rapid expansion of health insurance and inclusion of the poor (chapter 5). In only 39 years coverage rose from 15.4% in 1961 to about 90% in 2000. At first, only industrial workers were covered. A first extension added their dependents. By 1975 agricultural workers were covered, and by 1984 the self-employed were included. By 2000 coverage across income quintiles was fairly even, while remaining shares of the population not covered were relatively young, single, and educated—that is, individuals least likely to pursue health insurance due to good health.

The question addressed—almost accidentally because the authors did not expect the result—by the Costa Rica study is does it matter how you "cover the last mile?" It is well known in immunization programs that the cost of getting coverage above 80% rises astronomically, yet vaccines so reduce incidence of the immunizable disease that herd immunity may be achieved even if the last 20% are not vaccinated. Is it the same with insurance? In our 2006 data, 81% were covered by the national insurance system, and this has been the case for almost 20 years. To guarantee access to the 19% who were not affiliated, Costa Rican law prevents the insurance system from denying care to anyone and subsidizing those who cannot pay, extending the umbrella of catastrophic protection to everyone. The authors find that yes, indeed, the insured and uninsured seem to have similar access to health care and that they are both spared catastrophic expenditures.

Yet there are some troubling differences in behavior and health-related results. For example, health insurance contributes to completed schedules of immunizations among children ages 18 and younger. Health insurance is also conducive to more regular referred hospitalizations, rather than admissions through the emergency room, with an accompanying reduction in hospital length of stay among the insured. Health insurance substantially improves the care of diabetics—insured diabetics are far less likely than their uninsured counterparts to end up in the emergency room or inpatient ward of a hospital, and they use fewer medications. Generally, insurance coverage reduces the probability that conditions more appropriately treated in an outpatient setting result in a hospital visit. The uninsured are more likely to require intensive care and to die at the hospital. Imputed savings if the average length of stay for the uninsured could be reduced to that of the insured are estimated at about $8.5 million in 2006. Additional savings could come from the positive impacts of health insurance on timely treatment of diabetics, lower use of intensive care, and so on, raising the question of whether there might be healthier ways to cover the last 19%, even if the current approach adequately handles their financial protection and access risks.

Conclusion

We hope that because of this book policymakers interested in scaling up health insurance in low- and middle-income countries will be more informed about the likely impacts of health insurance on health outputs and outcomes, the important methodological factors that can obscure the measured impacts of health insurance, and the ways well designed health insurance might be harnessed to improve conditions facing poorer households within countries.

In reviewing the literature and conducting the case studies here, one thing is clear: health insurance is a complex subject. Its effects are conditional on initial design features and the efficacy of implementing them. If those design elements include sensible medical entitlements and cross-subsidies for the poor, health insurance will likely have equity-improving financial and health impacts. The goals of a health insurance reform should be clear and the design elements consistent with them.

In addition, measuring the effects of health insurance requires high-quality data as well as creative statistical modeling to assure robust empirical estimates. This applies particularly to retrospective analysis, which uses available historical data and is less demanding of time and resources than prospective analysis.

As mentioned earlier, European countries took 100 years and more to introduce, scale up, and repeatedly revise health insurance to achieve equitable universal coverage. The cases collected in this book suggest that low- and middle-income countries have the capability to shorten this gestation period substantially. With clear goals, designs compatible with the goals, and reasonable implementation, success can be achieved and generate tangible benefits for the population. But designs and implementation will have to be modified constantly to adjust to changing circumstances, technology, demands, and behavior. As an insurance program's impacts on equity, cost effectiveness, financial protection, provider behavior, and patient behavior become better understood, other modifications to the basic design and incentives created by the insurance system will have to be made. Knowing impacts and estimating the effects of changes requires an ability to monitor the performance of all elements of the system, including providers, patients, and administrators. We have only looked at patients in this book; the evaluation agenda is much broader. It is far better to build monitoring and evaluation systems into an insurance reform from the start so reform itself generates knowledge that automatically feeds back through institutional mechanisms to improve it.

References

Liu, X., R. Thomson, Y. Gong, F. Zhao, S.B. Squire, R. Tolhurst, X. Zhao, F. Yan, and S. Tang. 2007. "How affordable are tuberculosis diagnosis and treatment in rural China? An analysis from community and tuberculosis patient perspectives." *Tropical Medicine and International Health* 12(12): 1464–71.

Tang, S., and S. B. Squire. 2005. "What Lessons Can Be Drawn from Tuberculosis (TB) Control in China in the 1990s? An Analysis from a Health System Perspective." *Health Policy* 72(1): 93–104.

Wagstaff, A., M. Lindelow, G. Jun, X. Ling, and Q. Juncheng. 2007. "Extending Health Insurance to the Rural Population: An Impact Evaluation of China's New Cooperative Medical Scheme." Policy Research Paper 4150. World Bank, Washington, DC.

Wooldridge, J. 2001. *Econometric Analysis of Cross Section and Panel Data.* Boston, MA: MIT Press.

Zhang, T., S. Tang, G. Jun, and M. Whitehead. 2007. "Persistent problems of access to appropriate, affordable TB services in rural China: experiences of different socio-economic groups." *BMC Public Health* 7: 19.

Editors and Authors

An email address is included for the corresponding editor or chapter author for each group of authors.

Editors

Maria-Luisa Escobar is lead health economist and health systems program leader at the World Bank Institute. On leave from the World Bank as a senior fellow at the Brookings Institution, she worked on the Global Health Initiative from 2006 through 2008, when research for this book began. During the past 20 years at the Inter-American Development Bank and the World Bank, she has worked on health financing reform across Latin America, and she was one of a small group of designers and implementers of the Colombia reforms in the 1990s, led by Juan Luis Londoño.

Charles C. Griffin is senior advisor in the Europe and Central Asia Regional Office of the World Bank. Over the past 25 years he has worked on health financing policy in low- and middle-income countries around the world. Most recently he was director for human development at the World Bank in South Asia, then in Eastern Europe, before a leave of absence to join the Brookings Institution as a senior fellow from 2006 through 2008 (cgriffin@worldbank.org).

R. Paul Shaw is a former World Bank lead economist and previously an economist in the Canadian government, the International Labour

Organization, the United Nations Population Fund, and academia. At the World Bank he created the Health Sector Reform Flagship Program, which has supported more than 20,000 policymakers around the world in applying rigorous analytical techniques to support improved health policies and health system performance. He currently advises the Bill & Melinda Gates Foundation on health economics.

Authors

Chapter 2—Literature Review

Ursula Giedion is a health economist with 20 years' experience in Colombia, Latin America, and other developing countries. Her areas of expertise include the study of health sector reform and health sector financing strategies, the design and implementation of health prioritization policies, and the implementation of econometric health-related impact evaluation studies. In recent years she has carried out consultancies for the Inter-American Development Bank, the Economic Commission for Latin America and the Caribbean, the World Bank, the International Development Research Centre, and the Brookings Institution (ugiedion@gmail.com).

Beatriz Yadira Díaz is a PhD student at the University of Essex and holds an MS in economics. She has experience using quantitative methods for the design, analysis, and evaluation of the impact of public policy. She has 11 years' professional experience at several of Colombia's government agencies, including the National Planning Department, the National Statistics Institution, and the Ministry of Finance. As part of research teams for projects in developing countries, she has worked as a consultant for the World Bank, the Pan-American Health Organization, and the Brookings Institution.

Chapter 3—Namibia

Emily Gustafsson-Wright is a research fellow at the Brookings Institution and the Amsterdam Institute for International Development. Her work involves analysis of health risk and low-cost health insurance programs in Africa. Her professional experience includes consulting for the World Bank's Human Development Network, where she focused on education and child labor, conditional cash transfer programs, and risk and vulnerability in Latin America. She holds a PhD in economics from the University of Amsterdam/The Tinbergen Institute and an MS in applied economics and finance from the University of California (egustafsson-wright@brookings.edu).

Wendy Janssens, a research fellow at the Amsterdam Institute of International Development and the Vrije Universiteit Amsterdam, holds a PhD in economics from the University of Amsterdam/The Tinbergen Institute. Her research interests include health risk, financing and HIV/AIDS, early child development, and social capital. Her regional experience includes Africa, Southeast Asia, and the Caribbean (wjanssens@feweb.vu.nl).

Jacques van der Gaag is co-founder and co-director of the Amsterdam Institute for International Development and a distinguished visiting fellow at the Brookings Institution. Before serving as dean of the faculty of economics and business at the University of Amsterdam, he held various positions at the World Bank in Washington, DC, including chief economist of the Human Development Network. He has published widely in refereed journals and books and served on the editorial boards of the *Journal of Human Resources,* the *Journal of Health Economics,* and the *World Bank Economic Review* (jvandergaag@brookings.edu).

Chapter 4—Ghana
Slavea Chankova is an associate at Abt Associates, Inc., specializing in global health program evaluation and research, focusing on health systems and reproductive, maternal, and child health. She has worked on assignments for the United Nations Children's Fund, the United Nations Development Programme, and Analysis Group (slavea_chankova@abtassoc.com).

Chris Atim is a senior health economist working with the World Bank's Health Systems Strengthening program in Senegal and is executive director of the African Health Economics and Policy Association. He has worked as a senior health economist for the HLSP Institute and Abt Associates, Inc.

Laurel Hatt is a health economist and senior associate at Abt Associates, Inc., specializing in health financing, maternal and child health, and survey research. She has consulted for the Johns Hopkins School of Public Health and the World Bank.

Chapter 5—Costa Rica
James Cercone, founder and president of Sanigest International, is a mathematical economist from the University of Michigan with 20 years' experience in public policy and public sector reform in Latin America, the Caribbean, and Eastern Europe (jcercone@sanigest.com).

Étoile Pinder, consultant at Sanigest Internacional, holds a masters degree in the evaluative clinical sciences from Dartmouth College, working on public sector reform and modernization in Latin America, the Caribbean, the United States, Eastern Europe, and Southeast Asia. Ms. Pinder developed the technical and regulatory framework for the legislation of the Bahamas National Health Insurance Act.

José Pacheco Jiménez is director of the consulting division of Sanigest Internacional. He holds an MA in development economics from the Institute of Social Studies (The Hague) and in impact evaluation methods from the Massachusetts Institute of Technology's Abdul Latif Jameel Poverty Action Lab. He has worked on many aspects of health insurance in more than 20 countries in Latin America, the Caribbean, Eastern Europe, and Southeast Asia.

Rodrigo Briceño holds a masters degree in economics from the National University of Costa Rica. He specializes in financial and social sector data analysis of resource allocation and primary health care.

Chapter 6—Peru
Ricardo Bitrán is founder and president of Bitrán y Asociados in Santiago, Chile, a leading research and consulting group specializing in health economics. He teaches at the University of Chile and the World Bank Institute's Course on Health Sector Reform and Sustainable Financing. He graduated from the University of Chile with a degree in industrial engineering and earned both a PhD in health economics and an MBA in finance from Boston University (ricardo.bitran@bitran.cl).

Rodrigo Muñoz is an engineer specializing in health economics, social metrics, and evaluation. He has worked in Africa, Asia, Latin America, and the Caribbean. His expertise includes economic assessments of social and health programs, impact evaluations, surveys, and software design.

Lorena Prieto was a consultant at Bitran & Associates for six years and is an assistant professor at ESAN University in Lima, Peru. A health economist, she focuses on cost-effectiveness of health services and evaluation of reform programs, risk adjustment, and health policy impacts on households.

Chapter 7—Indonesia
Facundo Cuevas is an economist in the East Asia and Pacific Human Development Department of the World Bank, working on social protection, poverty, and

migration. He has conducted research in health and crime, including work for an article in the upcoming World Bank publication on crime and violence in Central America.

Susan W. Parker is professor of economics in the division of economics at the Center for Research and Teaching in Economics in Mexico City and an adjunct professor at the Rand Corporation. She has extensive experience in the design, implementation, and evaluation of programs, including both randomized controlled trials and nonexperimental methods, with numerous publications in the field (susan.parker@cide.edu).

Chapter 8—China

Winnie Yip is reader in economics for health policy in the Department of Public Health, University of Oxford. She holds a PhD in economics from the Massachusetts Institute of Technology and was associate professor of international health policy and economics at the School of Public Health, Harvard University. She leads several projects on large-scale health system interventions and evaluations in China (winnie.yip@dphpc.ox.ac.uk).

William Hsiao is K.T. Li professor of economics at the School of Public Health, Harvard University, and he holds a PhD in economics from Harvard University. He has published widely on U.S. health policy, comparative health systems, and health policy in developing countries.

Chapter 9—Colombia

Ursula Giedion is a health economist with 20 years' experience on Colombia, other countries in Latin America, and other developing countries. Her areas of expertise include the study of health sector reform and health sector financing strategies, design and implementation of health prioritization policies, and implementation of econometric health-related impact evaluation studies. In recent years she has carried out consultancies for the Inter-American Development Bank, the Economic Commission for Latin America and the Caribbean, the World Bank, the International Development Research Centre, and the Brookings Institution.

Carmen Elisa Flórez is an economist/demographer working on Colombia and other Latin American and Caribbean countries during the last 28 years. She has focused on social economics, particularly the impact of health system reform on access and use of health services and health status. She has carried out national consultancies for government institutions and international consultancies for the Economic Commission for Latin America and the Caribbean, the International Development Research Centre, and the World Bank.

Beatriz Yadira Díaz is a PhD student at the University of Essex and holds an MS in economics. She has experience using quantitative methods for the design, analysis, and evaluation of the impact of public policy. She has 11 years' professional experience at several of Colombia's government agencies, including the National Planning Department, the National Statistics Institution, and the Ministry of Finance. As part of research teams for projects in developing countries, she has worked as a consultant for the World Bank, the Pan-American Health Organization, and the Brookings Institution (yadiradiaz76@gmail.com).

Eduardo Alfonso is an economist engaged in research and the use of evidence to improve public policy. His areas of expertise include the design and implementation of public policy impact evaluations, analysis of health insurance market failures and regulation, and estimation of risk-adjusted health insurance premiums. In recent years he has worked for the Health Ministry and the National Planning Department in Colombia and carried out consultancies for the World Bank.

Renata Pardo, an economist, has worked as an advisor for the Ministry of Social Protection and for the Health Division at the National Planning Department on the Colombian health system. She has also participated in research projects assessing the impact of health insurance on financial protection and the determinants of catastrophic health expenditures. Currently, she works at the National Planning Department on issues related to poverty measures.

Manuela Villar is a public health specialist with experience working in Latin America and Africa. Her areas of expertise include health systems research, health policy design and implementation, and monitoring and evaluation. In recent years she has worked for the World Bank on health reform and health policy in Latin America.

Index

indigators

for country cases, 7

descriptive data for health service
demand, 110–112

health insurance impacts on, 182–183

of health status, 130, 131, 135

income and health finance for select country groupings, 3

indigents, NHIS means test for, 62

indirect members, in Costa Rica, 92

individuals, entering labor market for first
time, 130

Indonesia

case study, 9–10

gross national income, 122

health insurance distributional effects,
181, 184

health system, 123–124

impact of health insurance, 122, 183

summary data on, 7

Indonesian Family Life Survey (IFLS), 122,
126

inequality, of wealth in Namibia, 34

informal care

defined, 175

reduced prevalence of, 181

informal provider, proportion seeking care
from, 71

injury, reported prevalence of, 38

inpatient care, insured with higher rates of,
124

INS (National Insurance Institute), public
insurance monopoly in Costa Rica, 90, 93

Institute of Medicine, of the National Academies, 5

instrumental variables, selecting, 188–189

insurance. *See* health insurance

insurance enrollment, in Greater Windhoek,
35–39

insurance scheme, impact depending on
specifics of, 25

insurance status

changes in in Indonesia, 123–124

determinants of, 99, 100

unobserved characteristics affecting, 41

insured

appearing to have worse health status, 99

descriptive statistics in Indonesia, 124–125

experiencing shorter hospital stays, 101

having higher burden of disease, 96

higher rates of outpatient care, 124

more likely to report chronic illness, acute
illness, and hospitalization, 37

paying more out of pocket, 39

by state regime, 90

use of government health facilities, 38

insured children, differences from uninsured,
124

insured diabetics, self-perceived health status,
101

insured mothers, less likely to have babies
with low birthweight, 101

insured pregnant women, clear benefit for, 163

integral health insurance, 107–108

integrated risk-pooling, 195–196

intensive care unit, uninsured more likely to
end up in, 98

international conferences, on social health
insurance, 1

international insurance companies, in Costa
Rica, 93

intervention, designing to address the problem, 189

interventions, independent effects of aspects
of, 152

variables

explaining affiliation with the Caja, 95

weak instrumental, 188–189

Vietnam, health insurance program, 21, 23

village clinics, in China, 140

village doctors

as private practitioners, 138

RMHC screening and regulating, 141

selecting, 140–141

village management committee, checking

village clinics, 142

villagers, monitoring RMHC operations, 151

voluntary enrollment, for NCMS in China,

137

voluntary members, of insurance program in

Costa Rica, 92

W

wealth, differences within Namibia's popula-

tion, 34

wealth indexes, constructing for NHIS study,

83

wealth quintile, enrollment in NHIS increas-

ing with, 78

weight loss

consequences of, 44

in previous 12 months, 48

as proxy for advanced state of AIDS, 46, 48

World Bank Health VIII project in China

impact of, 19

mixed evidence of an impact on health

status, 23

reducing out-of-pocket payments among

the poorest, 20

World Health Organization (WHO)

advocating social health insurance, 2

estimates on financial catastrophe for

expensive emergency care, 1

Z

Zambia, impact of health insurance schemes,

21

Zhangjai Town

in China, 141